Interpersonal relations
and education

By the same author

Social Relations in a Secondary School (1967)
Social Rules and Social Types (1965)

Interpersonal relations and education

David H. Hargreaves
Department of Education, University of Manchester

Student Edition

Routledge & Kegan Paul
London, Boston, Melbourne and Henley

First published in the **International Library of Sociology** *in 1972*
First published as a student edition in 1975
by Routledge & Kegan Paul Ltd,
39 Store Street
London WC1E 7DD,
9 Park Street, Boston,
Mass. 02108, USA,
296 Beaconsfield Parade,
Middle Park, Melbourne,
3206, Australia and
Broadway House, Newtown Road,
Henley-on-Thames, Oxon RG9 1EN
Reprinted in 1976, 1978, 1980 and 1983
Printed in Great Britain by
Unwin Brothers Limited,
The Gresham Press, Old Woking, Surrey
A member of the Staples Printing Group

ISBN 0 7100 8081 6

Contents

Acknowledgments

The author and the publishers gratefully thank the following for permission to include extracts from their work: Evans Brothers Limited for extracts from H. F. Ellis: *The Papers of A. J. Wentworth*; Prentice-Hall Inc. for extracts from Solomon E. Asch: *Social Psychology* © 1952 the Publishers; Harcourt Brace Jovanovich Inc. and Jonathan Cape Limited for extracts from © 1968 Kingsley Amis: *I Want It Now*; Little, Brown and Company and A. D. Peters & Company for extracts from Evelyn Waugh: *Decline and Fall*; Scott Meredith Literary Agency, Evan Hunter & Constable & Company Limited for extracts from Evan Hunter; *The Blackboard Jungle*; Penguin Books Limited for extracts from Leila Berg: *Risinghill*; Peter Terson for extracts from his article in the *Guardian*.

Preface

In preparing this revised and abbreviated edition I have made a number of changes. Four of the original chapters—on friendship formation, youth culture, attitude change, and staff relationships—have been completely deleted, since these are topics of more specialized interest than the chapters that have been retained. The book is now divided into two distinct parts, the first of which is predominantly concerned with general social psychological theory and research, and the second of which is devoted to applications to education.

There have been extensive deletions in all parts of the book; no doubt the 'advanced' student can refer to the original edition if he seeks a more elaborate treatment of a particular topic. The revision has, however, allowed me to make a number of changes. I have rewritten certain sections to remove ambiguities or a lack of clarity; I have made additions to take account of books and articles that have been published since the original edition; and certain parts have been substantially rewritten in the light of my own changing views, especially in Chapter 7.

At the same time I have been unable to respond to the requests of some readers and critics that I should deal with a number of particular themes. Probably the most important of these is the topic of 'language'. This is certainly an area which is of considerable interest to social psychologists, as the textbooks of Brown (1965) and Lindesmith and Strauss (1949) attest. I have neglected this topic, especially the work of Basil Bernstein, quite intentionally; but not because I think it unimportant, but because the subject is fully treated in a wide variety of books and my own book was intended to complement the existing literature, not replace it.

The general aim of this edition remains unchanged; namely to introduce the reader to the social psychology of education in a style which I hope conveys the fascination and excitement of this relatively neglected field in education. The heart of the educational process is in the classroom; it is that world and the relationships within it that is of special interest to the social psychologist. If my analysis and prescriptive suggestions interest and challenge the reader, then I shall have succeeded. In the end, this remains a book, and for teachers and social scientists alike, it is worth remembering La Rochefoucauld's maxim: *Il est plus nécessaire d'étudier les hommes que les livres.*

part one

Theory

1 The self and symbolic interactionism

It would be easier to begin this book if the teaching and learning of social psychology could be approached in a similar way to the teaching and learning of mathematics or a language. In the case of these latter subjects there are fairly obvious simple and primary elements that must be mastered before moving on to more advanced areas. It would be unusual to begin a book on mathematics with calculus and end it with simple algebraic equations, just as it would be strange to teach the pluperfect of irregular verbs in French before teaching the present tense of regular verbs. The teacher of these subjects can assume in a broad way a linearity in the subject. All disciplines are really spherical rather than linear, for all the elements of a discipline are inter-related in complex ways, but some subjects are more readily adaptable to linear treatments than others. Social psychology does not lend itself easily to such an approach—the standard textbooks take very different starting points and paths through the subject.

Since the chapter structure of a book implies some degree of linearity, even though a spherical shape has no obvious beginning or end, some justification is required for entering the sphere at a particular point. We shall enter the discipline of social psychology by looking at a concept which is closer to the middle of the sphere than to its outer edge, or, to change to a more popular metaphor, by plunging the reader into the deep end. One of the more central conflicts within social psychology is the tension between the 'individual' and the 'social'. It is a conflict within other social sciences too, but there it is not so central. Sociology claims that its central concerns are with social phenomena, social facts and social explanations. The 'individual' aspect is of secondary importance. Thus Albert Cohen, whose book *Delinquent Boys* (1955) is one of the most important and influential sociological approaches to delinquency, writes: 'We are

3

not primarily interested in explaining why this boy adopts a delinquent solution to his problems and why another boy does not . . .
This book does, however, have implications for the explanation of
the individual case.' The task which Cohen dismisses is often regarded as the task of psychologists, for psychology is concerned with
the 'individual' rather than the 'social'. It takes as its central focus
individual phenomena (cognition, perception, motivation, etc.), and
their internal structure and dynamics. The research, theories and
explanations of psychologists are rooted in individual behaviour, in
its prediction and control. Psychologists recognize the importance of
the 'social' but they are interested in it not in its own right but in so
far as it affects the individual's behaviour.

The tension between the 'social' and the 'individual' is at its most
acute in social psychology, which takes as its central focus interpersonal relationships. Social psychology is social for it seeks to
analyse the relationship between two or more persons; it is individual
in that it takes account of what an individual contributes to a social
interaction or a relationship and how he is affected by it. The dicho-
tomy, between the 'individual' and the 'social' becomes largely artificial, though it remains a useful and convenient distinction.

We shall begin this book by trying to come face to face with (but
not with resolving) this central tension and it is nowhere more obvious
than in the concept of the 'self'. At first sight this seems to be an
'individual' rather than a 'social' concept, but on further analysis
such a simple view is immediately undermined and we are forced to
recognize the tension which is inherent in all social psychology.
Because the concept of the self is toward the centre of the sphere of
the discipline of social psychology, it is linked with all the other concepts in a very complex way. It is one of several threads that run
through all the chapters, implicitly or explicitly. It cannot be dealt
with and then dismissed in one chapter as if it were an isolated bit.
This is the danger of the implied linearity of books, a danger for the
author in his desire to carve up the field into convenient segments,
but an even greater danger for the reader who may come to perceive
these convenient segments as the inherent structure of the discipline.
For this reason the reader should perhaps re-read this chapter when
he has finished the book. He can then consider the concept of the
self from a more sophisticated position, recognize the oversimplification necessary in an early chapter, and, armed with greater understanding and insight, acknowledge that the imposed structure has
been convenient, arbitrary and tentative. In the end it is simply one
of many possible approaches.

Before we begin this exposition, it is crucial that the reader should
recognize that in taking the self as a central concept I am effectively
offering a particular brand of, or perspective on, social psychology.

Most people would acknowledge that social psychology is about the individual in social situations, about social relationships and about small groups. Yet these topics can be analysed in terms of very different perspectives. One can, for instance, approach social psychology from a behaviouristic position or from an experimentalist standpoint. Alternatively one might take a more eclectic position, basing one's analysis on selected central concepts. Thus Peter Kelvin's *The Bases of Social Behaviour* (1970), an outstanding brief introduction to social psychology, used the concepts of *value* and *order* to examine and evaluate the problems, theories and research findings of the field. For the most part I shall be following the perspective which is known as *symbolic interactionism*. This approach has been pioneered in successive editions of the textbook by Lindesmith and Strauss (1949) and its current popularization has been aided by the collections of readings by Manis and Meltzer (*Symbolic Interaction: A Reader in Social Psychology*, 1967) and by Rose (*Human Behaviour and Social Process: An Interactionist Approach*, 1962). The founding fathers of this perspective, writing in the first four decades of the century, made the analysis of the concept of the self a cornerstone for a much wider analysis of social relations; and in so doing, they provided a social psychological foundation for a distinctive perspective within sociology.

These writers have emphasized the fact that in a very fundamental sense the self is a product of a person's interaction with others. It is the *social* environment which is seen as fundamental. The central idea, in short, is that a person's self develops in relation to the reactions of other people to that person and that he tends to react to himself as he perceives other people reacting to him. That is to say, the self-system is not merely a function of a person's manipulation of the environment, but a function of the way in which a person is treated by others. The self is a social product. This line of thought is an important element in many of our great theorists, such as Piaget and Freud, but its most notable exponents come from another tradition.

The American sociologist Charles Horton Cooley (1902) coined the important phrase the *looking-glass self*. Just as a man considers his reflection in a mirror and uses the reflection to acquire information about his physical nature, so he uses other people's attitudes to him as a measure of what he is really like. The mirror provides 'feedback': he can corroborate by means of the reflection whether or not his appearance is acceptable to him. Similarly, the reactions of others provide a man with feedback on how he appears to them and he can then discover whether or not this is in accord with the way in which he perceives himself.

Cooley never fully developed this line of thought, but the task was taken up by another American, George Herbert Mead (1934). The major part of Mead's work was not published until after his death, but it has subsequently exerted a profound influence on many areas of thought in social psychology and sociology. Mead's great contribution was the recognition that the self is a social structure which rises through communication. In his terms, the primary element of communication is the *gesture*. For example, an animal in a state of anger will bare its teeth. In Darwinian terms such a gesture has adaptive value for survival, since the teeth are ready for action or for counteraction. This gesture is really the first part of a series of acts and can come to serve as a *sign* for the whole act.

The situation in which each of two animals responds to the actions of the other may be referred to as a 'conversation of gestures'. A good example is the instinctive mating behaviour of the three-spined stickleback as described by the ethologist Tinbergen (1951). The female with her swollen abdomen swims casually through the water. When the male sees her, he begins to perform his zig-zag dance. At this point, the female approaches the male, who goes to the nest he has previously built, closely pursued by the female. He demonstrates the nest to his prospective mate, who enters. At this moment, the male begins to quiver (with excitement?) which induces spawning in the female. Finally, the male fertilizes the eggs. This complex behaviour pattern is really a sequence of actions and reactions. The action of one is the stimulus to the other to respond in a certain way, and this reaction becomes a stimulus to the first fish to react in his turn. Each stimulus 'releases' a reaction which then becomes itself a stimulus 'releasing' another reaction, and so on. Courtship among the sticklebacks is a 'conversation of gestures'.

Yet a 'conversation of gestures' is not the same thing as communication. According to Mead, the 'conversation of gestures' becomes communication when the gestures become *significant*, that is, when they arouse in the organism making the gesture the same response that the gesture arouses, or is intended to arouse, in the other organism. Communication is considerably facilitated by the use of language. Communication does not demand language, for as John Macmurray (1961) reminds us, communication is not the offspring of language, but its parent. The process, however, is best illustrated by the use of speech. When I speak to another person, I am seeking to call out in him a response to my linguistic stimulus. At the same time, I call out the same response in myself. The value of language hinges upon the fact that I get the meaning of what I say. So if I make a request of another person I arouse in myself the very response I am trying to evoke from him. This is a very important step, because if I arouse in myself the response I am trying to evoke from someone else, then without the other having to respond at all I can anticipate the other's reaction to my behaviour and, by extension, I can anticipate my own reaction to the other's anticipated reaction. The individual can anticipate the other's reaction by the process which Mead calls *taking the role of the other*, by considering oneself from the standpoint of the other. Thus on Mead's view the self is essentially reflexive; it is a social structure. This is because the self can be both subject, which Mead calls the 'I', and object, which Mead calls the 'me'. There becomes possible a kind of internal conversation by which the individual can, without action, rehearse possible courses and conseqences of action. This means that the individual's behaviour ceases to be determined by the *actual* response of the other person, as was the case with our amorous sticklebacks. By anticipating the other's reaction to my action and also my reaction to his reaction, I am able to examine and evaluate several possible courses of action and from these choose one particular course of action. In a social interaction a person's behaviour is influenced not by the acts of the other as such but by the meaning (intentions, motives, etc.) which the person assigns to the other's acts. Individual action is constructed in relation to the other, not simply released by the other's acts. As Blumer (1962, 1966) has pointed out, Mead's argument means that the individual's behaviour is not simply determined by outside forces (as in some sociological views) or simply evoked by internal impulses (as in some psychological views).

In short, the self is not inborn, nor could it appear in the individual isolated from his fellows. The self arises from the social experience of interacting with others. The self has an important reflexive quality: it is both subject and object. In interaction, a man learns to respond to himself as others respond to him. He becomes object to himself when he takes to himself the reactions of others to him. He acquires a self by putting himself in the shoes of others and by using their perspective of him to consider himself. It is to this ability of man to take to himself the attitudes of others to him that Mead refers in his famous phrase 'taking the role of the other'.

On this view the distinctive attributes of man arise not so much from the superiority of his nervous system as such (the biological view) but from the kind of social relationships man holds with others of his species. A person is a being with a self, and that self arises through the social relationships of that being. Macmurray (1961) sums it up when he writes:

the unit of personal existence is not the individual, but two persons in personal relation; and . . . we are persons not by individual right, but in virtue of relation to one another. The personal is constituted by personal relatedness. The unit of the personal is not the 'I' but the 'You and I'.

The notion of the person totally independent of others is a fiction.

Mead's major contribution, then, rests on his suggestion that a self develops only when a person begins to 'take the role of the other', when a person takes to himself the attitudes that others take to him. One of the important ways in which the child learns to do this is in play, as Mead and Piaget have stressed. Whether the play is alone or with others, whether in fantasy or with toys, it serves the same function. Let us consider the case of a child playing at being another person, either a parent or some childhood hero. Frequently the child will play two roles in interaction, as in the game of 'house' where the child is both mother and father. In such play or fantasy situations the child is exploring the reactions of other people to one another and to him, as well as his reactions to them. It is in this way that the child learns to see himself from the perspective of others. The organization of the responses of others is an essential part of the process of self development.

In the early socialization of the child, then, the learning of roles and the development of the self are inseparably fused (cf. Maccoby, 1959, 1961). Both are achieved in the essentially social context of interpersonal relationships. But from the complex process of socialization let us tease out the strand of role learning for analysis. Clearly the young child's interpersonal environment usually consists of the home. It is with his parents that the child most frequently interacts and on whom he is so dependent. Mother and father are so important to the child that they may, in Sullivan's (1940) phrase, be regarded as his *significant others*. Kuhn (1964) has defined significant others as

(*a*) the others to whom the individual is most fully, broadly and basically committed, emotionally and psychologically;

(*b*) the others who have provided him with his general vocabulary, including his most basic and crucial concepts and categories;

(*c*) the others who have provided and continue to provide him with his categories of self and other and with the meaningful roles to which such assignments refer;

(*d*) the others in communication with whom his self-conception is basically sustained and/or changed.

Thus it is the parents who dominate the child's world, it is their role relationships with him that must be learned and also explored in fantasy and play, it is their concepts, categories and attitudes that the child must take to himself. As the child does take the attitudes of his parents to himself, he begins to acquire a conception of the role of the child. His parents expect certain forms of behaviour from him and when he conforms to these expectations he is rewarded by them either materially or with love and approval. If he deviates from these expectations, he is punished. The child is learning how a child should behave. He is learning the role of a *child* in relation to his *parents*, and then more specifically the role of a *son* in relation to his *mother* and his *father*. Concomitant with his understanding of the son role is his understanding of the roles of mothers and fathers. He is beginning to discover that relationships between people are *structured* and that the role structure is independent of particular individuals. In time he will appreciate the relationships that his friends have with their parents. He will be in a position to understand, and to respond appropriately to, other adults who also have children. They are mothers and fathers like his own parents, but their parent roles are held in relation to their own children, not to him. The learning of these roles and role relationships is slow and complex, and certainly slower than simply learning to name the roles correctly.

When the child learns the content of his own and other people's roles, he is also learning to facilitate his relationships with them. As he learns what his parents expect of him he also learns what he can expect of them. When he learns to take their attitudes to himself, he becomes capable of anticipating and predicting their reactions to him. This has at least two important consequences. Firstly, by anticipating the reactions of the others, the child learns how to reduce potential conflict by gearing his behaviour to the role relationship. In role learning we shape and oil the cogs so that the social machine will run smoothly. Secondly, by taking the attitudes of his significant others to himself, their expectations can be effective in their physical absence. For when the child takes the attitudes of his significant others to himself, he internalizes controls which were originally external. It represents a movement from 'Mummy will smack me (not love me) if I . . .' to 'I am a bad boy if I . . .' to 'It is bad to . . .' We all learn to make the jump from the specific 'Mummy will smack me (not love me) if I . . .' to the normative and conventional 'One does not . . .' which has cut free from its specific interpersonal origins. We become what others want and expect us to be by making *their* views and *their* rules and *their* ways *our* views, rules and ways. More than this, we can soon come to view our (i.e. theirs and mine) views, rules and ways as the *only* and the *right* ones.

Whilst role learning is one of the basic features of socialization within the family, it is by no means the only important feature. We have suggested that much of the basic role learning is acquired through the child's interactions with his primary significant others, his parents, because his dependence on them makes him sensitive to their expectations, their evaluations and their rewards and punishments. It is this same dependence and sensitivity in the child which makes the parents the primary source of the child's knowledge, beliefs and values. In short, the 'culture' of a society is initially bestowed upon the child through his parents, who channel and filter the culture to the child in their interactions with him. And among the attitudes which the child takes to himself from his parents are his

9

parents' knowledge, beliefs and values. The child's conception of 'reality'—what society, social institutions, his fellow men are like, what is 'important' or 'proper' or 'good' or 'right'—all this is socially mediated to the child, and in the first instance by taking over his parents' attitudes.

As the child grows older he moves out into a wider social environment and makes relationships with a wider range of people. The nature of the interaction, too, tends to change. One such situation is the organized game. The young child does not really play such games with other children, as Piaget (1932) has shown. Rather, he plays a private fantasy game alone but in the company of others. Knowledge of the rules is in itself not sufficient to ensure true game playing. An organized game represents a complex interactional system, for the roles of all the players have definite relationships with one another. To play the game requires a reciprocity and co-operation of which the ability to take the role of the other is an essential component. Indeed, the child can participate in the game only when he allows his own actions to be related to the actions of all the other players. For the fullest development of the self, according to Mead, a person must take to himself the role of the 'generalized other' or the attitudes of the group or community of which he is a member. Just as in an organized game the player learns to synthesize in a general way the attitudes of all the other players, that is the collective goals and attitudes of the team-as-a-whole, so the growing child synthesizes the attitudes of members of groups of which he is a part and to whose influence he is subject, whether the group be small, like the family or friendship group, of intermediate size, like the neighbourhood or religious group, or large like the nation or culture. In Mead's own words:

> The individual experiences himself as such, not directly, but only indirectly, from the particular standpoints of other individual members of the same social group or from the generalized standpoint of the group as a whole to which he belongs. For he enters his own experience as a self or individual, not directly or immediately, not by becoming a subject to himself, but only in so far as he first becomes an object to himself just as other individuals are objects to him or are in his experience; and he becomes an object to himself only by taking the attitudes of other individuals toward himself within a social framework or context of experience and behaviour in which both he and they are involved . . . If the given human individual is to develop a self in the fullest sense it is not sufficient for him merely to take the attitudes of other human individuals toward himself and toward one another within the human social process and to

bring that social process as a whole into his individual experience merely in these terms. He must also, in the same way that he takes the attitudes of other individuals toward himself and toward one another, take their attitudes toward the various phases or aspects of the common social activity or set of social undertakings in which, as members of an organized society or social group, they are all engaged.

In this way Mead brilliantly demonstrates the connection between learning to take the role of the other and the process of socialization, both in the sense of becoming what is distinctively human and in the sense of internalizing the norms and values of one's membership groups, both at the cultural and sub-cultural level.

Mead is regarded as the father of the important school of thought within the social sciences that is called Symbolic Interactionism because he first asserted that both human nature and the social order are products of communication. The implications of this assertion are far reaching, and will be felt throughout this book. The self is one of the most central concepts in social psychology because of Mead's fundamental contribution. For the moment we must content ourselves with a hint of the implications of a symbolic interactionist position. In Shibutani's (1961) words:

From this standpoint, behaviour is not regarded merely as a response to environmental stimuli, an expression of inner organic needs, nor a manifestation of cultural patterns. The importance of sensory cues, organic drives, and culture is certainly recognized, but the direction taken by a person's conduct is seen as something that is constructed in the reciprocal give and take of interdependent men who are adjusting to one another. Furthermore, a man's personality—those distinctive behaviour patterns that characterize a given individual—is regarded as developing and being reaffirmed from day to day in his interaction with his associates. Finally, the culture of a group is not viewed as something external that is imposed upon people, but as consisting of models of appropriate conduct that emerge in communication and are continually reinforced as people jointly come to terms with life conditions. If the motivation of behaviour, the formation of personality, and the evolution of group structure all occur in social interaction, it follows logically that attention should be focused upon the interchanges that go on among human beings as they come into contact with one another.

The perceptive reader may have noticed that in the above analysis of identity formation, role learning and socialization based on Mead's theory, the concept of 'taking the role of the other' has been used in an ambiguous way (Turner, 1956). In one usage, which can be called *identificatory role-taking*, the person takes to himself and makes his own the attitudes that the other—normally the 'significant others'—takes to him. He adopts the other's standpoint as his own; the attitudes of the other are transformed into self-attitudes. The other then becomes a source of a person's values, beliefs and standards. Further, since the other acts as a mirror, the person derives his self-conception from the reactions and evaluations—or what have been called the 'reflected appraisals'—of the other. Thus a person's identity (who he is) and his self-esteem (his feelings of worth) are socially derived. At the same time, this self-conception consists not only of what the person is, and what he has been in the past, but also of what he plans to do, of what his future goals and projects are, of what he would like to be. It is through identificatory role-taking that a person acquires an ideal self.

In the second usage of the concept 'taking the role of the other', which I shall call *facilitatory role-taking*, the person does not identify with the other at all. He retains a sharp distinction or separation between the attitudes of the other and his own identity. In facilitatory role-taking the person imaginatively constructs and anticipates the attitudes of the other so that he can facilitate his interaction with the other, by adjusting his conduct towards the other's own self-conception and the other's attitudes towards him. Facilitatory role-taking is most clearly demonstrated in the process of social manipulation. The confidence trickster succeeds precisely because he can accurately estimate the self-conception of the other and the other's attitudes to him without in any way identifying with those attitudes. It is also demonstrated in a relationship characterized by empathy, in which a person seeks to make an accurate estimate of the other's self-conception and attitudes, not in order to manipulate the other but in order to understand him.

With increasing age the child's social world expands and he comes into contact with many other persons outside his immediate family. An important step here is his entry into school, where he has to learn a new set of roles and the ability to interact within new role-relationships. Parsons (1959) has implied that the role of pupil may be learned with difficulty, for there are permanent and fundamental differences between the role of son or daughter and the role of pupil. Whilst mother and teacher are (usually) both women, the role relationships with the child are of a very different order. For example, it is part of the teacher's job that she should evaluate the pupils differentially on the basis of scholastic performance. The mother, on the other hand, is concerned primarily with offering emotional support to the child who is less likely to be evaluated in terms of his capacity for achievement. Any experienced nursery or infant teacher has a fund of entertaining and moving stories which illustrate the problems experienced by the child in learning to differentiate and adjust to the new role relationships required by the school and classroom situation. In school, moreover, the child has to learn to associate with many other pupils who are in the same class; the role of friend assumes a special significance.

Through childhood into adolescence and adulthood, the person is brought into contact with a great range of others with whom he assumes new role relationships. In so doing, he comes into contact with, and sometimes becomes a member of, particular *groups* of others. The study of groups and their impact on the individual—group dynamics—is a central topic for social psychology. At this point I merely wish to emphasize that these groups can come to constitute significant others for the person.

It may help to clarify some of the issues if we introduce the concept of *reference group*. The term was first introduced by Hyman (1942) and has subsequently been developed by social psychologists (notably Newcomb, 1950; Sherif, 1953; Shibutani, 1955) and sociologists (notably Merton, 1957). Traditionally, a reference group is a group in which a person seeks to attain or maintain membership or in whose terms he evaluates himself. Kelley (1952) has suggested two main functions of reference groups. The first function is *normative* and is specified in the definition just given. Here the person wishes to become a member of the group or to maintain his membership in it. To do this, he conforms to the group's norms, adopts its values and evaluates himself in these terms. The members of the group become his significant others. With respect to the normative function a reference group can be negative. A negative reference group is a group of which a person would like to cease being a member or of which he would have definite antipathy to becoming a member; he would not evaluate himself in the group's terms. The second function of reference groups is *comparative*. In this case a person uses the reference group as a standard of comparison with which to estimate his own position. For example, as a university teacher I might use schoolteachers as a comparative reference group when they are given a pay rise. I may have no interest in them normatively, i.e. I do not want to become a schoolteacher or to conform to their norms, but I may take their pay rise as a basis for estimating my own financial position. By comparing my position with theirs, I might feel economically deprived. Thus groups, whether or not one is a member, can be used as reference groups with one or both functions.

The concept of reference group is a useful analytical tool in the study of the processes of social influence and in the explanation of the uniqueness of individuals. A person does not merely take to himself the dominant attitudes of his culture and subculture (Mead's

13

'generalized other'), but from all the possible others available to him selects some others as significant others. Moreover, the reference group which is taken as a set of significant others need not be a group of which the person is a member. Social influence is not confined to those others with whom fate has put a person in immediate contact, nor even to those who are living, for reference groups can be taken from the past or from unborn future generations. As yet there is little research on the determinants of the selection of particular reference groups, but it is clear that we cannot account for individual action without considering both the groups of which a person is a member and the groups of which he is not a member, and then that person's orientation (positive, negative, neutral; normative, comparative) to these groups. The individual's perspective, with its complex processes of meaning interpretation through which action is constructed, is related to that individual's significant others. The concept of reference group can assist us in this endeavour.

In the final section of this introductory chapter I shall outline some of the main assumptions of the symbolic interactionist perspective. Every perspective in the social sciences makes some assumptions about man and the world; the differences between perspectives are fundamentally differences in assumptions. Only when we recognize these perspective assumptions—or what Gouldner (1970) has called 'domain assumptions'—can we begin to understand the conflicts between the different theories, models, methodologies and research findings offered by different social scientists. This means that these assumptions must be made as explicit as possible.

A basic assumption of the symbolic interactionist is that objects in the world do not have a fixed, pre-established character. They have no intrinsic meaning at all until human beings impose a meaning on them. In this sense objects are human constructs. In Blumer's (1966) words:

> the nature of an object is constituted by the meaning it has for the person or persons for whom it is an object. Second, this meaning is not intrinsic to the object but arises from how the person is initially prepared to act towards it.

Thus the meaning of a piece of chalk to a teacher depends on whether he wants to use it to write on the blackboard (writing implement) or to throw it at a pupil (missile). The object acquires its meaning in relation to a person's goal or plan of action. It has no meaning except in relation to that plan of action or to a plan of action imputed by that person to another person. And as a person's plans of action change, so does the meaning of the object.

The world is thus a social construction in which persons interpret or impute meanings to objects. Of course, each individual does not

14

work through this process *de novo* for himself, for human beings acquire what we loosely call 'culture' or the ready-made interpretations or meanings of those who have preceded him in society. Many objects are defined in the same or a similar way by groups of persons through the process that Sullivan (1940) has termed *consensual validation*. Many objects have the appearance of having an obvious, taken-for-granted and objective character because the members of the group have agreed to define them in a particular way. At the same time, these agreed definitions are not entirely identical between different groups, and quite often not even within the same group. The symbolic interactionist social psychologist, then, has a special interest in the processes by which persons interpret and categorize the world (perception) and the ways in which this is influenced by group membership. In particular, he is interested in the ways in which persons interpret and categorize *other persons* with whom he interacts (person perception).

In Mead's analysis of the self, the individual becomes a kind of society in miniature, for he can engage in a form of internal social interaction. When, through the process of taking the role of the other, the self acquires its reflexive quality and attains self-consciousness, the individual is no longer at the mercy of the forces of nature. He does not merely respond to those forces which play upon him from inside or outside, as is the case with objects or organisms that lack a self. In short, his behaviour is no longer determined. With a self, the individual ceases to be subject to the direct impact of other stimuli, for he can withhold his response to such stimuli and estimate their significance and consequences for particular lines of action towards them. His ability to anticipate makes several possible future lines of action available in the present; and from such future possibilities he can make a choice. The person thus constructs and chooses what he does; his acts are not predetermined responses. For this reason, the symbolic interactionist often prefers to describe the individual as an *actor*. The primary meaning of this term is that the individual can choose his line of *action*; its secondary meaning, using the dramaturgical analogy of the stage actor, is based on the first meaning, for one cannot pretend to be something unless we regard human beings as capable of choice.

In this perspective social interaction is a situation in which two or more actors orientate themselves to one another. Each actor has to treat the other person as an actor—namely as a person like himself, one who has goals, problems of interpretation and freedom of choice. Each member of the interaction, then, has to interpret the conduct of the other before he can react to it. Each has to interpret the goals and intentions of the other, and then evaluate them for his own goal or plan of action, and then construct his own responding action in

15

that light. Each member has to develop a *definition of the situation*—a definition of the identity and goals of both persons in relation to the specific context of the interaction. The relationship between each member's definition of the situation becomes a topic for analysis.

Every perspective within the social sciences carries its own methodological imperatives which spring from the basic assumptions of that perspective. In the case of symbolic interactionism, these have been neatly described by Blumer (1966).

> If human beings are, indeed, organisms with selves, and if their action is, indeed, an outcome of a process of self-interaction, schemes that purport to study and explain social action should respect and accommodate these features. To do so, current schemes in sociology and psychology would have to undergo radical revision. They would have to shift from a preoccupation with initiating factor and terminal result to a preoccupation with a process of formation. They would have to view action as something constructed by the actor instead of something evoked from him. They would have to depict the milieu of action in terms of how the milieu appears to the actor in place of how it appears to the outside student. They would have to incorporate the interpretive process which at present they scarcely deign to touch. They would have to recognize that any given act has a career in which it is constructed but in which it may be interrupted, held in abeyance, abandoned, or recast.
>
> On the methodological or research side the study of action would have to be made from the position of the actor. Since action is forged by the actor out of what he perceives, interprets, and judges, one would have to see the operating situation as the actor sees it, perceive objects as the actor perceives them, ascertain their meaning in terms of the meaning they have for the actor, and follow the actor's line of conduct as the actor organizes it—in short, one would have to take the role of the actor and see his world from his standpoint. This methodological approach stands in contrast to the so-called objective approach so dominant today, namely, that of viewing the actor and his action from the perspective of an outside, detached observer. The 'objective' approach holds the danger of the observer substituting his view of the field of action for the view held by the actor.

We cannot afford, therefore, to ignore or bypass the interpretative process. To do so would be to build a social science which is inherently unfaithful to the nature of man. Human society and internal impulses are sociological and psychological constraints within which human action is constructed, but they do not determine that action.

16

Our subsequent discussion of perception, role interaction and group dynamics must always be seen in this light.

Recommended reading

JEROME G. MANIS & BERNARD N. MELTZER, *Symbolic Interaction: A Reader in Social Psychology*, Allyn & Bacon, 1967.

GEORGE HERBERT MEAD, *Mind, Self and Society*, University of Chicago Press, 1934.

ARNOLD M. ROSE, *Human Behaviour and Social Processes: An Interactionist Approach*, Routledge & Kegan Paul, 1962.

TAMOTSU SHIBUTANI, *Society and Personality*, Prentice-Hall, 1961.

2 Perceiving people

An analysis of human interaction clearly involves a consideration of the ways in which persons perceive one another. It is the perception of just who the other person is, his identity, his characteristics and his intentions, which in part steers one person's conduct towards another. At a very elementary level the knowledge that I am going to interact with an old lady rather than a small boy is sufficient to inhibit certain lines of conduct. Interaction is also guided by our evaluations of others. We tend to accord a different treatment to our friends than to our enemies, to superiors than to subordinates, to those who are beautiful than to those who are ugly. So before we can turn to the more direct study of social interaction we must examine some of the basic dimensions and mechanisms of person perception.

Suppose we ask someone (whom we shall call Person) to go into a room to interview another person (whom we shall call Other). Person has not been told anything at all about Other. Person goes into the room and *sees* Other. Person's first action is to make a visual perception of Other. If we ask Person what he has seen, he will tell us that he has seen a young woman. If we ask him how he knows this he will tell us that it is obvious since Other is wearing a dress and has a well developed figure. Person did not use all the information at his disposal but *selected* certain aspects of the multiplicity of available data. He has selected information relating to Other's age and sex, but neglected information that might permit additional conclusions about Other. Further, he has not noted all the information that might be used as evidence for Other's femaleness. He can 'tell at a glance' that Other is female. The means whereby he has selected some information about Other is rapid and subconscious. He is not aware of his selection of some data as a basis for reaching a conclusion until we ask him how he reached that conclusion. The primary perceptual phenomenon is thus the selection of data. Some information passes through the filter and some information does not (Fig. 2.1). Data relating to the sex and age of Other are selected at once not only because they are the most obvious characteristics of Other that can be obtained through a visual inspection but also because they represent basic aspects of Other that will help Person to know how he should behave towards Other and how he might expect Other to behave towards him.

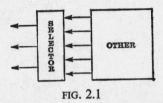

FIG. 2.1

Implicit in our illustration of the selection process is the process of *organizing* the data. In concluding that Other is a woman Person has organized his perception. In organizing the data, Person is trying to make sense of what he sees. Perception, to use the words of Bartlett (1932), is an effort after meaning. To organize the information is essentially to make *interpretations* and *inferences* about the information. It is because Other is wearing a dress that Person infers that it is a woman. The two processes of selection and organization are only theoretically distinct, for they are related in complex ways. It is the need to organize which leads Person to select in the first place. Once the data have been organized this may influence the selector by filtering in information which is congruent with the interpretation made and promote the selection of further data to confirm or resolve a tentative or ambiguous interpretation.

Most people are prepared to make interpretations and inferences on the basis of a very small amount of information. The knowledge that Other is wearing a dress is not sufficient in itself to make an inference about Other's sex absolutely certain, although it will be highly probable. We do not normally regard more extensive research for confirmatory evidence as necessary because we have learned that the wearing of a dress correlates highly with femaleness and that baldness and pipe-smoking correlate highly with maleness. Indeed normally there is such a superfluity of information available about Other's basic attributes that we need to pay attention to only a small number of cues which are sufficient to ensure correct inference making.

Suppose, however, that when Person went into the room to meet Other, Other was smoking a pipe. Person would notice, i.e. select, this information immediately because it would not be congruous with the other evidence, e.g. the wearing of a dress which could be used as the basis for inferring that Other was a woman. The process of organization and inference making would become more explicit in Person's thinking because one element has interfered with the normal process of making inferences at great speed. He would be forced to consider several possible inferences. Is this a woman who is exhibitionistic in her emancipation from conventional mores? Or is it really a man who for some reason is dressed to look like a woman? The inferences would now be tentative and could be resolved only through the selection of additional information. An active search for confirmatory evidence is now necessary (Fig. 2.2).

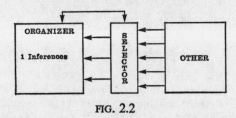

FIG. 2.2

It is because most people are prepared to make inferences on the basis of the most slender evidence that so many of our initial inferences about other people are misleading and sometimes completely false. The mistaken identity situation is a common result of false inference making. Who has not at some time mistaken a complete stranger on the street for a friend? An elderly teacher once boxed the ears of a student teacher on his first day of teaching practice for running along a corridor. He had inferred from the student teacher's age that he must be a sixth form pupil.

The actor in a social situation, then, uses in his perception what Schutz (1932) has called 'interpretive schemes' to make sense of the data. Some of these interpretive schemes are shared by all the members of a culture; others may be restricted to members of subcultures or groups; others may be unique to the individual, arising through his unique biography. Any experience is referred to these interpretive schemes as it occurs. The selectivity of perception hinges on the fact that not all the available data is *relevant* to the actor. Further some of the information that is relevant to the actor may not be available to him. Schutz (1970) speaks of 'systems of relevancies' which are related to the actor's interests, goals, roles and so on. For instance, in the example we have used so far, Person has to find out a number of things about Other before he can interact with Other in the light of his goal. It is this problem which becomes most relevant and he has to suspend his plan of interviewing Other. Having recognized this new problem, he then has to make interpretations about Other to resolve the ambiguities. To this end appropriate interpretive schemes are activated. When he has made the necessary interpretations and inferences, he can then return to his original goal, namely that of interviewing Other, and a new system of relevancies and appropriate schemes of interpretation are brought to bear.

The first step, then, is to gather as quickly as possible as much information about Other so that Person will have some basis on which to structure his relationship to Other. The primary information will be of physical order. Person will absorb instantly the basic cues of age and sex. This is such an automatic process that we rarely think about it at all unless we have the misfortune to find ourselves in a situation in which such information is not accessible to us. To be unable to determine the age and sex of Other, as occasionally happens in a telephone conversation, produces a sense of unease and an uncertainty about how to proceed with the interaction.

Once Person has acquired the basic information about Other's age and sex, which is in itself enough to provide quite an elaborate structure for their interaction, Person will seek out more subtle information about Other from the cues that Other gives off. The facial expression of Other is a major source of further information. From the face Person can discover whether Other is friendly or hostile, happy or sad. Other aspects of Other and his behaviour are selectively used by Person. Posture, gestures and other physical movements offer a rich source of information. Clothing reveals much more than Other's sex, for it can give indications about taste, wealth and social background, personality, sexual attractiveness, occupation. Uniforms convey information of one's profession and often of one's status within that profession.

When a person speaks, the richest source of potential information becomes available. The voice can convey much, purely in the way the words are spoken. Tone and volume can reveal important clues about the emotional state of the speaker, and accent may yield information about a person's origins, both regional and social, as well as his educational level. The principal source of information comes, of course, from the content of what is said. In the words he speaks Other discloses much of what Person wants to know about Other. In a new interaction it is customary for Other to provide Person with certain basic facts about himself. When Other introduces himself to Person he is giving a basic structure to the early phases of the interaction and unless Other is willing to furnish Person with relevant verbal information the interaction is unlikely to proceed smoothly.

The process of inference and perceptual organization has been brilliantly demonstrated by Solomon Asch (1946), who showed that from a list of isolated traits we experience no difficulty in describing the sort of person who is purported to possess these traits. In this classic experiment Asch read to his subjects a list of traits which were said to belong to an unknown person. One such list contained the following terms: energetic—assured—talkative—cold—ironical—inquisitive—persuasive. These subjects were then requested to write a short characterization of the person to whom these traits belonged. It is interesting that the subjects readily organized and integrated these discreet characteristics into a unified whole. One subject described the unknown person as follows:

> He seems to be the kind of person who would make a great impression upon others at a first meeting. However as time went by, his acquaintances would easily see through the mask. Underneath would be revealed his arrogance and selfishness.

The subject not only converts the bare terms into a rounded portrait, but also makes inferences about characteristics which are not actually mentioned in the original list. He does not seem to be satisfied with the pieces of evidence at his disposal but goes beyond the evidence in elaborating a more complex whole.

In a second experiment by Asch the subjects were given the following list of traits: intelligent—skilful—industrious—warm—determined—practical—cautious. Another group of subjects was given the same list except that 'cold' had replaced 'warm'. Changing one of the traits made an enormous difference to the portraits painted by the subjects. One subject given the 'warm' list wrote: 'A person who believes certain things to be right, wants others to see his point, would be sincere in argument and would like to see his point won.' In contrast, one subject with the 'cold' list wrote: 'A rather snobbish person who feels that his success and intelligence set him apart from the run-of-the-mill individual. Calculating and unsympathetic.' A change in just one of the stimulus traits can produce a deep and pervasive change in the whole impression. Indeed Asch shows that the subjects with the 'warm' list are much more likely than the subjects with the 'cold' list to see the person as exhibiting such characteristics as wise, humorous, popular, imaginative, humane, generous, happy, good-natured and sociable. It seems that knowledge of the warmth or coldness of a person leads one to make inferences about temperament (e.g. happy—unhappy) and about relations to others (e.g. popular-unpopular). All these inferences go beyond the known information.

From what has been said it is clear that people have an 'implicit personality theory' or a tendency to believe that certain traits go together (Bruner and Tagiuri, 1954). It is the implicit personality theory which is brought into action when we make inferences and when we organize our perceptions and impressions of other people. It is possible that different persons have different theories about what traits go together and develop implicit personality theories both from the common elements of our culture and from the various forms of social learning peculiar to the individual. If it is true that people vary in their theories of what traits hang together—and there is very little research on this topic—then this would have important effects on any single Person in his inferences about Other.

The second element in the organization of our perceptions of others is the process of *attribution*. On the basis of the inferences he makes about Other, Person tends to attribute certain qualities to Other. Paul Secord (1958) using photographs showed that from certain facial characteristics of Other, Person is prepared to make judgments about Other's emotional state and personality. For example, if Other is a woman with a full mouth and considerable lipstick, Person infers that she is sexy and attributes the trait of sexiness to her. If Other is a man with a dark skin, Person makes inferences which lead him to attribute to Other such qualities as hostility, boorishness, conceitedness, dishonesty, shyness and unfriendliness. Thus from cues given off by Other, Person attributes to Other what Fritz Heider has termed 'dispositional properties' or stable characteristics such as personality traits, attitudes and abilities.

The process of attribution can take place at various levels of complexity. On the simplest level Person attributes to Other one central trait such as 'reserved' or 'aggressive' which somehow seems to sum up Other. On the next level Other is described in terms of a number of traits which are congruous, which somehow seem to 'hang together'. For instance, to describe a person as having the following characteristics:

aggressive
cold
ambitious
self-confident
shrewd
mean

is likely to bring to mind a definite sort of person whose qualities are meaningfully consistent. At the most complex level Other is described in terms which are, to the outsider but not to Person, incongruous. In this case the properties of the person do not seem to 'hang together' in any obvious way. To describe a person as

kind
cautious
quick-tempered
sociable
blunt
wise

is to offer a picture of a person which is not easily conjured up in the imagination.

It seems to me rather doubtful whether people possessing a large number of completely incongruous traits actually exist. If they did, they would be monsters of inconsistency and unpredictability. The level at which we describe people is probably a function of how well we know them: the deeper our knowledge of a person, the higher will be the level of complexity with which we describe him. With someone we have met for but a few moments, for example at a party or on a bus journey, we are often left with the impression of just a single dominant trait. In the case of people we know rather better, our appreciation of the complexity of their personalities is limited by the formality of the relationship and the specificity of the situation in which we interact with them. But the people whom we know intimately can be perceived as possessing traits which are not entirely congruous because we see them in a variety of social situations and conditions in which different aspects of their personalities are brought into play. People are probably much less congruous than we imagine, in spite of the tendencies towards consistency operating on the self, for there is a strong tendency within every Person to oversimplify every Other, to try to make sense of Other in an economical and meaningful way by stressing those elements which give him consistency and by ignoring those aspects which are at variance with our picture of him.

In this respect E. M. Forster's (1927) distinction between 'flat' and 'round' people is of interest. Characters in novels he divides into these two types.

> Flat characters were called 'humours' in the seventeenth century, and are sometimes called types, and sometimes caricatures. In their purest form, they are constructed round a single idea or quality: when there is more than one factor in them, we get the beginning of the curve towards the round. The really flat character can be expressed in one sentence such as 'I will never desert Mr. Micawber.' There is Mrs. Micawber—she says she won't desert Mr. Micawber: she doesn't, and there she is.

From this description it is clear that 'flat' characters are at the lowest two levels outlined above. And flat characters, like persons who are perceived in terms of a single dominant trait or a cluster of congruous traits, have, as Forster points out, the advantage of being easily recognized and easily remembered. In novels, and perhaps in life too, such characters never need re-introducing and never need to be watched for development. They move through life unaffected by the chances and changes of this fleeting world. From the writer's (or perceiver's) point of view, all but the two or three dominant facets of them are disregarded. The recipe for their construction involves a small number of very obvious ingredients. In Forster's view almost all the characters in the novels of Charles Dickens and H. G. Wells are essentially flat.

'Round' characters, in contrast, cannot be summed up in a neat phrase (or a few traits). They wax and wane as they pass through life and they are constantly modified by their experience of it. In Forster's words: 'The test of a round character is whether it is capable of surprising in a convincing way. If it never surprises, it is flat. If it does not convince, it is a flat pretending to be round. It has the incalculability of life about it.' Forster regards Jane Austen and Russian writers such as Tolstoy and Dostoyevsky as specializing in round characters. In the works of such writers even the minor parts are essentially round.

The dispositional properties which Person attributes to Other do not consist only of personality traits. Of rather greater importance is the fact that from his inferences Person may attribute to Other certain *motives* or *intentions*. If Person sees a man rushing towards him with a dagger in his raised hand, Person is likely to attribute to the man not only the trait of anger or aggression but also certain motives such as murderous intentions. It is from these dispositional properties which Person imputes to Other that Person feels that he can 'explain' Other's behaviour. To work out a motive or intention behind Other's behaviour is to explain that behaviour. To be unable to attribute a motive or intention to Other makes Other's conduct somewhat puzzling to Person. Thus he may say, 'Other is crazy: I don't understand him at all.' We search for possible intentions and motives in order to make other people's behaviour comprehensible and meaningful. Most of the time we are able to impute definite intentions and motives to other people and most of the time our attributions correspond to Other's actual motives and intentions. But such is not always the case. One of the most common sources of the 'misunderstandings' which arise in human relationships is the attribution to Other of motives and intentions which are incorrect. The art of the confidence trickster is based on his ability to lead his prey into making false inferences and attributions of intent.

It is through the attribution of dispositional properties such as personality traits or intentions that Person is able to perceive Other's behaviour as consistent. When Person ascribes an enduring and persistent personality characteristic to Other he is drawing together and unifying a wide variety of past incidents in Other's behaviour. And once Person has created a consistent picture of Other by attributing certain dispositional properties to him, then he will tend to acquire expectations of how Other will behave in new situations in the future. Other's behaviour becomes, within limits, predictable. It is in this way that the attribution process can structure and facilitate future interaction between Person and Other. If Other has lied to and stolen from Person on several occasions, then Person will infer that Other is dishonest and he will tend to impute to Other the general characteristic of dishonesty, and expect this characteristic to manifest itself again, even though the time, place and form of its expression may be different. The attribution of dishonesty may exert a strong influence on future interaction between Person and Other in that Person may treat Other as untrustworthy.

Once Person has developed a fairly consistent picture of Other he will tend to resist new information which threatens this consistency. First impressions may be important precisely because on the basis of the initial information we create an impression of another person which is not easily changed. When Person is faced with information about Other which does not seem consistent with his impression, Person can resort to some common methods for resolving the psychological strain involved. Person can assume, for instance, that some factor unknown to Person must be influencing Other, a factor which has upset Other's normal pattern of behaviour. Person can say to himself, 'Other would never behave like that of his own free will. Someone else must be making him behave in this way.' Thus when a prisoner-of-war condemns his own side and eulogizes his captors in an enemy broadcast, his countrymen can dispel their psychological discomfort by assuming that his conversion is not genuine but the result of pressures exerted by the enemy on the prisoner. Alternatively, Person can maintain his consistent picture of Other by concluding that Other's behaviour is only apparently inconsistent and that Person himself must have misperceived or misunderstood Other's actions. It is also possible for Person simply to ignore those aspects of Other's behaviour for which he is unable to account, either because it appears to be inconsistent or because it does not appear to be governed by rational principles.

A further aspect of the attribution process is the tendency to see persons as origins of actions, to which Fritz Heider (1944) has drawn our attention. In this respect we tend to overestimate the contribution of a person to his actions and underestimate the other factors at work. Thus we tend to see the causes of a person's success or failure in his personal characteristics ('because he worked so hard' or 'because he is just bone idle') and to ignore other contributory factors in the environment. Nietzsche made the same point when he remarked that 'Success is the greatest liar.' One of the most useful contributions by sociologists of education has been to increase our knowledge of the role of the home in providing values and conditions conducive to academic attainment. Yet many teachers still hold their pupils wholly and personally responsible for their attitudes and achievements.

In his perception of Other, therefore, Person constantly attributes to Other a range of mental factors, such as traits, goals, motives, intentions and purposes, without which it is quite impossible to assign meaning to Other's conduct. This range of mental factors has been given the general name *sens* by Franz From (1971) in his most illuminating analysis of person perception derived from some ingenious experiments. In the early stages of an interaction, the *sens* may be very indefinite to begin with, requiring confirmation from subsequent actions of Other as they unfold. The *sens* frequently gains precision and confirmation in this manner, but it may happen that Person's actions cannot be given any adequate meaning with the *sens* that was first imputed. As events unfold, the *sens* may become very indefinite as it increasingly proves less valid as a means of making sense of Other's conduct. Ultimately a new *sens* emerges—often quite suddenly—and then this acts backwards, as it were, so that the earlier actions of Other are now interpreted in the light of the new *sens*. The old *sens* was preserved as long as possible; the appearance of the new *sens* provokes retrospective reinterpretations of actions which were puzzling under the old *sens* but which become entirely meaningful under the new *sens*. But the old *sens* is often not abandoned completely; rather, it is kept aside for possible future use.

On the basis of Person's selection of certain data about Other and the means by which these data are organized and interpreted through inference and attribution, Person creates what might be called his conception of Other. Whenever Person thinks of Other or interacts with him, this conception of Other is activated. This conception of Other is constructed slowly as Person's perception of Other becomes more extensive and complex. When Person believes that he knows Other very well, this conception becomes relatively stable and influences the selection and organization of any further information about Other. It is used as a basis for predicting Other's future behaviour. In its most primitive form Person's conception of Other is based on his 'first impressions' of Other. First impressions are really a temporary working hypothesis about Other. As interaction proceeds or as additional information about Other becomes available from other less direct sources, this working hypothesis can be accepted and refined or rejected and replaced (Fig. 2.3).

A crucial problem for the psychology of interpersonal perception is not simply the processes which underlie the nature of first impressions of others, but the impact these impressions have on extended interaction. Most laymen believe that first impressions count. The research on this rather basic question is limited, but there does seem to be some evidence to support the widely held belief that first impressions may have repercussions on the ensuing interaction. In this respect an experiment by Harold Kelley (1950) is particularly relevant. At the beginning of a psychology class some students at the

27

Massachusetts Institute of Technology were informed that their usual instructor was out of town and that a substitute would take his place. The students were then given, in the form of a note, some pre-information about the replacement instructor.

> Mr. —— is a graduate student in the Department of Economics and Social Science here at M.I.T. He has had three semesters of teaching experience in psychology at another college. This is his first semester teaching Ec.70. He is 26 years old, a veteran, and married. People who know him consider him to be a rather cold person, industrious, critical, practical and determined.

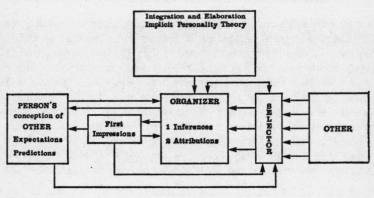

FIG. 2.3

The last set of traits in this pre-information recall the lists used by Asch in his experiments. This is indeed the source of the pre-information. For half the students in the class the pre-information contained the words 'very warm' instead of 'rather cold'. At the end of class the students were asked to rate the instructor on a number of traits and it was found that the original Asch findings on the warm–cold variable were substantially confirmed. Once again the 'warm' instructor was rated as more considerate, more informal, more sociable, more popular, better natured, more humorous and more humane than the 'cold' instructor. In this experiment the power of the warm–cold dimension to influence impressions in an interactional situation is fully supported.

But did the impression the students gained of the instructor influence their behaviour towards him? This is an important question, for if the impression we have of another person does *not* influence our behaviour towards him in any way, then the study of impression formation may be much less significant than the other experiments have indicated. Since the psychology class took the form of a leader-centred discussion, Kelley was able to record the number of times any student initiated verbal interaction with the instructor. Fifty-six per cent of the students with the 'warm' pre-information participated as against only 32 per cent of the 'cold' students. It is a striking fact that two words in the pre-information should influence the students' perception of and interaction with the instructor to such a remarkable extent. It shows that under certain circumstances our expectations about Other may be much more influential in determining our behaviour to him than Other's actual characteristics.

In the Kelley experiment a comparison of the data from two different persons who played the part of the instructor revealed that, although the warm–cold variable produced differences in the same direction for both, there were also differences in the ratings which reflected differences in the actual personalities of the instructors. It is as if the subject were making a compromise between the pre-information and the actual behaviour of the instructor. In real life it is probably true that first impressions count in the short term, but in the case of an interaction which extends over a period of time it seems likely that Person's assessments of Other are subject to constant revisions as he gains more information about Other. Probably the revisions get progressively smaller as Person consolidates his picture of Other, unless Other behaves in an unexpected way or is seen by Person in a new situation. For most of us, first impressions of another person are no more than a working hypothesis to which we temporarily subscribe, but which we are prepared to alter in the light of new information. In this sense we are all detectives of the human personality.

Impressions of others serve an important function in preparing the ground for and thus facilitating human interaction, but they also serve the function of organizing a vast amount of information that is available about others. Person cannot possibly remember all the details about Other's appearance and behaviour: to do so would be extremely wasteful. So he condenses what he has learned about Other into an 'impression' of him. In this way, impression formation has an important *economic* function. One of the most basic labour-saving devices of the human mind is the ability to organize all the incoming data into *categories*.

> To categorize is to render discriminably different things equivalent, to group the objects and events and people around us into classes, and to respond to them in terms of their class membership rather than their uniqueness. (Bruner, Goodnow & Austin, 1956)

Unless we invented categories, we could have no concepts at all. No two apples are exactly alike, but unless we invent the category of 'apple' then we must react to every apple as a unique object. Once we invent the category of 'apple' we can identify examples of the category, and thus reduce the complexity of the environment and the need for learning. Knowing that an object belongs in a category also gives advance direction of our behaviour towards an object. To know that an object is an apple is to know its physical appearance and that it is edible.

It is the same with people. When Person meets Other for the first time Person seeks to discover the information on the basis of which he can categorize Other. Is Other in the male or female category? in the young or old category? in the friend or enemy category? Once we have made these basic categorizations, we are to some extent prepared for a particular sort of interaction with Other.

Roles, which we shall examine in the next chapter, are really categories of human beings. Person's interaction with Other is considerably facilitated if he can discover the roles of Other. In fact in normal interaction we respond to others as unique persons much less frequently than we imagine, but more in terms of the mutual expectations controlling the role relationship. When Person is playing the role of customer in a store and Other the role of the assistant behind the counter, both Person and Other are unlikely to possess, or want to possess, information about the personality or the motives of each other. (Some intentions and motives are, of course, relevant within the role relationship. The customer may believe that the sales-girl is anxious to sell him a tie to increase her commission and thus suspect her comments that the tie suits him. Whether or not the sales-girl has such a motive, she will, if she infers that the customer is attributing such a motive to her, have to behave in such a way that the customer's fears are allayed.) They are able to carry on a satisfactory interaction if both customer and assistant are aware of and conform to the rules which govern their role relationship. It is the roles which structure and guide the interaction. So seeking out information about other people's roles is typical of the early stages of an interaction between strangers. The correct perception of the role relationship is often facilitated for the participants. In our example, the store assistant may wear a label on her lapel which states her own name or the name of the store so that her role is easily perceived by the customer. Uniforms of various kinds are a common method of revealing roles. Where there are no indications of role, the participants in an interaction will actively seek information about each other's roles by subtle probes or even direct questions.

Earlier we used the 'mistaken identity' situation to illustrate a point about person perception. This same situation was used by Abravanel (1962) to illustrate the importance of role factors in perception. In this experiment, subjects listened to one end of a telephone conversation. Some of the subjects were told that the speaker was a college student and others were told that he was the chairman of an academic department. The person at the other end of the line, who could not be heard, was supposed to be a college instructor. It was clear that the speaker was unhappy about the instructor's teaching. The subjects who thought that the speaker was a student thought him aggressive, ambitious and egotistical; those who thought the speaker was the chairman of the department termed him hesitant, compassionate and indecisive. This experiment is a clever demonstration of an obvious point with which we are all familiar in experience. Our categorization of Other in terms of roles exercises a profound influence on the way in which we assign meaning to Other's behaviour and attributable personality traits or motives to him. The content of Other's communication is interpreted in relation to Other's roles.

It is because of the universal human need to place other people in categories that the phenomenon of *stereotyping* arises. A social stereotype refers to a set of characteristics which are held to be common to members of a category. For example, to say that 'Germans are arrogant and aggressive' or 'Negroes are lazy and dirty' is to suggest that by virtue of his membership in an ethnic or national group a person is likely to possess certain characteristics. To say 'Professors are absent-minded' is to do the same with an occupational group.

Stereotypes are one form of categorization and generalization among humans. Like any form of categorization they may serve an important and useful function in that they reduce the need for learning and help a person to anticipate how he might react to a member of the category. The ability to categorize is one of the fundamental aspects of human intelligence and it is important that he categorizes people as well as things. The categories of 'Negroes' and 'politicians' are as essential as the categories of 'apples', 'fruits' and 'edible things'. The stereotype goes beyond categorization for it ascribes certain characteristics to members of the category and the drawback is that in so doing stereotypes become neither totally true nor totally false. To suggest that 'Spinsters are sexually frustrated' is as dangerous as saying that 'Fruits are edible'. Because one cannot put the word 'all' before most social stereotypes, they have a limited value, unless it can be shown that it is true for the vast majority of the members of the category. But since we have little evidence on the truth or falsity of most social stereotypes, they are potentially dangerous generalizations. Some stereotypes do contain some truth. For example, the stereotype that 'Jews are ambitious and industrious' could to some extent be supported by the fact that Jews, as against Protestants and Roman Catholics, are more likely to have higher achievement motivation, to be over-achievers, to enter further education, and to have higher rates of social mobility. But at the same time

31

it is doubtful whether the differences between Jews and other religious groups are of a sufficient magnitude to give the stereotype any great value in facilitating human interaction between particular individuals.

Another phenomenon of person perception, in some ways similar to stereotyping, is that of the 'halo effect'. This refers to the tendency to be generally favourable or unfavourable in one's reaction to others. Once Person has decided that Other has certain favourable characteristics, this impression misleads him into giving Other a very high rating on many other characteristics. On the other hand if Person's initial impression of Other is unfavourable, Person is likely to under-rate Other on other dimensions. The 'halo effect' is really another example of the tendency of persons to overestimate the homogeneity of other people, to perceive consistency at the expense of reality. It is also an illustration of the tendency of persons to see certain characteristics as belonging together, to see people in essentially 'flat' terms as a bundle of congruous traits. The 'halo effect' is particularly strong in interviews and rating scales, though its repeated demonstration does not seem to have affected the addiction of most organizations to the interview as the basis of selection. I can only conclude that the interview as a selection device serves a highly important function for the interviewer himself, in that it convinces *him* that he has chosen the best person, even though it may do nothing of the kind. Most interviewees are aware of the 'halo effect'. I have seen many undergraduates waiting for interviews with Unilever and I.C.I. in clean white shirts, formal ties and dark suits instead of their usual hoary sweaters and ragged jeans. Presumably they hope that their spruce appearance will lead the interviewer to attribute intelligence, efficiency, reliability, etc. to them. I don't suppose the interviewer is so easily taken in: the 'halo effect' can operate in much more subtle ways. But of course if the interviewee is an attractive member of the opposite sex, the 'halo effect' may not be so subtle after all (Fig. 2.4).

One important link in our model of person perception, which is clearly implied in the earlier exposition, must now be made explicit. Person's conception of Other is one of the most important factors affecting Person's behaviour towards Other. With reference to an interaction between Person and Other the model must be completed with the mirror image of the model—a similar model involving Other's perception of Person. Only then can we be said to have a model of *inter*personal perception. We shall consider this more fully in a later chapter devoted to a more specific analysis of social interaction processes. This chapter has been relatively little concerned with a direct discussion of the impact of perception on behaviour or with illustrations from educational situations. So it is appropriate to conclude this chapter with the examination of a concept which relates perception to behaviour and which has significant applications to teacher–pupil relations. It is the concept of the self-fulfilling prophecy.

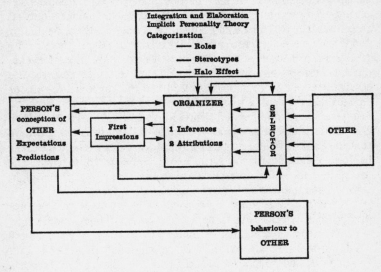

FIG. 2.4

The concept of the self-fulfilling prophecy is not new, though the most famous exposition and analysis is that of Robert Merton (1949). It is related to a wide variety of other ideas and concepts within the social sciences. Certainly interpersonal perception is highly relevant, though most analyses do not emphasize this aspect. In a memorable sentence W. I. Thomas (1928) once said, 'If men define situations as real, they are real in their consequences.' What counts in human behaviour is not so much the objective features of a situation but the way in which we perceive or define situations. For instance, it may not be true that you dislike me, but if I believe that you dislike me it will have important repercussions on my behaviour towards you. In Carl Rogers's words, 'It is the perception, not the reality, which is crucial in determining behaviour.' The relationship between perception and reality is very complex. It is not simply a question of perception being accurate, i.e. a true reflection of reality, or inaccurate, i.e. having no foundation in reality. As Lemert (1962) has shown in a brilliant paper, the beliefs of the paranoid person that he is being persecuted and excluded are by no means groundless.

We have observed that one important aspect of person perception is the development of a conception of Other which is used as a basis for developing expectations or predictions about Other's future behaviour. If we make predictions with respect to objects the predictions do not influence subsequent events. If I predict that it will rain tomorrow, my forecast does not and cannot affect the weather. In the social world, however, it may be that under certain circumstances my expectations and predictions about Other's behaviour will exert some influence on Other's subsequent behaviour. In the self-fulfilling prophecy the prediction so influences events that the prophecy comes true as a direct result of that prophecy. For example, a bank is conducting business as usual. The bank's directors and manager are confident about current business and future prospects. A rumour spreads that the bank is in difficulties and in danger of being declared insolvent. Large numbers of clients hurry to the bank to withdraw their deposits before the rumoured collapse. Because so many believe that the bank is failing and try to withdraw money at one time, the bank does indeed collapse. Or, a man is about to get married. The teasing remarks of his male friends arouse anxieties that he might prove to be impotent on his wedding night. His fears are really quite groundless but he becomes so worried about his sexual competence that he does indeed prove to be impotent on his honeymoon.

There have been a number of studies of the self-fulfilling prophecy in educational contexts, but the most famous study is that of Robert Rosenthal & Lenore Jacobson (1968), social psychologists at Harvard University. Rosenthal is concerned with the positive self-fulfilling prophecy, that is, when children improve as a result of a prediction that they will do so, though the *negative* form, whereby pupils deteriorate in work or behaviour as a result of the teacher's expectation, is obviously of at least equal educational significance. The results of Rosenthal's experiment are very complex in detail, but the main findings can be briefly summarized. The pupils of an American elementary school were given the 'Harvard Test of Inflected Acquisition'. The teachers were told that this test would single out those pupils who could be expected to make dramatic academic progress. Actually the test was simply an intelligence test. Rosenthal selected at random 20 per cent of the pupils, who, the teachers were informed, were the spurters. After the teachers were given the names of the alleged spurters no further action was taken until the pupils were all re-tested for intelligence at a later stage. If the teachers believed that the alleged spurters would indeed bloom academically then they might so influence events that the prophecy would come true. We would then have a self-fulfilling prophecy. The results supported such an interpretation. After one year the children nominated as spurters did make marked gains in intelligence. Spurters in the first grade gained on average fifteen IQ points more than did other pupils and in the second grade the spurters gained on average nine IQ points over the rest of the pupils. In these two grades one fifth of the pupils who were not nominated gained over twenty IQ points whereas al-most half the spurters did so. The spurters also made marked gains in reading as assessed by the teacher.

To demonstrate the existence of the self-fulfilling prophecy we must exclude at least two alternative explanations. First, we must exclude the possibility of coincidence or correct prediction. A child might gain in IQ not as a result of the teacher's prediction but for a wide variety of reasons quite unconnected with the teacher's predic-tion. The fact that the teacher predicts such a gain accurately does not of course mean that the prediction caused the gain. This possibi-lity seems excluded by the fact that the spurters had been nominated at random yet the gains were statistically significant. Second, we must have evidence that the children did in fact bloom. It is possible that the teacher, believing that the pupil would make dramatic academic progress, might be led to interpret the child's behaviour in line with the prediction and evaluate the child and assign grades accordingly. The possibility seems excluded by the fact that the intel-ligence test score was independent of the teacher and could not be falsified by the teacher's perception. The superiority of the spurters in reading could be explained in terms of teacher misperception, but there is little evidence in support of such bias. As Rosenthal reports, the teachers' gradings seemed to show a negative halo effect. In other words, the special children were graded by the teachers more severely than were the ordinary pupils.

We cannot take Rosenthal's finding entirely for granted in the light of methodological and statistical criticisms that have been levelled at his work (Snow, 1969; Thorndike, 1968; Taylor, 1970) and in the light of the failure of at least one replication (Claiborn, 1969). On the other hand a number of further studies are supportive of the notion of the educational self-fulfilling prophecy (Shrank, 1968 and 1970; Palardy, 1969; Burstall, 1970; Nash, 1973). For the rest of the discus-sion, however, we must assume its existence, for if such self-fulfilling prophecies do arise in educational contexts, then the real problem is the mechanics and dynamics by which the process of the self-fulfilling prophecy operates. Two main alternatives are available. It could be that the teacher, accepting the prediction that the spurters would bloom, altered her behaviour to these pupils by according them special and differential treatment, for example by devoting more of her time and attention to them. We have good reasons for supposing that once the teacher perceived the spurters in a new way she would bring her behaviour into line with her perception. The pupil might then respond to this special treatment by an appropriate improve-ment in performance. Alternatively, the explanation could be that the teacher communicates her beliefs and expectations about the spurters' ability to the pupils—and the communication of the prophecy could be achieved in very subtle ways—so that the pupils change their own beliefs about themselves and alter their behaviour in line with these new beliefs and so improve. These two alternatives are not mutually exclusive and may well occur in combination.

Rosenthal himself cannot be sure how the self-fulfilling prophecy was effected, nor can he explain why some of the nominated children made very high gains (up to sixty-nine IQ points) whilst other spurters did not (one actually lost six IQ points). Any explanation of the self-fulfilling prophecy must account for individual differences which are masked in the reporting of the average gains of the spurters. Rosenthal was unable to test the differential treatment hypothesis directly, though he cleverly uses indirect evidence to show that more time was not devoted to the spurters. Certainly the teachers themselves in their reports about the time spent with individual pupils gave no evidence for such an explanation. Rosenthal himself is inclined to the view that it is quality of the teacher–pupil interaction that varies between the two groups, for example by the teacher being more friendly and encouraging and by watching them more closely. Probably both are involved. Recent work by Silberman (1969) shows that teachers give more positive evaluations and are more receptive to pupils whom they like, whereas children who are rejected by the teacher receive a larger number of negative evaluations. Further, where the teacher expresses concern for the child there is a definite tendency to greater contact with the child, whereas when the teacher feels indifference towards the child contact is significantly reduced.

Recent support for the differential treatment hypothesis is available in the work of Brophy and Good (1970) in an intensive inter-action analysis of the behaviour of teachers and first grade elementary school pupils of whom the teacher has high expectations ('highs') or low expectations ('lows'). The highs tend to receive much greater praise, whereas the lows receive greater criticism from the teacher. The highs also initiate greater contact with the teacher. One of the most significant findings was that

the teachers consistently favored the highs over the lows in demanding and reinforcing quality performance. Despite the fact that the highs gave more correct answers and fewer incorrect answers than did the lows, they were more frequently praised when correct and less frequently criticized when incorrect or unable to respond. Furthermore, the teachers were more persistent in eliciting responses from the highs than they were from the lows. When the highs responded incorrectly or were unable to respond, the teachers were more likely to provide a second response opportunity by repeating or rephrasing the question or giving a clue than they were in similar situations with the lows.

Conversely they were more likely to supply the answer or call on another child when reacting to the lows than the highs.

Whilst there were notable individual differences between teachers in conforming to this pattern, it is still very striking that such differential treatment should emerge in relation to pupils of six years of age. As the authors comment: 'If the differential teacher treatment leads to differential reciprocal behaviour by the children, the classroom behaviour of highs and lows should become progressively more differentiated as the school year progresses.' The expectation may soon become established into a more general reputation, and as we shall discuss shortly, be formally institutionalized within the school.

As to the communication to the pupil of the teacher's changed beliefs and expectations Rosenthal has surprisingly little to say. Yet from our knowledge of social psychology certain conditions under which we might expect the prophecy to be communicated and accepted can be suggested. Following symbolic interactionism, we might hypothesize that it is those pupils who regarded the teacher as a 'significant other' who would be the ones most inclined to take to themselves the teacher's attitude to them. It is known that many pupils do see the teacher as a significant other. Wright (1962) for example, has shown that fourth-year secondary modern children, who are not usually thought to be the most teacher oriented of pupils, do see the teacher as closer (than parents) to their ideal self in such dimensions as clever, skilful, persevering or knowledgeable. Brookover, Thomas & Patterson (1964) show that pupils perceive teachers' estimates of their general ability as closer to their own than the estimates of parents or peers. We might predict, then, that the more a pupil perceives the teacher as a significant other, especially with reference to his ability, the more likely he would be to accept those expectations communicated by the teacher. Thus given that the prophecy is communicated we have a means of explaining the differential response of pupils to that communication.

A second hypothesis to explain the acceptance of a communicated expectation would involve the pupil's conception of his own ability and the teacher's conception of the pupil's ability. We might hypothesize that where the teacher has a clear and stable conception of the child's ability he would be less susceptible to accepting new ideas about the child's ability. The situation in Rosenthal's experiment is very unusual in that psychologists intrude and give an authoritative statement about the pupil's ability to develop intellectually at a dramatic rate. Information of this sort and with such authority is not usually given to teachers. But it does not seem unreasonable to suppose that where the teacher did not have a fixed conception of the child's ability, the more readily the teacher would accept such information. We have no evidence on the degree to which the teachers accepted Rosenthal's own communication of the prophecy about the spurters. The prophecy may well not have been accepted with reference to all the spurters *in toto*. We might further hypothesize that where the child's conception of his own ability is relatively unstable, he will be more open to accepting the teacher's belief about him once it is communicated. Rosenthal recognizes these possibilities, though he does not develop them, for he introduces them as an explanation of the fact that the self-fulfilling prophecy was much more effective among the younger children in the first two grades (six to eight years of age). He argues that the experimental conditions may have been more effective in the case of the younger pupils simply because their youth makes them easier to change than older ones. Later, he suggests that the younger pupils would also have less well established reputations in the school. This would mean that the teacher would be more susceptible to accepting the prediction from Rosenthal in the case of these children than in the case of pupils about which the teacher had firmly established views.

On this basis we can hypothesize the conditions in the Rosenthal experiment under which the self-fulfilling prophecy is most likely and least likely to be effected. It is most likely to occur if

(*a*) the teacher has an unstable conception of the pupil's ability (or a stable conception that is congruent with Rosenthal's prediction);

(*b*) the pupil has an unstable conception of his own ability (or a stable conception that is congruent with the teacher's conception of his ability);

(*c*) the pupil perceives the teacher as a significant other.

The self-fulfilling prophecy is least likely to occur if

(*a*) the teacher has a stable conception of the pupil's ability and this conception is incongruent with Rosenthal's prediction;

(*b*) the pupil has a stable conception of his ability and this conception is congruent with that of the teacher and incongruent with Rosenthal's prediction;

(*c*) the pupil perceives the teacher as a significant other.

The concept of the self-fulfilling prophecy is open to further refinements. Merton himself noted the 'suicidal prophecy' or the anti-self-fulfilling prophecy—a prophecy which accurately predicts its own opposite. Rosenthal also recognizes this possibility, but does not develop it in educational terms. Yet it may be a very important variant form. Let me illustrate from my own experience. At school I was not very able in Latin, a subject which like most of my fellow pupils I disliked. The teacher believed that many of us would fail in the 'O' level examination, so as examination day drew near, he divided us into two groups. A third of the class was felt to have a chance and were seated at the front for special tuition. The rest, who seemed certain to fail, were relegated to the back to get on with their own work. I was a member of this latter group. But I was extremely annoyed at the teacher's treatment of me, feeling that I had been unjustly rejected and insulted. I was determined to pass the examination, to prove to myself that I could do it. In the event I passed. I suspect that if I had not been put in the failing group I would indeed have failed. In a very real sense the teacher's prediction that I would fail caused me to pass.

Our analysis of the processes of person perception and the self-fulfilling prophecy have some clear educational implications. When Person perceives Other a process of categorization is involved and on the basis of this categorization Person develops expectations and predictions about Other's future conduct. When teachers perceive pupils they inevitably categorize them. We shall examine the basis of this categorization in a later chapter. Here I wish to stress that whenever a teacher categorizes a pupil as 'good' or 'succeeding' or 'bad' or 'failing', he is making a prediction that congruent behaviour is to be anticipated in the future. Teachers then have to beware of two dangers. The first consists in the process of categorizing itself and the second consists in the communication of the predictive element of the categorization with its potentiality for stimulating a self-fulfilling prophecy.

One of the principal dangers of categorizing is that once the teacher has categorized a pupil he is likely to resist having to re-categorize the pupil. This is normal and natural in that most categorizations are reasonably accurate and economical and permit the development of a stable conception of Other which will facilitate interaction. We need large amounts of corrective information before we are willing to allow some of the incongruent information which does not fit our conception of Other through the filter and set about the necessary revisions in our conception of Other. Teachers are no exception. Once a pupil has been categorized as 'good' or 'bad' then it may require marked deviation on the part of the pupil from the teacher's conception of him before the teacher is willing to revise this conception. When teachers appoint a Head Girl they do so on the grounds that she has been firmly categorized as 'good' by certain criteria. She will have to misbehave very seriously before the teachers will change their view and revise their categorization. Early evidence that she is not living up to expectations will be misperceived or discounted. As we say, allowances are made. In effect, she 'gets away with things'. A similar process affects 'bad' pupils. Once categorized, the bad pupil can be caught in a heads-I-win-tails-you-lose situation. The consistently rude boy who is now being polite is regarded with suspicion by the teacher; his intentions and motives come under

39

scrutiny. His politeness may be interpreted as 'taking the mick' out of the teacher or as evidence that a crime is being concealed. His motives are regarded as ulterior motives. The boy who turns in a first class piece of work when normally his work is appallingly poor is suspected of copying. When such pupils behave 'out of character' and thus 'out of category' the teacher's reaction may well be inhibiting the process of change which superficially the teacher is anxious to promote. What could be more devastating for a lazy pupil to find that, when he does respond to the teacher's appeal for change, his efforts are greeted with suspicion and disbelief? Would it not be reasonable for the pupil to conclude that the effort is not worth making since this is a game he can never win?

The teacher, then, should try to avoid making categorizations of pupils which are premature or too sharp and final. He must constantly be open to the possibility of re-categorization. Also he must be suspicious of those forces which encourage him to categorize or seem to confirm categorizations to the point where the categorization becomes virtually permanent. Staff-room gossip about pupils, record cards, intelligence quotients, all these can easily be used as evidence in support of a categorization which, however 'accurate', may become static. For once the categorization becomes static it influences the teacher's behaviour in a profound way and is easily communicated to the pupil with the obvious danger of initiating a self-fulfilling prophecy. All information which is at the teacher's disposal and which from one point of view serves to assist the teacher in helping the pupil to learn is information which can potentially have the reverse effect. There was once a Psychological Myth which suggested that knowledge of a child's IQ would be a valuable aid to the teacher. The dangers of making unwarrantable inferences from the IQ were soon forgotten. An IQ tells us that this child can do at least as well as this on a particular test at a particular time under specific conditions. In practice the IQ was not treated as such. In more recent years we have become prey to what I call the Sociological Myth. Sociologists have amassed a considerable amount of evidence which demonstrates how many factors in the home and community affect the child's capacity to profit from education. The research is usually taught in some depth to student teachers, in the hope that such knowledge will broaden their understanding of the environmental influences affecting the child's behaviour, attitudes and attainments in school. It may serve as a counter-weight to the teacher's tendency to ascribe the pupil's difficulties in learning to 'laziness' or 'awkwardness' which may pay insufficient attention to the child's background. But the way in which teachers use this knowledge is not by any means always in accordance with the intentions of the sociology lecturers. In the Sociological Myth the evidence is distorted by teachers into two propositions: that if the child comes from a 'bad' home, this is a sufficient explanation of the child's difficulties in school; and that because these environmental factors are beyond the school's control, there is little the teacher can do to help the child. Once the teacher has accepted the Sociological Myth he is led to undervalue the extent to which he can rectify deficiencies originating in the child's home environment and to ignore the contribution which life in school may itself make to the child's difficulties.

The teacher must also beware of those organizational devices of schools which are associated with categorization. Streaming is obviously one such device. Once the pupil is assigned to a stream the teacher tends to perceive him on occasions in terms of the collective category of the stream rather than in terms of his individual charactersitics. The streaming system encourages the making of generalizations about streams which are then applied to individual pupils in that stream. Expectations about streams soon become expectations of individuals. As has been indicated in several studies (Douglas, 1964; Jackson, 1964; Partridge, 1966; Hargreaves, 1967; Lacey, 1970) children in the top streams are expected to work and behave well whereas children in lower streams are expected to misbehave and to make little academic progress. Sometimes this is associated with differential treatment of different streams, especially when the 'better' teachers are assigned almost exclusively to the higher streams and these pupils are given privileges and status which is denied to the pupils in lower streams. In such a situation it is hardly surprising if the pupils take to themselves the attitudes, expectations and predictions exhibited by the teachers and institutionalized in the organizational structure. A self-fulfilling prophecy seems almost inevitable. Nor are these matters easily rectified. Ability grouping within an unstreamed class poses exactly the same sort of dangers. Indeed they may operate here in a much more subtle way.

This has been well documented in Rist's (1970) observational study over a two-year period of the pupils in the early grades of an American kindergarten. When these children arrived at school, the teacher made a series of subjective evaluations of them in terms of each pupil's likelihood of becoming a 'success' or a 'failure' in school. This affected the assignment of the pupils by the teacher to one of three tables, with the 'fast learners' at table 1 and the 'slow learners' at table 3.

Those children who closely fit the teacher's 'ideal type' of the successful child were chosen for seats at Table 1. Those children that had the least 'goodness of fit' with her ideal type were placed at the third table. The criteria upon which a teacher would construct her ideal type of the successful student would rest in

41

her perception of certain attributes in the child that she believed would make for success. . . . Those attributes most desired by educated members of the middle class became the basis for her evaluation of the children. Those who possessed these particular characteristics were expected to succeed while those who did not could not be expected to succeed. Highly prized middle class status for the child in the classroom was attained by demonstrating ease of interaction among adults; high degree of verbalization in Standard American English; the ability to become a leader; a neat and clean appearance; coming from a family that is educated, employed, living together and interested in the child; and the ability to participate well as a member of a group.

Once the pupils had been categorized or typed, the typical pattern of differential treatment ensued. The pupils at table 1 sat closest to the teacher, occupied the majority of her teaching time and received more rewarding comments. As these pupils internalize and identify with the teacher's attitudes, they begin to despise and reject those pupils at the other tables, who are 'failures' in the teacher's eyes, and begin to refer to them as 'stupid' and 'dumb' (see Hargreaves (1967) for a secondary school equivalent). In a study of British primary schools, Nash (1973) has shown that pupils quickly recognize the hierarchical structure of within-class groupings and pick up their relative academic status in comparison with other pupils.

The more extreme a categorization is, the more dangerous it becomes. Once the teacher has concluded that the pupil is exceptionally 'bad' or 'good', the more likely the teacher is to convey his conviction and its associated expectations to the pupil with the attendant risks of fulfilment. Further, extreme categories like extreme attitudes are the most resistant to change. Rosenthal notes this effect in his own research.

After one year it was the children of the *medium* track [i.e. stream] who showed the greatest expectancy advantage, though the children of the other tracks were close behind. After two years, however, the children of the medium track very clearly showed the greatest benefits from having had favourable expectations held of their intellectual performance . . . It was the children of the medium track who showed the greatest expectancy advantage in terms of reading ability . . . Children of the medium track were the most advantaged by having been expected to bloom, this time in terms of their perceived intellectual curiosity and lessened need for social approval.

and further:

It seems surprising that it should be the more average child of a lower-class school who stands to benefit more from his teacher's improved expectation.

It is not at all surprising when we remember that it is the average child in the middle stream who escapes extreme categorization in the teacher's estimation and in the organizational structure. On the basis of our earlier theorization we would expect the teacher's conception of the pupil's ability to be more open to suggestion from Rosenthal in the case of the middle track. Also the middle stream pupil does not place himself in an extreme category, so it is this pupil rather than the high or low stream pupil who will be most open to the acceptance of a new expectation communicated by the teacher.

Rosenthal also has evidence of the teacher's unwillingness to revise categories when the change in the pupil is incongruent with the categorization. Again, we should expect the pupils in the extreme categories to be most affected. Rosenthal reports that the more pupils in the highest stream who had been nominated as spurters gained in IQ score, the more favourably they were rated by the teachers. Their nomination as spurters and their high stream status were congruent with the teachers' expectations of them, so when they improved they were rated favourably. By contrast the low stream pupils who had not been nominated as spurters met with a different teacher reaction. The more they gained in IQ the more negatively they were viewed by their teachers, for such change was quite incongruent with the teachers' expectations of them. It seems that when teachers categorize their pupils either in their own minds or as part of an organizational differentiation they must make a special attempt not to consolidate or communicate such categorizations. All teachers are committed to the improvement of their children. It seems that improvements can occur, even dramatically and contrary to the evidence, if the teacher can go on believing that the potentiality for improvement is always there within the child waiting to be released. And an important part of promoting the release of these potentialities consists in the teacher's communication of his faith in the pupil to the pupil.

Recommended reading

FRANZ FROM, *Perception of Other People*, Columbia University Press, 1971.

D. A. PIDGEON, *Expectation and Pupil Performance*, N.F.E.R., 1970.

R. C. RIST, 'Student social class and teacher expectations: the self-fulfilling prophecy in ghetto education', *Harvard Educational Review*, vol. 40, 1970, pp. 411–51.

R. ROSENTHAL & L. JACOBSON, *Pygmalion in the Classroom*, Holt, Rinehart & Winston, 1968.

3 Roles

A few years ago when I was having a drink in a pub on a hot summer's evening I struck up a conversation with another man at the bar. The conversation turned to a recent case of a murderer who, the court had decided, was insane. The man informed me that in his view all psychologists were outright charlatans, using as evidence the part played by psychologists at this trial. As a psychologist, I was interested in his opinion, especially as up to this point I had regarded him as an intelligent and interesting person. The threat to my self-esteem was simultaneously a threat to my favourable first impression of him.

'The trouble with psychologists,' he said, 'is that they always dehumanize human beings. They don't treat people as people at all. To the psychologists, a person is nothing more than a *type*—a neurotic, a psychopath and that sort of thing. They are so busy putting us all into little boxes that we cease to be responsible and unique individuals.'

I sympathized and we discussed the nature of the human sciences for some time. Several drinks and two hours later we were generally in agreement, though I suspect it was more a function of the drink than of our arguments. Initially the man had taken a very narrow view of human behaviour. Although each individual is indeed unique he does possess certain characteristics which he shares in common with all or many other individuals. Further, human behaviour is, within limits, regulated in a number of ways. Social scientists, whether they be psychologists, sociologists or anthropologists, look for these regularities. One aspect which my drinking companion failed to take into account is that human behaviour takes place within structured situations and it is very doubtful whether we can say much about the unique individual unless we can analyse the structures within which such a person thinks, feels and acts. The individuality of a man is achieved within a social environment, so to explain the individual we must, amongst other things, consider the structure of the social system in which he operates.

All social systems, from the small unit such as the family to the large unit such as a nation, consist of a complex structure of inter-related *positions*. These positions are really categories of persons with certain similar attributes who hold certain structured relationships with members of other positions. To say 'mother' is to describe how a certain position which can be occupied only by females is related in a particular way to another position, 'child'. Some of the positions occupied by people are *ascribed*, that is to say, a person occupies a position quite independently of his wishes or accomplishments. For example, age, sex, family and race are ascribed positions. Most people cannot change their age, sex, family or race, however much they might like to do so. It is very rare for a person to be able to change his sex and it is unknown for a person to change his age or his biological parents. It is equally impossible for a person to change his race, though he may sometimes be able to convince others that his race is not what it actually is, as in the case of the light-skinned Negro who can 'pass as white'. Other positions are *achieved* and depend on the qualities or abilities of the individual. A man's occupation, for example, may be largely a reflection of his own attainments. In practice, of course, it is difficult to make a clear distinction between ascribed and achieved positions, because many positions are the result of a fusion of the two elements. A person's occupation in Western society is related not only to his personal accomplishments but also to the social class of his parents, his age, his sex and his race.

These positions are quite independent of particular individual persons. The term 'doctor' is quite meaningful without thinking of 'Doctor Smith'. The position persists despite particular incumbents. Individuals become old and die, but the position of 'old woman' is not very much affected by them. That is why we speak of people *occupying* a position, as if it were a seat in a waiting room being constantly filled and emptied by widely different individuals over time. Most people occupy a very large number of positions both simultaneously and consecutively. In addition to the basic positions of age, sex, social class and race, we occupy a multiplicity of positions such as neighbour, colleague, friend, committee member, driver, customer, patient and so on. Some of these positions are much more important to the incumbent than others. Age, sex, family and occupational positions are obviously much more central to a person's self-identity than others, such as the positions of neighbour or patient, because they are much more pervasive and permanent in that incumbents spend more of their lives in direct occupation of the positions. One is a woman all the time, but only a small proportion of one's time is likely to be spent in the position of committee member.

The concept of position is a fundamental one in sociology, where one major concern has been to examine and codify the ways in which these positions are inter-related in various social systems, such as families, organizations, tribes and nations. Another problem of interest to the sociologist has been the *functions* of these positions, or the part they play in, and the contribution they make to, the social system as a whole. The findings and theories of sociologists are of great importance to social psychologists, but as we shall see shortly, the social psychologist has interests of a rather different sort.

The concept which is closely allied to that of position is the concept of *role*, which is perhaps the main concept which offers a potential link between the too frequently estranged disciplines of sociology and psychology. Like many basic concepts in the human sciences, role lacks any clear definition to which the leading writers subscribe. In this book we shall use the concept of role in a broad way to refer to behavioural expectations associated with a position. That is to say, attached to any position are a set of expectations about what behaviour is appropriate to the person occupying the position, who is often referred to as the actor. Thus the concepts of position and role are bound together by definition and one might use the term position-role to refer to the whole complex, the position itself and the behavioural expectations attached to it. Consider the position of *mother*. In our society there are a number of expectations which most people share about how a mother should behave. It is expected, for instance, that she will love her children, look after their bodily and emotional needs to the best of her ability, take care of them when they are ill or in need, encourage them to acquire moral values appropriate to the culture and so on. There are also expectations about what she should not do—a mother is not expected to be cruel to her children or to neglect them.

Role, then, refers to prescriptions about the behaviour of a person occupying a given position, a set of guide-lines which direct the behaviour of the role incumbent or the actor. Roles consist of sets of expectations. But what of the actual behaviour of the actor? We shall call the behaviour of an actor in a given position-role his *role performance* which, as we shall see, may or may not conform to the expectations associated with the position. There are mothers who do indeed neglect their children. It is because some individuals do not conform to the expectations that we must distinguish role from role performance.

The fact that all positions within a social system are related to other positions has important consequences for the position-role complex. Many positions have what may be termed a *complementary role* with which the position is specially related. A mother, for instance, is primarily linked with the complementary positions of sons and daughters. Likewise, husbands have wives, doctors have patients, teachers have pupils. In each case the two form a role partnership; the positions make sense only in terms of the complementary position. Can we conceive of a doctor without the concept of a patient, of a teacher without pupils?

The occupant of a complementary position-role, the role partner, plays a very important part in defining the role associated with a position. It is his expectations which make a highly significant contribution to the content of a role. There are three basic reasons for this. First, it is toward the complementary position-role that an actor principally directs his role performance. A doctor spends most of his time performing his role as a doctor in relation to his patients. Similarly, a teacher directs most of his role performance to his pupils. So the expectations of the main role partner tend to assume a special significance. Second, because much of an actor's role performance is directed to him, the role partner can, to varying degrees, constrain the actor to fulfil his expectations by rewarding him when he conforms to the expectations and punishing him when he deviates. For example, a patient whose doctor fails to fulfil his expectations can seek medical attention elsewhere. Third, the nature of the role relationship between role partners is so structured that the two actors are bound together in a special way. Associated with every position are *duties* (or obligations) and *rights* (or privileges). But the duties of the actor are the rights of his role partner, and the rights of the actor are the duties of his role partner. For example, a doctor has a duty to his patient to give him the best possible medical attention and advice, and it is the patient's right to expect this. The doctor has a right to expect the patient to follow his advice scrupulously and this is the duty of the patient.

Yet the complementary role partner is not the *only* role partner, nor the only or necessarily the most important source of role expectations. Most roles are linked to a number of other position-roles, referred to by Merton (1957) as the *role-set*. The teacher's complementary role partner is the pupil, but the teacher is linked to other role partners, such as the headteacher, colleagues, pupils' parents, the chief education officer, the school governors, the education welfare officer, the school caretaker. When the teacher interacts with such persons he does not cease to be performing his teacher role. For the teacher, in common with many position-roles, has an extensive role-set which involves him in a wide range of social relationships. With each different role partner he behaves in a readily distinguishable way. In all of them he is performing his teacher role.

Every role partner from the role-set has expectations about how the teacher should behave towards him. Headmasters and pupils do not expect to be treated in the same way by the teacher. But in addition each role partner usually has expectations about how the teacher should behave towards the other role partners. For example, a head-teacher has not only expectations about how the teacher should behave towards him, but also expectations about how the teacher is supposed to behave toward the pupils, other members of staff, parents, governors and so on. It is unlikely that all members of the role-set will have precisely the same expectations concerning each of the teacher's role relationships. Each member of the role-set is likely to have more elaborate expectations for some role relationships than for others. A related phenomenon is that the expectations of some role partners will exert more influence on the teacher's conception of his role performance than will other role partners. (And it does not follow that the role-set members with the most elaborate expectations exercise the greatest influence.) Three of the main role relationships that make up the teacher role and their connection with the principal role partners in the teacher's role-set are outlined in Figure 3.1. If we charted all the teacher's role relationships in relation to a more complete role-set it would be clear that the concept of the 'teacher's role' is remarkably complex.

A position-role, then, is linked to a number of other position-roles, the incumbents of which have expectations about the actor's be-

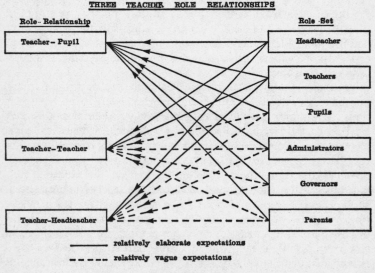

THREE TEACHER ROLE RELATIONSHIPS

FIG. 3.1

haviour towards all the other role partners. It is obvious that the whole body of expectations making up the role is likely to contain some conflicting elements. For this, and other reasons, most actors do not and cannot entirely fulfil the expectations associated with the position they occupy. It is in considering the situations in which an actor experiences difficulty in conforming to the expectations that make up his role that we discover one of the principal values of the concept of role. All these situations can be subsumed under the term *role strain*, or its alternative name of *role conflict*. It is not possible to discuss the innumerable types of known role strain—and there are doubtless many types still to be discovered—but we shall confine ourselves to some basic forms.

One form of role strain arises when an actor simultaneously occupies two positions whose roles are incompatible. A good example is the military chaplain. He is occupying the position of priest and officer at the same time. An officer is expected to be rather distant from the enlisted men with whom his relations must be rather formal. But a priest is expected to be a highly approachable person with whom one can discuss personal problems in a warm and familiar relationship. The military chaplain has the problem of reconciling the incompatibility between the two roles. Another example is the teacher whose own son or daughter is in his class. As a father he is expected to be warm and personal in his relationship to his children, but as a teacher he is usually expected to hold a more formal relationship with his pupils.

Role strain of a different sort arises when there is a lack of consensus among the expectations that make up a role. Such dissensus takes a variety of forms. One of the most important contributions to the content of a role is the actor himself. Yet it is not uncommon to find a lack of role consensus among the occupants of a position themselves. Among teachers there exists a variety of opinions about certain basic aspects of the teacher's role, such as the nature of the relationship between the teacher and his pupils. 'Traditional' and 'progressive' are examples of the ill-defined labels we attach to different role conceptions within the teaching profession. Musgrove & Taylor (1965, 1969) have shown that there are different role conceptions of teachers working within various segments of the educational system. The teachers involved in this research were asked to rank six objectives as they valued them. These aims were Moral Training, Instruction in Subjects, Social Training, Education for Family Life, Social Advancement, and Education for Citizenship. Grammar school teachers were found to have a much more restricted conception of their role than teachers in modern schools, in that they tended to reject a greater number of the educational objectives as 'none of their business'. Although teachers in all types of schools conceived their role primarily in intellectual and moral terms, placing greatest weight on Instruction in Subjects and Moral Training, there were some interesting differences between grammar and modern school teachers. Eighty-six per cent of the male grammar school teachers ranked Instruction in Subjects first or second compared with 63 per cent of the Modern school teachers. The modern school male teachers were much more likely to include 'social' elements in their role than their grammar school colleagues. Forty-two per cent of the modern school men rated Social Training first or second and 74 per cent put Moral Training first or second. The relevant figures for the grammar school men are 20 and 60 per cent respectively. These differences in role conception among teachers probably reflect differences in the *ethos* of different types of secondary school, differences in the characteristics of the pupils they serve, and differences in the background and training of the teachers.

A different type of role strain emerges when the lack of consensus is not among the actors but among one of the role partners. Musgrove (1961) has shown that parents in different social classes have different conceptions of certain aspects of the teacher's role. One of the areas which Musgrove investigated was parental expectations of the teacher relating to the child's behaviour. Working-class parents are much more likely than middle-class parents to place responsibility on the school for training the child, especially in respect of good behaviour, obedience, respect for elders, manners, honesty, truthfulness and cleanliness. Middle-class parents tend to emphasize the responsibility of the home in such training.

A particular severe form of role strain has its roots in a conflict between an actor's conception of his role and a role partner's conception of that role. In short, A and B have divergent conceptions of A's role. Often this conflict is bilateral: A and B have different conceptions of both A's role and B's role. In such circumstances it becomes very difficult for either actor to sustain a very adequate role performance toward his role partner. A good illustration of such role strain is provided in Leila Berg's (1968) study of the famous Risinghill School affair. The headmaster, Michael Duane, had a 'progressive' conception of the roles of headteacher and teacher which conflicted with the role conceptions of some of the teachers on his staff, and with other role partners.

Mr Duane felt his duty was more to his pupils than to his staff. Sometimes a teacher became upset, and wanted to be put first; then the teacher didn't want impartial fairness, but comfort.

many of the staff did not want discussion—they wanted to be 'told'; and secondly they wanted to be led in a completely different direction from the way Mr Duane was going.

The administrators wanted someone who would keep a school quiet and orderly, a man who would only have to stroll through the playground and you could hear a pin drop; and the politicians wanted someone who could be manipulated or who at least would show he was grateful to be chosen.

The inspector cold shouldered the child-centred approach, which since this policy is rarely applied in state schools, needed help, and spent considerable time with the traditionalists, whom he approved of and with whom he sympathized.

How could Inspector Macgowan ever co-operate with Mr Duane without going against his own convictions? Wasn't there bound to be antagonism—manifest antagonism—between a man who believed that 'six of the best would cure almost any disciplinary problem' and a man who believed corporal punishment was brutal and encouraged brutality, between a man who disapproved of informality between head and staff, and between head and children, and a man who thought life could only be lived on terms of friendliness . . . ?

Sometimes role strain may arise because the expectations of different role partners conflict with one another. The deputy head-teacher is particularly susceptible to this form of role strain. The head may expect the deputy to be loyal to him; to be his executive officer who carries out the head's policies among the staff; to be an informer on staff gossip. The staff, on the other hand, may expect the deputy to be loyal to them; to fight for their views and policies with the head; to be their informer on the head's intentions.

Another variation of this theme is the role strain which derives from incompatible expectations held by a single role partner. This sounds a rather unlikely situation, in that the role partner must be to some extent inconsistent to make conflicting demands. Yet it is a common occurrence. In the teaching situation the pupils usually expect the teacher to help them to pass the examinations successfully but they also expect to be set minimal amounts of homework. Sometimes this strain takes the form of the 'heads-I-win-tails-you-lose' game, as in the case of teachers who complain that the headmaster is autocratic and domineering, but when he becomes more democratic accuse him of failing to make important decisions or to give a lead or to take responsibility.

Role strain of a different sort arises when the expectations are unclear. Where there is a lack of clarity in the role expectations the actor is uncertain how he ought to behave. Roles vary in the degree of clarity of the expectations, but even in the case of roles where the expectations seem very explicit and specific the actor is likely to find himself in an unexpected or novel situation where the expectations become unclear, diffuse or ambiguous. Many of the expectations of the teacher's role are of a very general order and it is often unclear which expectations should apply in a given situation and which expectations should be given priority.

Many roles, which may not in themselves be usually lacking in clarity, are perceived as unclear when the actor assumes the position for the first time. When a child first enters school he may lack even a basic knowledge of the expectations of the pupil role, especially if he has received no nursery education and if he comes from a working-class home where, relative to the middle-class child, he is less likely to have received preparation for this new role. For a time he will call his teacher 'mother' and expect maternal treatment from the teacher. Part of the child's early reluctance to go to school may derive from the strain he experiences in learning and adjusting to this new role. The difficulties arising from lack of role clarity are often mitigated by the introduction of special training courses or orientation sessions.

The last type of role strain we shall discuss has its roots in the personal qualities of the actor which make it difficult for him to perform the role. An actor may lack an attribute which is essential to an adequate role performance. A man with little dexterity is likely to be an unhappy and unsuccessful watchmaker. Similarly a teacher who never got beyond 'O' level Latin is unlikely to make a success of teaching classics to the sixth form. As a person with neither ability nor interest in any form of sport, I was horrified to discover on arrival at the school of my first teaching appointment that I had been appointed House Athletics Master. Often the actor's values, attitudes and personality may interfere with role performance. Many agnostic and atheist teachers consent to teach religious education only because they are pressured to do so by the headteacher. A lack of organizing ability or interpersonal skills in a headteacher is likely to produce administrative chaos or frictions with his teachers because of his inability to meet their role expectations of him.

Essentially this form of role strain is a conflict between the self and the role. This is a complex area since we know that roles often contribute to and form part of one's self-image. In general we strive towards maintaining congruence between self and role, so when we move into a new position-role we often change or modify certain aspects of our self-image in order to bring self into line with role. Attitudes are one important link between self and role that can be modified to enhance self-role congruence. Liebermann (1956) has shown that when industrial workers become foremen or shop stewards they change many of their attitudes accordingly. The workers who became foremen became more favourable to management and less favourable to the Union. New shop stewards followed the reverse trend. Interestingly when some of the foremen had to be demoted because of reduction in staff they reverted to their original attitudes.

Most teachers teach those subjects which they have chosen to teach and for which they are qualified by their training, and throughout their careers they maintain an expertise in their subject which makes them superior in achievement to their pupils. An exception, however, is the teacher of physical education. As he grows older, he may discover that his physical skills are on the decline and that he is rapidly being surpassed by his pupils. He loses the attributes which he regards as necessary to an adequate role performance. Thus we meet the tragedy of the worn-out games teacher as described by Terson (1967).

I'll tell you how it happens. You're eighteen, you were in the school cricket team, or football team, or this and that team, or you were a genius at every sport except snooker. You were clean living and healthy, you could swim the 100 metres in some time that is good for the 100 metres, or you could bowl spinners or dribble down the left wing at outside left. The world was open. You could have played for Newcastle United Reserves, or been on the ground staff of Hampshire, or gone in for boxing; but no, you had intelligence as well and your father was a pitman or railway clerk and wanted his son secure and 'professional', so you went into teachers' training college. Here you had three blissful years; you jumped about in the gym, you somersaulted on the trampoline, you were watched for style, under water, through the observation glass in the swimming pool, you got drunk, sang Rugby songs, you jeered at the History students or English specialists, you were banned from the college drama festival for jeering at something you did not understand, you brought back pub signs from Bristol, Cheltenham, or Wolverhampton when you played away, you gloried in your strength, you got all the girls. You usually left with a pregnant girl.

. . . Then you were among the kids. They didn't care for your bygone feats, you were an old man with them anyway. You tried to keep up the Saturday afternoon football, but that wore off with your worries and pram-pushing. In two years you refereed 63 major football matches and 184 house matches. You jeered because the school records on Sports Day were not a patch on what you could do at their age.

. . . Then suddenly, last summer, you weren't as fit as you used to be and you won't retire until you're sixty-five and the other blokes in the other subjects are streets ahead. One day soon, that kid in 3A is going to outrun you, or beat you to a tackle, or knock you for six, and jeer 'Come on, Sir?' And you'll say, 'Ah, but I'm an old man, I'm past it.'

It is for this reason that many teachers of physical education like to keep one foot in the 'academic' subject departments, in which they can spend an increasing proportion of their time as their physical skills wane. It may also account for the disproportionate number of physical education teachers who apply for courses leading to an Advanced Diploma or a Master's degree in Education. For to change his expertise is one of the best ways of changing his role, and a further qualification in educational studies is the most obvious means by which he can gain entry to a College of Education as a lecturer in education. Such a role change would also solve the P.E. teacher's restricted career mobility, since it is well known that the P.E. teacher's 'Head of Department allowance' is invariably of a less substantial order than in the case of 'academic' subjects.

To summarize, we have distinguished eight basic types of role strain. An actor may be said to be in a situation of role strain when:

1 he simultaneously occupies two positions whose roles are incompatible.
2 there is a lack of consensus among the occupants of a position about the content of a role. ($A_1A_2A_3$ ... lack of consensus about the role associated with position A.)
3 there is a lack of consensus among the occupants of one of the complementary role positions. ($B_1B_2B_3$ ... lack of consensus about role A.)
4 his conception of his own role conflicts with the expectations of a role partner. (A and B have different conceptions of A's role.)
5 the various role partners have conflicting expectations. (B, C and D have conflicting conceptions of A's role.)
6 a single role partner has incompatible expectations.
7 the role expectations are unclear.
8 he lacks the qualities required for adequate role performance.

Role strain is obviously a very common occurrence and there are probably very few roles which are not to some degree liable to one or more of the conflicts we have examined. As an actor performs his role he is likely to be involved in several types of role strain, and sometimes to experience several forms simultaneously, though the type and severity of the role strain concerned will vary with the situations in which the role is performed. Why, then, are we not constantly suffering from the dilemmas, confusions, and conflicts which the various types of role strain seem to imply?

The main reason which accounts for our ability to perform roles with little discomfort despite the role strains involved is that there are various mechanisms which an actor can use to resolve or reduce role strain. If an actor is simultaneously occupying two positions with roles which are likely to conflict he can solve such a conflict by giving one of the roles a priority over the other. Thus a working mother will usually give priority to her mother role when her child is sick, and her occupational role takes second place. When a teacher has his own son in his class he may treat his son like any other pupil and thus give the teacher–pupil role relationship priority over the father–son relationship. Even within a single role there is likely to be a hierarchy of obligations which dictate which expectation is to be accorded priority. Thus a teacher will tell his class that he is sorry that he cannot spend the lesson reading a play, which he knows the children want, because he must give them practice in comprehension passages to prepare them for the examination.

A common solution is to conform to the expectations of the role partner with the greatest power. If the actor were to conform to the least powerful role partner then he would have to forego the relatively larger rewards and incur the relatively greater punishments at the disposal of the most powerful partner. To conform to the expectations of the most powerful role partner is common sense in that it is the path of maximum gain and minimum cost. Thus a teacher is more likely to conform to the expectations of the headteacher rather than the pupils' parents, since the parents have very little power over the teacher, but the headteacher is able, amongst other things, to exercise a great influence over the teacher's career prospects.

Should there be no power differential between two conflicting role partners, the actor can still resolve the strain by regarding one partner's expectations as more legitimate than the other. When an actor regards one role partner as possessing no right to prescribe behaviour for him, then he frees himself from the need to conform to his expectations and from the strain that is induced by nonconformity. But if, of course, the role partner who is regarded as having illegitimate expectations is also a person with power over the actor, the role strain is not so easily resolved, as many teachers who regard the expectations of their headteacher as illegitimate ('unfair' 'unrealistic' 'theoretical' 'autocratic') will testify.

It is very costly to ignore the role partner who can invoke numerous sanctions. One possible solution is to insulate the role performance against (simultaneous) observation by conflicting role partners. This is in fact the mechanism by which the teacher is protected from the potential role strains inherent in his position. None of his major role partners but the pupils normally observe his role performance in the classroom. The headteacher, the inspectors, Local Authority officials, governors, parents, other teachers, etc., have limited if any opportunity to see whether or not the teacher is in fact conforming to their expectations in the way he conducts himself in the classroom. But at times these members of the role set may have a right of entry into the classroom. If the teacher is failing to abide by their expectations, then the teacher must develop defensive ploys to conceal this non-conformity. Since Miss Jean Brodie, the heroine of Muriel Spark's (1961) novel, believed in unorthodox methods, by no means approved by the headmistress, she would keep a long division sum permanently on the blackboard or have the pupils prop up history books in front of them. These provided useful cover in the event of unwelcome and unexpected intrusions by the headmistress in the classroom. Indeed, as the novel shows, the headmistress had great difficulty in collecting firm evidence of Miss Brodie's mal-practices and in the end was forced to rely on the betrayal of a pupil informer.

All teachers do deviate from the expectations of the headteacher, colleagues, parents, etc., to some degree, but the surprising thing is the extent to which they conform to such expectations. This is partly because their general expectations have been codified into a set of professional norms and partly because they are perceived as more legitimate and more powerful exponents of expectations of the teacher's classroom role. They can promote conformity to many of their expectations even when the teacher is not under their surveil-lance. They can, in the very apt term of Getzels & Thelen (1960), be regarded as 'invisible participants' in the classroom. Should the head-teacher or an inspector be present during his lessons for a short period, it is an easy matter for the teacher to create a special temporary role performance which will meet the expectations of the observer. On a 'Parents' Evening' the teacher may present himself to a parent as a charming, friendly and gentle person who has been completely mis-represented by the pupil in his accounts at home, and then return to the classroom the following morning as a bad-tempered autocrat. When a parent complains about a teacher's behaviour, many head-teachers will not on principle allow the disgruntled parent to meet the teacher concerned. The teacher could hardly be more insulated than he is from simultaneous observation by different role partners. His role performance tends to consist of different performances to different role partners, who are carefully segregated from one an-other. A typical reaction of a teacher in a situation where his class-room insulation from observation is invaded is given in Evan Hunter's *The Blackboard Jungle* (1955). Rick Dadier, the teacher, is visited by the Department Chairman, Mr Stanley. The intrusion has interesting effects on both teacher and pupils.

The class filed in, spotting Stanley instantly, and behaving like choir boys before the Christmass Mass. There'd be no trouble today, Rick knew. It was one thing to badger a teacher, but not when it led to a knock-down-dragout with the Department Chairman. No one liked sitting in the English Office under the cold stare of the Stanley man.

The cold stare showed no signs of heating up during the lesson. Rick gave it all he had, glad he'd prepared a good plan the night before, able for the first time actually to follow the plan because the kids kept their peace in Stanley's presence. He called primarily on his best students, throwing in a few of the duller kids to show Stanley he was impartial, but he steered away from Miller and West, not wanting to risk any entanglements while Stanley was observing . . .

Nor was this the last visit. Stanley began stopping by frequently, sometimes remaining for the full period, and sometimes visiting for ten- or fifteen-minute stretches, and then departing silently.

In the beginning, Rick resented the intrusions. He would watch Stanley scribbling at the back of the room, and he wondered what Stanley was writing, and he felt something like a bug on the microscope slide of a noted entomologist. Why all this secrecy? What the hell was this, the Gestapo?

With the growth of team teaching and similar developments, perhaps teachers will be less sensitive than at present about the private world of the classroom.

If insulation against observation by role partners is not feasible, an actor may try to reduce the role strain by reaching a compromise between the two conflicting expectations, by partially meeting the expectations of both in his role performance. Alternatively, he may try to bring the conflicting expectations into the open and arrange a conference between the role partners in which some sort of consensus may be achieved. Conferences of various sorts are also means of giving greater clarity to roles for persons assuming the role for the first time. Some schools open a day earlier for new pupils so that they may familiarize themselves with the physical arrangement of the school and receive some preparatory induction into their new roles within a new social organization, largely through talks from the headteacher and his staff. Training courses of all sorts tend to socialize the members into the roles for which they are being trained so that the eventual transition is facilitated. The work of Nash (1973) shows how the teachers of the last year in the primary school seek to prepare the pupils for life in the secondary school, and the teachers of the first year in the secondary school try to ease these pupils into their new school. Unfortunately, in the case of the schools in this study, the lack of contact between the teachers and their consequent misconceptions of the routines in the other school produced two training programmes which were contradictory and misdirected.

It is generally assumed that role strain is 'bad', a state of affairs which, whether it is objective, subjective, or both, must have negative and undesirable effects for persons, relationships and social systems. We have devoted too little attention to the potential positive effects of role strain. It could be argued that a certain mount of role strain can have beneficial effects under certain conditions. For persons, relationships and social systems, the benefit might reside in a valuable and necessary corrective to acquiescence, conformity, conservatism and resistance to change. Friction and conflict may be essential ingredients for the promotion of health and change.

These are not by any means exhaustive lists of the varieties of role strain or of role strain resolution, nor can it be claimed that they include the most basic forms. Lists of different types of role strain or of role strain resolution are simply products of the academic's attempt to elaborate distinctions within the over-all and inclusive concept of role strain. Such attempts on the part of social scientists serve important purposes in the development of the concept, since, it is argued, with each distinction and clarification our understanding of the concept is enhanced. Yet paradoxically the more elaborate our typologies of role strain become, the less easy it is to place a particular example of role strain drawn from 'real life' into a particular category. Role strains taken from 'real life' are often complex and multiple, so that we have to place the role strain concerned into several categories simultaneously or we are not sure how to classify it at all. It is when our formulations become too cumbersome that we recognize the need for new formulations and conceptualizations and this point has probably been reached in role theory.

A good example of what might be termed a 'complex of role strains' is available in the role of the student teacher and his transition to the full teacher role. During his professional training the student teacher formulates his conception of the teacher role. It would not be true, of course, to say that the student *acquires* his role conception during training, for his own lengthy experience as a pupil and his decision to become a teacher suggest that he will already hold a fairly elaborate conception of the teacher's role. The influence of training on his role conception is basically two-fold: the influence of his tutors and lecturers, and the influence of the pupils and teachers he meets on teaching practice. Several strains are likely to arise. For example, the student may have been educated in a traditional grammar school and then find that most of his tutors hold progressive views about education. In such a case the models provided by his own school education may inhibit his acceptance of the tutors' conception of the teacher's role in which they are seeking to train him.

When the student goes on teaching practice, he is likely to find some conflicts between his tutors' and the school's teachers' conception of the teacher's role, a problem which is not infrequently exacerbated by the (albeit veiled) hostility between the tutor and the supervising teachers, each of whom regards the other as holding 'wrong' ('unrealistic', 'reactionary') views on the nature of the teacher's role. Moreover, the student may find that the views he has acquired from his tutors are not easily put into practice because of the pupils as well as the teachers. The student has to face problems which were not considered in the safety of the college seminar and to which he feels he has no answers. And these problems sometimes never allow him the opportunity to try out his new ideas and beliefs. Finlayson & Cohen (1967) have demonstrated the deep differences in role conception between student teacher and headteacher. They report:

> Headteachers are much more strongly in favour of interpreting right and wrong for the child, using punishment, being stricter in their discipline, and insisting on immediate conformity from children than are the students. On the other hand they are more inclined to reject activities in which the children formulate their own rules of behaviour, opportunities for children to learn from their own experiences and for them to discover their personal difficulties with teachers. In all of these items, the head teachers' greater concern for good order and discipline and outward conformity is clearly manifested.

A number of studies have shown that there is a distinct change in the teacher's conception of his role as he moves from being a student, to a student on teaching practice, and then finally to a fully-fledged teacher. Wright & Tuska (1968) have conceived of this as a transition from 'dream', the student's conception of the teacher role before practice, through 'play', the student's conception of the teacher role after teaching practice, to 'life', the full teachers' conception of his role. The same writers have shown that after one year of teaching the woman teacher sees herself in her role very differently from the way she originally thought she would be. She sees herself as less happy, relaxed, perceptive, confident and inspiring but as more blaming, demanding and impulsive than she had imagined at the beginning of training. Similar disillusionments have been reported by others. Rabinowitz & Rosenbaum (1960) tested student teachers during training and after three years' full-time teaching on the M.T.A.I. They report a major change in score (and thus in attitudes), especially in the area of discipline.

> in the three years between testings the teachers became less concerned with pupil freedom and more concerned with establishing a stable orderly classroom, in which academic standards

59

received a prominent position. The change was accompanied by a decline in the tendency to attribute pupil misbehaviour or academic difficulty to the teacher or the school.

Similar findings are reported by Wallberg (1968) Jacobs (1968), Muss (1969) and Hoy (1969). Finlayson & Cohen reported that the peak of radical and liberal educational attitudes is in the second year in the College of Education, followed by a distinct decline in the third year. It seems that the teacher must in the first few years of his career come to terms with the 'harsh realities' of life in school. It is not possible at present to state how much of the changes in attitudes of a teacher after training is attributable to the influence of the attitudes and norms of other teachers (as revealed in the research of Finlayson & Cohen reported above) to which as a member of the school and staff-room he is pressured to conform, or to the practical problems of classroom management which damage the ideals of education which he has acquired in training. But all this research does seem to suggest that there is truth in the charge that tutors in Colleges and Departments of Education are 'unrealistic' either in their views of what teachers should be doing and/or in failure to prepare students for the difficulties of putting their views into practice in school. It seems doubtful whether this situation will be solved until lecturers are more ready to listen to the charges levelled against them and until the supervising teachers in schools are more ready to give a sympathetic ear to new ideas and experiments. This is unlikely to take place until there is much more co-ordination between tutors and supervising teachers and until the tutors are willing to give much more responsibility for training the student to the supervising teachers. Perhaps the best solution would be to make tutorial posts in Colleges and Departments of Education short-term appointments. Without such radical innovations it is difficult to see how a flow of personnel between schools and Colleges, which would be beneficial to both, could be effected.

Some of the student teacher's role strains arise directly within his training institution. Many student teachers see the function of their course as essentially practical; they want to learn to be good classroom practitioners. Thus they like the curriculum and method courses and teaching practice since they directly serve this objective. The staff, however, believe that students should acquire some knowledge of the more theoretical aspects of education and require students to follow courses in the major educational disciplines of history, philosophy, psychology and sociology. The students often feel that these theoretical aspects of the course are irrelevant. The content of these courses is learned reluctantly merely to pass the final examination. It is very doubtful whether we can make a clear distinction between theory and practice in the training of teachers, but there is little doubt that training institutions alienate some students from the more theoretical aspects by making them a compulsory part of the course without making the basic rationale for their inclusion explicit to the students. Conflict seems inevitable unless the staff make the justification both clear and acceptable to the students.

A further strain resides in the student's relationship with his tutor. With respect to teaching practice the tutor tries to enact the role of friendly help and guide to the novice teacher. But at the same time he must evaluate the student's performance by grading it as part of the practical examination. These two functions of helper and evaluator may not be inconsistent to the tutor, but they frequently are to the student. He may, for instance, be reluctant to confide his problems to the tutor for fear that he will give the impression that he is incompetent. When his teaching is being observed by the tutor he will try to give an idealized performance in order to boost his practical teaching grade. The observed lesson will be carefully planned and elaborately staged with a wide variety of fashionable teaching aids. Paradoxically we find that it is the student in the greatest difficulties who is least willing to betray his weaknesses to the tutor and is thus inhibited from gaining the help and advice and support which he may need so desperately at this crucial stage in his career as a teacher.

Recommended reading

B. J. BIDDLE & E. J. THOMAS (eds), *Role Theory: Concepts and Research*, Wiley, 1966.

G. R. GRACE, *Role Conflict and the Teacher*, Routledge & Kegan Paul, 1972.

N. GROSS, W. S. MASON & A. W. MCEACHERN, *Explorations in Role Analysis*, Wiley, 1958.

R. RUDDOCK, *Roles and Relationships*, Routledge & Kegan Paul, 1969.

4 Interaction

The concept of role and many of its allied concepts are drawn from the world of the theatre. The language of role theory relies heavily, though not exclusively, on the language of the drama. Of greater importance is the tendency of role theorists to develop a conception of man in terms of a dramaturgical analogy, an analogy which contrasts with psycho-analytical or behaviourist psychologists' conception of man. To speak of a person as an actor performing a role is to see human behaviour as analogous to a character in a play. In Shakespeare's words:

> All the world's a stage
> And all the men and women merely players;
> They have their exits and their entrances;
> And one man in his time plays many parts.

This analogy has been extremely useful in providing a set of concepts with which we can describe and analyse the conduct of man, but we must also be prepared to examine the limitation of the analogy and the dangers inherent in this dramaturgical conception of man. For unless we are prepared to admit the shortcomings of role theory we shall be unable to create a more refined set of concepts with which we can describe and analyse human behaviour more adequately. More specifically, we need to show why the concepts of role theory are not in themselves sufficient to provide us with a theory of interaction.

One of the most basic ideas in role theory is that the role is quite independent of a particular actor. The words that Hamlet speaks and the ways in which he speaks them are fairly fixed and survive the various interpretations of the actors who may play the role on stage. Whilst it is true that Sir John Gielgud and Ian McKellen give very different interpretations of the part, what is common to the two versions is greater than the difference between them. Both are clearly recognizable as Hamlet. It can be argued that in the same way a social role, such as that of the teacher, has fairly fixed elements within it and we can recognize the role despite the differing interpretations of Mr Smith and Mr Jones.

Yet when we look at the details of two teachers performing their roles and try to make sense of their behaviour, there seems to be comparatively little that they have in common. This is still true even if we take, say, the role performances of two male teachers of science, with similar qualifications and background, teaching children of the same age in the same school. The differences in role performance are quite as striking as the similarities. But if we contrast the role performances of these teachers with the role performance of a doctor, we are then impressed much more by the similarities of the two teachers. In other words, role theory consists of a valuable set of concepts for distinguishing between role performances associated with *different* position-roles, but these concepts are much less useful for distinguishing different performances of the *same* role.

It is in the nature of roles that they consist of a modicum of prescriptions with which the actor and his principal role partners agree. Yet it is important to recognize that this consensus about how the actor should behave is limited to a relatively small number of aspects of the actor's role performance. There is a high level of agreement about a few things the actor *must* or *must not* do. In many more areas there is a prescription for *preferred* behaviour. Then there is by far the largest area in which there are no prescriptions at all—the actor may do as he pleases because these behaviours are irrelevant to the performance of the role. Thus it is generally agreed that teachers are obliged to have some sort of qualification to teach and are forbidden from propagating extreme political opinions among their pupils. If a teacher is known to deviate from these role requirements, various sanctions will be invoked against him, including dismissal. There is less agreement about whether or not a teacher should have received a professional course of teacher-training, should administer corporal punishment, should give up his spare time to supervise extracurricular activities, or should supervise school meals, though there is probably some consensus about a preferred course of action for teachers in these respects. Teachers may, and do, deviate from the preferred course without much recrimination, because these are preferred 'optional extras' rather than basic role requirements. Finally, there is a wide spectrum of behaviour in which the teacher is totally free to choose his own course of action, for example whether or not he makes jokes in the lessons to amuse the pupils, or marks his books at home or during a free period. This view does rather oversimplify the issue, since many role expectations are related not so much to the behaviour *per se* but to the situation or context in which the behaviour is displayed. For example, it is generally agreed that teachers should not smoke in the classroom in the presence of pupils, but there is less agreement about whether or not the teacher should smoke on a school visit, and there are no expectations about whether or not the teacher should smoke in his own home, even though he may be performing his role, by preparing a lesson for instance.

Further, much of the behaviour that occurs within a role relationship is governed by expectations and norms that are not role-specific at all. Many norms are what may be termed general social norms, expectations about how we should behave in all situations and role relationships. For example, we expect teachers to be punctual and to be honest. But these are not role-specific expectations, for it is expected of most adults that they should be punctual and honest whatever particular occupational role they happen to be performing.

A related point is that in real-life role performances, behaviour is influenced by the actor's other roles as well as by general social norms. Roles are separable and distinct only in theoretical analysis. Let us consider a teacher interacting with a headteacher. One is performing the role of teacher, and the other the role of headteacher. Yet it is not as simple as this, for each actor's performance of this particular role is influenced by other position-roles that he occupies, such as age and sex roles. A young male teacher performs his role differently than an old female teacher. Roles spill over and *fuse* into one another, and this nowhere more evident than in interaction. An old female headteacher interacting with a young male teacher is very different from a young male headteacher interacting with an old female teacher.

The general nature of the role expectations, the existence of pervasive general social norms, and the fact of role fusion make it difficult to conceive of role performance as simply a matter of interpretation by an actor parallel to the interpretation of the stage performer. These difficulties are easily reinforced by further consideration of matters we have already discussed. Role expectations do not affect an actor directly. He must perceive them and organize them into something which might be called his conception of the role, which then becomes an important determinant of his role performance. This role conception derives largely from the role partners in the role set. Yet we have seen that a single role partner is likely to conceive some of these expectations in an idiosyncratic way; consensus about the role expectations will be far from perfect among the role partners; the clarity and force with which these expectations are expressed by the role partners will be very variable. Further, the way in which these expectations are *perceived* by the actor is of crucial significance, and this perception will be influenced by many idiosyncratic elements within the actor himself. The analogy between a social role and the Shakespearean text begins to be rather strained.

What we have said so far makes nonsense of a crude sociological view that suggests that human behaviour is essentially role-determined. This view has been superbly characterized by Peter Berger (1963). Society, in this view, provides the script for all the actors and the social play can proceed if all the players will learn and conform to the roles that are assigned to them. The role thus shapes the actor and the action. The actor, unlike the actor on the professional stage of the theatre, actually becomes the part he plays.

> Role theory, when pursued to its logical conclusions, does far more than provide us with a convenient shorthand for the description of various social activities. It gives us a sociological anthropology, that is, a view of man based on his existence in society. This view tells us that man plays dramatic parts in the grand play of society, and that, speaking sociologically, he *is* the masks that he must wear to do so . . . The person is perceived as a repertoire of roles, each one properly equipped with a certain identity. The range of an individual person can be measured by the number of roles he is capable of playing. The person's biography now appears to us as an uninterrupted sequence of stage performances, played to different audiences, sometimes involving drastic changes of costume, always demanding that the actor *be* what he is playing.

In reality social roles, including the teacher's role, are not Hamlet-like theatrical roles, for none of the words or specific actions are fixed. Social roles require not just an interpretation, according to the actor's personality, of set lines and actions, but rather lay down some very general guide-lines of how the actor is expected to behave. The actor of the social role has, relative to the stage actor, very little to guide his conduct. There is no fixed script, no stage directions, no definite plot, no stage director. There is not enough substance to the social role to give a detailed guide to the actor's behaviour in specific interactional situations. So for the actor of a social role it is not so much a question of interpreting a role as of *improvising* and *constructing* the behaviour we call role performance. The role provides a loose prescriptive framework within which the actor must to a large degree make up the lines and action as he goes along. Thus the role performance becomes unique and idiosyncratic to the actor within a specific interactional context. Performing a role is a highly creative act. As Turner (1962) suggests, we should speak not of role-taking but of role-*making*.

Social behaviour takes place within situations, usually interactional ones. Normally the situation itself imposes constraints which a person must take into account in performing his role. To say the very least the role performance has to be adapted to those situational conditions. As Yablonsky (1953) pointed out:

> Few roles are so explicitly defined for an actor that he can mechanically act out its specifications within a situation. Even when certain roles are most explicit a shift in the structure of the situation has an effect on the actor and requires some measure of spontaneity.

People are not simply actors performing roles. It is true that most of us spend a large proportion of our lives performing various roles, but to see a person as nothing more than a collection and amalgamation of roles is a dangerous oversimplification. Much of our behaviour is indeed *within* various roles, and these roles structure the way we behave. But then to argue from this that our behaviour is role-*determined* is an unjustifiable distortion of role theory's potential contribution to our understanding of human behaviour. For the truth is that no role can in itself dictate the detailed step-by-step behaviour of the actor.

The limitations of a role analysis are most striking if we consider our relationships with the people we know best. We do not interact with people we know well purely or even largely in terms of roles. We regard them and treat them as persons. With people we do not know as individuals and with whom we have a highly specific and very short relationship (e.g. an encounter between a customer and a sales assistant in a shop) we do interact almost entirely in terms of a role relationship. It is all that we require to satisfy our needs. Indeed, we may actively resist any sort of 'personal' involvement. In this respect it is worth noting that the training for many occupational roles involves strong advice to avoid such personal involvement with clients as inimical to adequate role performance. (Teachers are, of course, particularly prone to such problems.) Yet for the most part we do not regard brief or formal relationships as our most important relationships. In short, I wish to suggest that the more we interact with another person, the less our relationship can be executed or analysed in role terms.

Even when sociologists have managed to avoid a crude deterministic conception of role, they have, with a few notable exceptions, suffered from a tendency to analyse role performance and social behaviour in terms of the formula role-plus-personality. This is epitomized in the famous Getzels & Guba (1957) model (Fig. 4.1). Goffman (1961) has drawn attention to that area which

> falls between role obligations on the one hand and actual role performance on the other. This gap has always caused trouble

for sociologists. Often, they try to ignore it. Faced with it, they sometimes despair and turn from their own direction of analysis; they look to the biography of the performer and try to find in his history some particularistic explanation of events, or they rely on psychology, alluding to the fact that in addition to playing the formal themes of his role, the individual always behaves personally and spontaneously, phrasing the standard obligations in a way that has a special psychological fit for him.

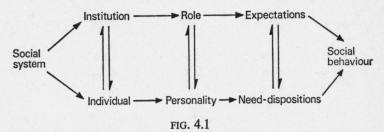

FIG. 4.1

To ascribe social behaviour, or even mere role performance, to an interaction between role and personality is either a gross over-simplification or, taking 'role' and 'personality' as synonyms for 'social' and 'individual', merely a statement of the obvious. Attempts have been made to link the concepts of role and personality by such concepts as that of *role style*. This, as we shall see later, offers at best a marginal advance. From a social psychological point of view the main weakness of this approach is that it ignores the interactional nature of role performance and social behaviour. We have learned from G. H. Mead and symbolic interactionism that every actor needs to take account, minute by minute, step by step, of the behaviour of the other as it unfolds by constantly assessing and assigning meaning to the other's behaviour. No theory of interaction can be regarded as adequate unless it builds in this idea.

The Getzels and Guba role-plus-personality model seems to over-look the simple fact that when human beings act they are seeking to achieve certain goals (objectives, projects). The strength of the concept of role is that it emphasizes that these goals are not just personal to the individual actor but are frequently *socially* mediated. In this sense the teacher's role consists of a set of goals which the teacher sets himself in relation to the goals that various other persons or groups, namely role partners, expect him to achieve. Conceptualizing roles as socially mediated goals can help us out of the difficulty of the inadequacy of role expectations in providing the actor with a detailed guide to conduct. This becomes clear in Kelvin's (1970) analysis, where he defines roles as *tasks* which is very close to my conception of role as a form of *goals*.

When we talk about the behaviour associated with a role we do not refer to this or that pattern of observable movements or words: we refer to the more or less adequate performance and *completion of a task*. The role specifies *what* is to be done, it rarely specifies precisely *how* it is to be done. The dominant factor in determining the expectations of a role is the task with which it is associated. It is the achievement of the task which is expected. . . . In some respects, therefore, it would be better to consider roles as sets of task expectancies associated with a position, rather than as sets of behavioural expectancies, with apparent implications about behaviour in the strict sense . . . The essence of 'role' therefore comes down to this: the position having specified the task, the role of the occupant is to use the demands of the task as criteria in evaluating and deciding between his possible courses of action.

If actors have goals, then they must also develop *means* by which these goals can be realized—or in Kelvin's terms, the *how* of task accomplishment. The means by which actors achieve certain goals is in essence by following sets of *rules* or rule-governed procedures. It is here that we can see the value of Alfred Schutz's concept of the *recipe*, developed in his essays 'The stranger: an essay in social psychology' (1944) and 'The problem of rationality in the social world' (1943). A recipe specifies what is going to be cooked or baked (the goal) *and* the ingredients, the way and order in which they must be combined, the cooking time, etc. (the rules).

It is possible then to conceptualize roles as recipes or goals-plus-rules which are socially mediated, that is transmitted, learned and negotiated by social processes, in relation to the position occupied by the actor. As Harré and Secord, in their recent critique of social psychology (1972), suggest:

A role, then, is a set of actions a person of a particular type or category is expected to perform . . . and knowledge of role consists of knowing the rules which enjoin these kinds of actions in the proper order and in the appropriate circumstances.

This allows us to make a real advance on traditional role theory in that we can now see that what we call a role expectation involves a social expectation related to a social position that sometimes specifies the full recipe, that is both the goal and the rules; but quite often it specifies only the goal and leaves to the discretion of the actor the question of the rules which then have to be devised or constructed by him. At the same time it is clear that a great deal of our conduct which is allegedly within the role is affected by the use of recipes where neither the goal nor the rules are the subject of social expectations.

The distinctions I have made shed light on the inherent ambiguity of the term *expectation*. Sometimes expectations are *normative*, that is we expect someone to do something in the sense that we feel he *ought* to do it. There is a moral force to a normative expectation. At other times expectations are what I can call *probabilistic*, that is we expect someone to do something or to do something in a particular way because we have learned from experience that this is what he normally does. There is no moral force here at all; our expectation is based on our past experience of observing what he does typically in certain situations. Role theory is about normative expectations, but not about probabilistic expectations. Yet the latter cannot be ignored. If a person fails to conform to probabilistic expectations, we are merely *surprised*; we wonder why he has changed from his typical pattern or recipe, but we do not make a moral judgment on him. If a person fails to conform to normative expectations, however, we are *affronted* and make efforts to see that he conforms to the recipes we feel he ought to be following.

In short, action can be conceptualized in terms of recipes, as goals and as rules for realizing these goals. Some of these recipes are normative (position-roles) and others are probabilistic (individual-typicality).

I am convinced that role theory will rapidly pass into disuse in contemporary interactionist social psychology, just as did the concept of instinct in earlier social psychology. As weaknesses are exposed (e.g. Turner, 1962), the concept becomes elaborated and massively over-stretched (e.g. Biddle and Thomas, 1966) and new concepts begin to enter the field (Harré and Secord, 1972; Cicourel, 1970). The concept increasingly becomes redundant (cf. Coulson, 1972) and current trends suggest that *rule* will become the substitute concept, because it offers much broader conceptual, analytic and explanatory power. Whilst we are in the period of transition, the wise student will treat the concept of role with a degree of open-minded scepticism. Now we must look much more closely at the detailed dynamics of interaction, something which classical role theory never did.

Interaction is a dynamic concept. An interaction involves at least two people each of whose behaviour is orientated towards the other. If we think of two people in interaction, we imagine two people in conversation in the same place and at the same point in time. This is the most common, but not the only form, of interaction. The participants can interact from widely different locations, as by telephone, and even from different points in time, as in written correspondence. Interaction can be non-verbal, as in letter-writing, playing a game of chess, or in making love. How then can we define interaction? Asch (1952) has described interaction well in the following way:

> The paramount fact about social interaction is that the participants stand on common ground, that they turn *toward one another*, that their acts interpenetrate and therefore regulate each other . . . In full interaction each participant refers his action to the other and the other's action to himself. When two people, A and B, work jointly or converse, each includes in his view, simultaneously and in their relation, the following facts: (1) A perceives the surroundings, which include B and himself; (2) A perceives that B is also oriented to the surroundings, that B includes himself and A in the surroundings; (3) A acts toward B and notes that B is responding to his action; (4) A notes that B in responding to him sets up the expectation that A will grasp the response as an action of B directed toward A. The same ordering must exist in B.

This can be summarized under *the principle of reciprocally contingent communication*. To express this more simply, in every form of interaction the participants must communicate, that is transmit symbols with a shared meaning, in such a way that the behaviour of each is in part a response to the behaviour of the other. Interaction is a process of reciprocal influence and mutual dependence.

This can be clarified by examining different types of interaction (cf. Jones & Thibaut, 1958). Some interactions may be termed *pseudo-contingent*: the contingency principle appears to be in operation, but is not really so. The interaction appears to be contingent, because each actor synchronizes his speech so that it does not overlap with the speech of the other. When we go to the theatre to watch a play, the actors time their lines in such a way that they appear to be interacting, though the lines have been pre-determined. To create the illusion of reality, each actor must wait for his cue, then speak his lines as if he had just had the thoughts which lead him to speak. If the actor does not look as if he is responding to the other actors, if he 'fluffs' his lines so that it is no longer credible that he is reacting to the others, or if he misses his cue and the temporal synchronization goes awry, then the illusion of the play breaks down. A similar pseudo-contingent interaction occurs in many religious rituals. The priest chants, 'O Lord open thou our lips', and the congregation responds, 'And our mouth shall show forth thy praise.' Now the congregation has not given a spontaneous response to the priest. They have no choice in the matter but to give the fixed reply. If they decided to respond with 'O Lord make haste to help us', then the service would soon be reduced to chaos. In such an interaction the only problem for the participants is to know the lines and make the right response at the right time.

Another form of interaction can be described as *asymmetrically contingent*. This arises when the behaviour of one participant is highly contingent on the other, but the behaviour of the second participant is only partially contingent on the other. A good example is the interview situation. The interviewee has to respond to the (unknown) questions of the interviewer, and what he says is very much dependent on the questions. The interviewer's questions, however, do not always depend on the interviewee's replies, though they may do so in a 'follow-up' question. The interviewer is likely to have a predetermined schedule of questions, and when he has received a satisfactory reply to one question, he will non-contingently turn to the next question. Teachers often behave in asymmetrically contingent ways, as when they are asking questions of children in the classroom. All the pupils' answers will be related to the teacher's questions, but not all the teacher's questions will be related to the children's answers.

In truly reciprocally contingent interaction, each participant reacts to the other, and the behaviour of each is in part determined by the other. It is not more than *in part* a function of the behaviour of the other, because each participant has to create a response. The actual content of the response and the manner in which the response is made are both functionally related to a number of factors additional to the immediately preceding behaviour of the other. One of the most important influences on content and manner will be the expectations deriving from the roles of the two participants. In a teacher–pupil interaction, for example, the response of the pupil to a teacher is influenced not only by the behaviour of the teacher but also by the norms governing the appropriate behaviour, both content and manner, on the part of the pupil. Thus in interaction we have to make some sort of compromise between the response we might wish to make, our own personality, needs and goals, and the limitations on our creative response which accrue from social norms, from the role partner's expectations and from the nature of his preceding behaviour.

The definition of the situation

Interactional situations vary along a continuum of the degree to which there is a structure inherent in the interaction. This structure concerns the mutual orientation of the participants and their awareness of how they should behave in the situation. When the structure is high, the participants are in no doubt about the roles each is going to perform; how the actor is going to perform his role, and how his role partner is going to perform his role; the goals of each participant in the interaction; the contribution and timing of each. Examples of high structure interactions would be a bus conductor collecting fares from the passengers, or priest and laymen saying Mass together. In both these illustrations, at least in normal circumstances, the roles of the participants are very clearly defined and there is an awareness by both participants about who should do what, when and for what reason.

When the structure of an interaction is low, we find the reverse situation. There is considerable uncertainty, confusion or ambiguity about the roles the participants are expected to play, the goals of the actors, the contribution each is going to make, and the way in which these contributions will be meshed together. The most common instance of interactions with low structure is the meeting of two strangers in a situation where few clues to a potential structure are available, such as on a beach or in a pub. Another common example is a situation where one actor is unaware of the structure but the other actor is, such as the person who becomes a patient of a psychiatrist for the first time.

When the structure is low, either because it is lacking or because it is not explicit, the interaction will have two outstanding features. The first is a certain psychological distress for each actor, marked by such thoughts as 'Who is this?' 'What does he want?' 'What am I supposed to do now?' 'God, how can I get away?' The second feature is a tendency to what might be called the interactional jerks, namely awkward silences or both participants speaking at the same time. This stage will in most cases be temporary, since the dissatisfactions experienced by the participants exert a pressure towards resolution. Typically, a 'probing session' in which each actor tries to clarify the situation and to discover the roles and purposes of the other ensues. If little progress is made, or if results of the probing session are distasteful to one or both of the participants, withdrawal will occur and the participants will leave each other's company or turn their attention elsewhere (a book, another person) in order to terminate the interaction.

In most teacher–pupil interactions, the structure is high rather than low. When a new teacher takes a class for the first time, or when an experienced teacher meets the new intake of a school for the first time, then the structure will be much weaker. Even in such a situation there will be some structure, for in most cases the teacher will have some previous experience of children in school and the children will have some experience of teachers. The most extreme case of low structure, then, would be that of a quite inexperienced teacher with a class of children who were coming to school for the first time. We shall be concerned with more typical teacher–pupil situations and interactions, but we shall have to consider the process of structural development if we are to have an adequate understanding of teacher–pupil interactions as they occur in an ordinary classroom.

We shall investigate and clarify this structure of an interaction by using the famous phrase of W. I. Thomas (1928, 1931) the *definition of the situation*. Thomas used this phrase or concept to examine the impact of definitions and meanings on the structure of human action. What sociologists call culture can be seen as a set of collective definitions. In spite of the contradictions that are evident within cultures, social interactions can proceed only when to a large degree the participants have a common definition of the situation. As Asch puts it:

> A conversation can proceed only when (a) the same (or a similar) context is present in the participants *and* (b) when the context possesses for each the property of being also the context for the other. This reference on the part of each participant to the other is the condition of psychosocial events; action in the social field is steered by phenomenal fields which are structurally similar in these respects. Only individuals who encompass their common situation in this way can produce social-psychological acts . . . It is individuals with this particular capacity to turn toward one another who in concrete action validate and consolidate in each a *mutually shared field*, one that includes both the surroundings and one another's psychological properties as the objective sphere of action. This relation between psychological events in each of the participants makes possible the sharing of actions feelings ideas and mutual acknowledgement. We cannot take a step in practice without presupposing this understandability; we cannot take a step in theory before clarifying it.

Alfred Schutz in defining interaction in terms of a 'reciprocal Thou-orientation' makes a very similar argument to those of Thomas and Asch, but he speaks of a *communicative common environment* rather than a 'mutually shared field'. Schutz points out that the world of one's daily life is by no means a private world of one's own making, but rather an intersubjective world that is shared with one's fellow men. The sociocultural world in which one exists is also the social environment of others, shared, experienced and interpreted by them. A man's fellow men are part of his environment as he is of theirs. A man acts upon others and others act upon him. This mutual relationship implies that all experience the world that is common to all and experience it in a way that is substantially similar. The mutuality of the definition of the situation springs in part from social norms, mores, customs and all those aspects of the cultural pattern which provides by its recipes typical solutions for typical problems available to typical actors. These recipes serve both as a common scheme of action, indicating to an actor how he is to proceed to attain a goal and as a common scheme of interpretation by which we can make sense of action.

In the chapter on role we considered the reciprocity of rights and duties in a role relationship, the rights of the actor being the duties of the role partner and vice versa. Schutz, noting that the participants in the common communicative environment are given to one another not as *objects* but as *counter-subjects*, is led to the concept of the *reciprocity of perspectives* in interaction. Both Person and Other must assume that each is taking broadly the same things for granted. Each participant assumes an interchangeability of standpoints, by which things would be broadly the same if each participant were to change places with the other.

Both Asch and Schutz, recognizing the unique individuality of each participant, stress that the participant's definitions of the situation must be similar or congruent rather than absolutely identical. At any point in time, argues Schutz, a man finds himself in a 'biographically determined situation' with the consequence that no two persons can ever view the situation in quite the same way. The unique biography gives a person a unique 'stock of knowledge at hand' which will serve as a scheme of interpretation for past and present experience and influence his goals and projects for the future.

The definition of the situation with respect to an interaction has shared elements that are common to both participants; these spring largely from various cultural recipes, including social norms and social roles. Yet each actor is unique, with his own biography, schemes of interpretation and purposes which he brings to bear in the interaction. Some elements of the definition of the situation are *given*, and come to constitute the agreed and taken for granted over-all definition of the situation. Other elements are unique to the individual participant, who has his own version of the definition of the situation, overlapping with but not identical with his partner's definition of the situation. Over time these individual definitions of the situation need, especially if they are not highly congruent, to be *negotiated* and agreed if the interaction is to proceed to the satisfaction of the participants. In many of our habitual interactions the situation has already been progressively negotiated in past interactions. We take the over-all definition of the situation for granted because it does not have to be negotiated *de novo* every time. But this should not blind us to the process of progressive negotiation and modification that has taken place. In order to facilitate the analysis of the process whereby the definition of the situation is established we shall consider the major segments separately. Later we shall draw all the segments together into a more coherent and dynamic model of interaction.

Typically each participant enters the interactions with a relatively clear set of goals. Rather than entering the interaction without purposes or objectives, he has some definite notions of what he wants to get from the interaction. Obviously the range and variety of these goals is endless. Secondly, each participant has a relatively clear conception of the role he expects to perform in the interaction. This role conception is, as we have seen, derived in complex ways from Person's perceptions of the expectations of his role partners in the role-set and from his own needs, personality and background. It is Person's goals and roles—and the two are usually inter-connected—which form the major contribution to Person's conception of how the situation should be defined. Sometimes Person may enter an interaction without any clear goals and roles. In this case the roles and goals will be progressively formulated in the early phases of the interaction. In the present analysis we shall be more concerned with the more typical case where each participant has a relatively clear conception of his goals and roles, though it is useful to recognize at this point that each participant is likely to modify his goals and roles in the light of subsequent interaction.

On entering the interaction, and sometimes, prior to it, each participant has the important task of *deriving information about Other*. This involves trying to find out as much as possible about Other that is likely to be relevant to the interaction. Among the most important questions that Person asks himself, though not always explicitly or consciously, are:

What is Other's role?
How does Other perceive his role?
What are Other's goals?
What does Other expect to gain from the interaction?
What are Other's intentions?
How is Other going to behave towards me?

In other words, Person comes to the interaction with his own goals and roles and has the immediate task of assessing Other's roles and goals. This raises once more the problems of interpersonal perception that we have already discussed at length. Each participant will select information from Other's behaviour and make inferences and attributions about Other's roles, goals, intentions, motives, personality and so on. Each participant must do this in relation to the other participant. Each will conclude with a conception of Other which will influence his behaviour towards Other.

In the chapter on person perception we were in the main concerned with Person's perception of Other. It was essentially a one-sided view for we were concerned with what happened in Person and ended up with a model of Person's perceptual processes. When we consider social interaction we are forced to come to terms with the facts of *inter*personal perception. Other himself is also a perceiver of Person. Person's behaviour towards Other is influenced by Person's conception of Other; Other's behaviour towards Person is influenced by Other's conception of Person. It becomes more complex when we realize that Person also has a conception of Other's conception of Person and that Other has a conception of Person's conception of Other. Whenever we get to know someone quite well, we become fascinated by this person's conception of us. When we say 'What do you really think of me?', we are asking for information which will allow us to develop or clarify our conception of the other person's conception of us. In short, Person's behaviour towards Other is influenced not only by Person's conception of Other but also by Person's conception of Other's conception of him. So Person asks himself two sets of questions. The first set, by which he creates his conception of Other, we have already dealt with. The second set, by which he creates his conception of Other's conception of him, includes such questions as:

What does Other think my role is?
What does Other think my goals are?
How does Other think I am going to behave towards him?
What motives and intentions is Other going to attribute to me?

In addition to deriving information about Other, Person has, on entering his interaction with Other, to face another important question: what sort of person do I want Other to think I am? Since Other has the task of deriving information about Person, Person is in a position to control to some degree the release of information which Other is seeking. Person may be able to influence Other's conception of him and Other's conception of Person's conception of Other by giving away information in his own behaviour towards Other. This is the task of *self-presentation*. Thus deriving information about Other and self-presentation are opposite sides of the same coin. Each derives information about the other through the other's self-presentation.

The writer who has contributed most to this field is the American Erving Goffman, especially in his fascinating book, *The Presentation of Self in Everyday Life* (1959). In our discussion we shall draw heavily upon the concepts and ideas of Goffman. In presenting himself each actor has to behave, intentionally or unintentionally, in such a way that he *expresses* himself by words, gestures, facial manipulations and so on and that the other receives an *impression* of him. This recalls our work on person perception. My expressions are the raw data on which, through selection, inference and attribution, you build up an impression of me. This means that I shall have to control my expressions in order to make sure you get the right rather than the wrong impression of me. For you to have the right impression usually means that you have interpreted my expressions accurately, that is, you have received an impression which is very close to the impression I wanted you to form. A wrong impression arises when you make inferences and attributions which are an incorrect reflection of my (actual or projected) roles, goals and expectations. In this case, you have 'misunderstood' me and I will attempt to alter your impression if I become aware of the impression I have made. Sometimes, of course, I may try to express myself in a way that is intended to mislead you. A pupil, for example, by keeping his eyes riveted on the teacher who is explaining some problem to the class may wish to give the impression that he is paying attention, when in reality he is thinking about his girl-friend. If the teacher suspects that he has the wrong impression, he may ask the pupil a question as a check on whether or not the pupil's expression is a genuine representation of his mental state. If it becomes clear that the pupil was not paying attention, then the pupil's misleading expression is 'seen through'.

Goffman demonstrates that the techniques required in self-presentation are extremely elaborate. There is a subtle art in managing our expressions to create impressions on others. Many of these techniques are so common-place that they are regarded as 'natural', though in fact considerable learning has taken place. One of the most important clarifications made by Goffman is the distinction between an expression that is *given* and one that is *given off*. The first concerns mainly verbal communication to convey information. The second includes a wide range of cues, often not easily controlled, that may or may not be in support of the expression given. For example, the pupil who is lying to the teacher may blush, and the teacher may regard the blush as an indication that the truth is not being told. Similarly a teacher who is having a 'mock rage' in order to bring the class to order may reveal his deception by the twinkle in his eye. So a participant in an interaction must make sure that the expression given off is consonant with the expression given if he is to make the right impression on the other.

A related distinction made by Schutz (1932) is that between the 'expressive act' and the 'expressive movement'. In an expressive act an actor intentionally communicates or seeks to communicate his subjective experience, whereas in the expressive movement there is no communicative intent on the part of the actor, even though it may be taken by Other as an indication of the actor's subjective experience. Other may have difficulty in distinguishing an expressive movement from an expressive act, especially when an actor seeks to control his self-presentation by turning what would normally be an expressive

77

movement into an expressive act yet at the same time seeking to leave Other with the impression that it is an expressive movement not an expressive act.

Goffman calls the expressive equipment employed by the individual during his performance 'front'. This is the part of the individual's behaviour which serves to define the situation for the other. In creating the appropriate front the actor may use props and scenery in addition to insignia, clothing, speech, posture and facial expressions. The use of the academic gown by teachers in English grammar schools is a good example of a prop which indicates that the wearer is both a member of the teaching staff and a superior, qualified expert in a particular discipline. It is often possible to detect the headmaster from among a group of teachers by his special front— a dark, formal suit, an impeccable appearance, a haughty, self-confident manner. In creating a front an actor helps to define the situation by giving the other information about his role and goals and the way he intends to behave during the interaction.

Frequently actors try to give others the impression that their performance is *idealized*, that their behaviour is an exemplification of what is expected by others. Thus on Open Days in schools the premises are made especially clean and tidy and both staff and pupils are better dressed than usual. Teachers may, in the presence of parents, refer to pupils by their first names rather than by their surnames as is customary in the classroom. I know one headmaster who, in his 'briefing' before Speech Day, gave detailed advice on the idealization of performance in the presence of parents and visitors. 'It doesn't matter if you are bored by speeches', he would say, 'but try to *look* as if you are interested'. During a general inspection of a school by Her Majesty's Inspectors, the teachers may use an unprecedented number of audio-visual aids and unheard of amounts of coloured chalk. In all these instances the actors are presenting themselves as closer to the ideal than is really the case. Practising teachers may try to idealize their performances in the presence of student teachers. As one of my own students reports:

A student teacher watching a teacher in action is often given an idealized performance. Several members of staff in the schools where I spent my teaching practices admitted that they had prepared careful lesson notes for the first time in years for the lesson I was to observe.

Often we try to avoid being given an idealized performance. The same student continues:

Many students, including myself, found the strain of expecting a tutor's arrival to observe a lesson was considerable. Although we were assured that it was only because of the pressing time-table arrangements that we could not be forewarned of a visit, we felt that it was because the tutors themselves were afraid that otherwise we would be able to prepare and give an elaborately staged and idealized performance.

In order to sustain a front or performance, especially an idealized one, the actor must ensure that in his self-presentation no action or cue is expressed that might discredit the performance. If we wish to give a boring friend the impression that we are interested in his stories, we must stifle our yawns. Similarly, the teacher who wishes to maintain his front as an 'expert' may be led to cover up behaviour which is discrepant with this front. The teacher who makes an error which is recognized by the pupils may try to retain his front by saying, 'I'm glad you spotted the deliberate mistake. I put that in specially to see if you were all wide awake this morning.' In face of an awkward question, the expert front can be maintained by such diversionary tactics as, 'That's a good point. We'll discuss it next week', or 'Now why don't you look up the meaning of that word in the dictionary?' or 'Can we have questions at the end of the lesson?'

In our discussion so far it has been implied that problems of self-presentation are a matter for the individual actor. This is not so, since actors are often members of teams who have a common front. The teacher is part of a team which by mutual agreement, co-operation and collusion fosters and sustains a front against the pupils. Thus teachers in conversation in the presence of pupils will often refer to each other by formal surnames. A teacher enters another teacher's classroom and smiling asks, 'Can I have a word with you, Miss Smith?' and in the privacy of the corridor demands, 'What the hell have you done with my register?' Most school staff frown upon a teacher who talks to the children about other teachers. To do so is 'unprofessional'; it threatens the image as well as the unity of the team front. For a similar reason many schools will not allow student-teachers to wear mini-skirts on teaching practice.

Within the team there is considerable trust between members. The front can be openly discussed—'I just don't seem to be able to look angry when I really want to laugh at the pupils' misdemeanours'—and confidences can be exchanged without fear of the content being reported back to the other team. Teachers and pupils are alike in their intense dislike of team members who 'tell tales' or give 'leaks' to members of the other team. Sometimes teams which are typically in opposition may combine against a third team. On Speech Day the teachers and pupils may co-operate in presenting an idealized performance for parents and visitors. To refuse to join in this co-operative venture is regarded as 'letting the *school* down'.

79

In creating an idealized performance, there is a dishonesty of intent. Most of us are ready to acknowledge that we frequently use a variety of techniques to misrepresent ourselves to others. But we also feel that in most of our performances our self-presentation is 'genuine'. We are, we might say, 'being our true selves'. Yet the art of self-presentation does *not* refer merely to the skills that are necessary to the creation of a contrived, essentially false performance. It refers just as much to being 'true' as to being 'false'.

We have to learn, in other words, to be sincere, because sincerity—like insincerity—has to be expressed in such a way that the other is appropriately impressed. A person who pretends to be sincere tries to use precisely the same self-presentation techniques as the person who is really being sincere. The very fact that one can pretend to be something one is not demonstrates that certain self-presentation techniques are essential to being genuine. Simply because much of the material of the writing on self-presentation is drawn from contrived performances should not mislead us into regarding self-presentation as the art of pretence. If such were the case, it would be of only peripheral relevance to the study of interaction. In fact self-presentation is at the very roots of an understanding of interaction.

Goffman's writings are rich in ideas on self-presentation. One review of *The Presentation of Self in Everyday Life* described it as 'one of the most trenchant contributions to social psychology in this generation'. This is not an unjustified claim. It is a book to be read. The concept of self-presentation is fundamental to a study of interaction, because it extends the dramaturgical perspective that is implicit, but undeveloped, in 'classical' role theory. Moreover, it allows role theory to become dynamic and thus more relevant to the study of interaction.

The further aspect of defining the situation concerns *situational proprieties*. This is a term coined by Goffman in another of his books, *Behaviour in Public Places* (1963). One of the difficulties with role theory from an interactional point of view is that it does not sufficiently allow for situational factors in an interaction. The concept of situational proprieties is a useful element for considering the impact of situational variables upon interaction. The basic idea can be best expressed in Goffman's words, that the rule of behaviour which is common to all situations is the one which obliges the participants to 'fit in'. They must not, in other words, make a scene or cause a disturbance or be out of place. They must not be too withdrawn from what is going on, but neither must they thrust themselves on the other people who are present. Many situational proprieties are really norms or rules which govern the participants' involvement in the interaction. *Autoinvolvements*, the tendency to be too much involved with oneself rather than with the other, are improper. Picking one's nose, cleaning one's fingernails are autoinvolvements that imply too little attention to and respect for the other is being paid. To be 'away' in a daydream or to doodle are similarly frowned upon. Goffman suggests that in interaction both the participants must show *civil inattention* to the other. By this term he means that we must not stare with constant eye contact at the other. This would be 'rude'. At the same time, it would be equally impolite to make no eye contact at all with the other. As Goffman puts it:

> one gives to another enough visual notice to demonstrate that one appreciates that the other is present . . . while at the next moment withdrawing one's attention from him so as to express that he does not constitute a target of special curiosity or design.

In the last decade some experimental social psychologists, notably Exline and Argyle, have undertaken research on eye contact in interaction. We know that in conversation most people look at one another for between 30 and 60 per cent of the time; that there is more eye contact while listening than while speaking; that women engage in more eye contact than men. Argyle (1967) has summarized the main functions of eye contact as a social technique. It may be used as a device to try to initiate interaction with another.

Goffman also draws our attention to many of the proprieties of everyday life, such as those of leave-taking. In interactions between superiors and subordinates the superior may give many cues that the interview is over, by standing up and moving towards the door or by saying directly, 'Thank you for coming to see me.' In interactions, especially informal ones, between equals the matter may prove to be more difficult as every host, weary of his guests at a late hour, knows to his cost. The host's hints that he would like to go to bed may have to be made very overt before the guests realize they are no longer welcome. Many of these proprieties have to be learned. For instance, a teacher who has called a young pupil to the desk to examine an exercise book may, at the end of the examination, turn the pupil round and propel him back to his seat to terminate the interview.

Consensus and modification

Each participant in an interaction is trying to establish a definition of the situation. If then the interaction is to proceed smoothly, there must be some agreement between the participants in the definitions of the situation they are trying to project. Such consensus about the definition of the situation involves a recognition and acceptance by each of the roles and goals of the other, an agreement about how each will treat the other, and the formulation of rules that will regulate conduct. For the consensus to be high, the definitions of situation projected and intended by each participant must be similar or compatible. In Goffman's (1959) view, absolute consensus is rare.

> Together the participants contribute to a single over-all definition of the situation which involves not so much a real agreement as to what exists, but rather a real agreement as to whose claims concerning what issues will be temporarily honoured. Real agreement will also exist concerning the desirability of avoiding an open conflict of definitions of the situation.

Typically, then, the consensus is a *working* consensus. Where the consensus about the definition of the situation is low, the interaction is subject to conflict and strain, which can be removed by the withdrawal of one or both participants in order to terminate the interaction, or by modification and compromise. In everyday life most interactions involve some degree of modification of the definition of the situation by one or both participants.

In reaching a consensus about the definition of the situation, each participant is constrained towards compromise by the demands of the other. Each can perform his role in the way he wishes, fulfil his own goals, and satisfy his needs only in so far as the other will allow him to do so. Unless Person has great power over Other, Person cannot force Other to accept his definition without demur. Both participants must be satisfied by the interaction; the satisfaction of each depends on the satisfaction of the other. If Person behaves in a way which conforms to Other's expectations and allows Other to realize his own goals, then Other will be gratified and disposed to reward Person in a variety of ways. If Person behaves in a way which conflicts with Other's expectations and inhibits Other's realization of his goals, then Other will be angry and disposed to withhold rewards and support from Person. There are very good reasons, then, why Person should try to please Other, for pleasing Other is instrumental to the attainment of his own goals. The problem is that in pleasing Other, Person may be led to behave in ways which prevent him from attaining his own goals. Thus it is that both Person and Other must reach some consensus about the definition of the situation, which is a compromise between 'having it all my way' and 'having it all your way'. The consensus is approached in terms of maximizing one's own satisfactions; the closer one can get to 'having it all my way' the better. Neither participant is usually prepared to settle for less. Thus the consensus concerning the definition of the situation is *negotiated* by the participants, and an obvious aspect of this is the negotiation of roles. In other words, often roles are not simply a *given* aspect of the situation but have to be agreed upon by the participants. It is difficult for me to perform the role of leader (benefactor, rebellious adolescent son, etc.) unless you are willing to perform the role of follower (beneficiary, unbendingly authoritarian father, etc.).

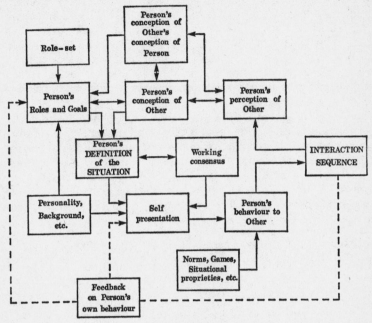

FIG. 4.2

We are now in a position to construct a rough model of the process of interaction (Fig. 4.2). The interaction sequence is made up of the contingent behaviour of each participant towards the other. For simplicity we shall deal with the interaction from a single participant's point of view. Person's behaviour towards Other is determined by two elements. The first concerns his roles and goals, which are influenced by his role-set and by his personality, needs and background. The second element is his conception of Other and his conception of Other's conception of him. These two elements influence one another and both contribute to Person's definition of the situation. Once formed, the definition of the situation arouses self-presentation techniques which need to be employed to translate Person's definition of the situation into actual behaviour towards Other, which is also conditioned by social norms, situational proprieties, games, etc. When Person behaves towards Other in a given way he gets feedback on the effect of his behaviour on Other, which may cause Person to modify his roles and goals, and thus all the other

83

elements of the model into which roles and goals feed, especially of course the definition of the situation and self-presentation. Other's reaction to Person's behaviour also influences Person's perception of Other, with consequent reinforcement or modification in the elements of the model to which this is connected. As interaction proceeds, Person's original definition of the situation has to be modified into a working consensus, which then becomes an intermediary link determining his behaviour towards Other. Eventually the working consensus may come to replace his original definition of the situation. In other cases Person's original definition of the situation may remain unimpaired even though his behaviour is effectively conditioned by the working consensus.

Finally, let us try to illustrate how all these concepts—defining the situation, perception of the other, self-presentation, working consensus, negotiation tactics and so on—look together in social interaction. The example is taken from Kingsley Amis's novel *I Want it Now* (1968). Ronnie Appleyard, a young television personality, is invited to a society party. When he arrives, the hostess, Mrs Reichenberger, is talking to a man in boots. When she sees Ronnie, she calls over to him.

'Mister-Heart-Throb in person. TV's Young Lochinvar. Nice of you to come, Mr. Appleyard.'

The possible satirical edge to these words was absent from her tone and manner. Actually she could have done with a bit of it in her manner; it was disturbing to think that all that breastwork might be for real. But, of course, Ronnie was overjoyed at this reception. Now that the need to gain her attention and fill her with a proper sense of his importance had been met in advance, all he need bother about was showing her that he was much too amusing and unspoiled by success not to be asked again very soon. Ten minutes' work at the most, after which he could get down to the more challenging tasks of (1) closing with and exploiting some of the other significant people here and (2) homing in on some unattended or incompetently escorted bird.

In the event it took nearer twenty minutes than ten, but promised proportionate gains. After the man in boots had been sent packing—not, Ronnie noted approvingly, without just the right amount of how fascinating it had been and how a proper get-together simply must be fixed up when everybody was back after the holidays—there was suddenly talk of an art-student son whose difficulties Ronnie might be the very man to understand. As described, the difficulties turned out to be nothing that being less of a talentless loafer would not cure, but he gave a full demonstration of himself being the said very man without having to offer the smallest help. As prelude, he had done some hypocritical surprise about any child of Mrs. Reichenberger's being of an age to have difficulties. Now, by way of epilogue, he did some eyes and tone of voice to suggest that he would not mind going to bed with Mrs. Reichenberger. The risk of being taken up on this total falsehood was as nothing compared with the certainty of being asked to more of the bag's parties.

Ronnie took himself off when a tiny painter and his rather large bird moved in among the pampas. The chap was up-and-coming all right, but had been at it for a decade. It was time he either came or went down again; anyway, he was not for Ronnie. Nor was his bird, who wore rococo spectacles and appeared to have white-washed her face before coming out.

. . . Ronnie went in the other direction, past an actor in a shiny green suit, a woman who was absolutely terrible at talking to kiddies on TV, a disc-jockey carrying in his arms a wriggling toy poodle, some young crap or other in Victorian army Officer's uniform, some little bitch or other dressed as a Spanish Lady, a food-and-drink pundit who was vigorously keeping up with both his subjects on the spot. None of these were any use to Ronnie. He left them behind . . .

Finally, Ronnie finds a girl who interests him.

As she stepped forward Ronnie noticed rather muzzily that her feet were bare and streaked with dirt. She spoke in a husky undertone.
'Hello, will you get me a drink?'
'What? Uh . . . what would you like?'
'Scotch and water. No ice.'
'Right.'
While he saw to this, Ronnie was wondering who the hell she was. And what she was. Not that it really mattered. He would forgive somebody who looked like that anything in the world. Even if she turned out to be a folk singer he was going to screw her.

He forced the whisky out of the bottle as quickly as was consistent with good manners, but by the time he got back to the girl with the face two other men had zeroed in on her: a television don and a little bastard in a four-button denim jacket and a very-queer-film-producer's trousers.

85

> 'Sorry chaps,' said Ronnie putting his arm through the girl's and walking her away, 'I'm afraid something's come up . . . nothing I can do about it . . . sorry . . . pity it's turned out like this . . .'

They go through the ritual of introductions and discover that they are both unmarried. Then Ronnie senses rivals. The girl shows interest in a colleague of Ronnie's who is also at the party. Ronnie decides to strike at once.

> Ronnie put sincerity, plus the merest dash of intimacy, into his gaze at Simon Whatsername. The . . . snuff-coloured ? . . . eyes gazed opaquely back at him.
> 'What about skipping out of here? Going and having dinner somewhere?'
> 'I'd rather go to bed,' she said in her habitual monotone.
> 'If you're tired some food'll perk you up.'
> 'I don't mean that. I don't feel tired. I mean sex.'
> This was exactly the sort of thing that Ronnie, in his role as a graduate student of Britain's youth was supposed to know all about. But, for the moment, his reaction was a simple, though uncomfortable mixture of lust and alarm, with alarm slightly to the fore. 'Okay,' he said reliably. 'Fine. Nothing I'd like better, love. We'll grab a taxi and go to my flat.' 'I can't wait,' droned the girl, 'I want it now.'

This is what is known as being hoisted by your own attempt to define the situation.

Recommended reading

M. ARGYLE, *Social Interaction*, Methuen, 1966.

E. GOFFMAN, *The Presentation of Self in Everyday Life*, Doubleday Anchor, 1959.

G. C. HOMANS, *Social Behaviour: Its Elementary Forms*, Routledge & Kegan Paul, 1961.

R. D. LAING, *The Politics of Experience*, Penguin, 1967.

5 Groups

Though by common consent the social psychological study of groups is referred to as 'group dynamics', it is surprisingly difficult to say precisely what is meant by the term *group*. It would not be very profitable to enter too deeply into the question of definition, but we must take the first few steps into this difficult terrain if we are to be clear what it is that social psychologists are seeking to study. One important kind of group is what might be called a sociological group or a *category*. We can group people together, in an infinite variety of ways, by members' common possession of a given characteristic. In this sense, all the following are groups or categories—males, adolescents, doctors, cricketers. Here people are classified according to a criterion of sex, age, occupation, and leisure activity respectively. But these categories are clearly not groups in the same sense of the term group as used in the following.

A group of friends met in the coffee bar.
A new cure for influenza has been discovered by a group
of research scientists.
The pupils asked Mr Smith to be in charge of the Political
Discussion Group.

These are examples of what the layman would call 'real' groups, whereas categories are logical groups. Sometimes they have a very real existence and members may be aware of their membership in a category, as in the case of doctors, but this need not be the case as in Sprott's (1958) example of 'red-haired archdeacons'. Groups of this latter variety exist only on paper, though these categories are often of major importance in sociological analysis. Social psychologists are little interested in categories as such, except in so far as membership in a category may affect the relations of members in a small group of interacting persons.

Groups as studied by social psychologists can also be distinguished from *social organizations*, such as a school, a factory, a village, a political party. These social organizations consist of complex networks of small groups. Sometimes they have a common spatial location (e.g. Dartmoor prison) but sometimes they do not (e.g. the Quakers). In becoming a member of a social organization one usually, but not always, also becomes a member of a small group. A teacher who joins the National Union of Teachers does not only belong to the massive social organization of thousands of teachers but he also belongs to a local branch and a small group of members within his own school. It is very difficult to say when a group develops into a social organization or to distinguish a large group from a small social organization. For the most part social psychologists have left the analysis of organizations to sociologists, though often the groups which social psychologists study are a part of a social organization.

The group, in the sense used by social psychologists in the field of group dynamics, has five basic characteristics. Unless all five criteria are met, there is no group, and we might refer instead to a 'collectivity' or 'aggregate' or 'near-group'.

1 *A group is a plurality of persons*. That is, two or more persons are needed to form a group. Some authorities would insist that a group must consist of at least three persons, since there are very fundamental differences between the dyad and groups of three or more persons. The criterion of plurality has another limitation; it does not state the upper limit to the plurality. The importance of the upper limit is clear when we consider how size affects the number of member relationships. In a dyad there are only two relationships (A–B and B–A). In the triad there are six (A–B, A–C, B–A, B–C, C–A, C–B). In a group of twenty persons, there are 190 relationships. At some point, then, there is an upper limit to the group, partly because beyond a certain point it will become rather like a social organization with sub-groups within it, and partly because beyond a certain size the group will fail to meet the remaining four criteria. The size of a group is in fact of major significance, since size affects all the group properties which follow. The reader might like to suggest in what way.

2 *The members are in face-to-face relationship, and aware of their common membership*. This is really tantamount to saying that the members must interact, that is, their behaviour must be reciprocally contingent. It is not easy, though not impossible, for persons to interact if they are not in regular face-to-face relationship.

3 *The members have common goals or purposes*. Groups have one or more goals that are common to most members. It is the goal which unites and draws them together as a group. Of course, members often have additional and personal goals. An adolescent may join a youth club not only because he wishes to follow the group goal of enjoying

his leisure in certain ways but also to achieve his private goal of becoming a powerful officer of the group or of keeping his Probation Officer quiet.

Because the members share common goals they are attracted to the group. Groups obviously vary in their attractiveness to members. Groups which satisfy the members' needs will be very attractive. If the group fails to attain any of its goals or does not meet members' needs then its attractiveness will fall, and if the attractiveness declines below a certain point, members will leave the group where this is possible. Usually the attractiveness of groups is referred to by social psychologists as their *cohesiveness*. This is a good term since it suggests the degree to which members will stick together. Cohesiveness can be measured in a variety of ways, such as the resistance of members to leaving the group.

4 *Members subscribe to a set of norms.* Norms are standards of behaviour which specify the conduct expected of members. They determine what is 'proper' within the group. Norms are required to regulate the behaviour of members and one of the most important functions of norms is to allow the members to achieve the group goal. Behaviour which is in line with the norms is rewarded; behaviour which deviates from the norms is punished. One of the reasons why persons who join groups for an individual goal come to share the group goal is that the norms spring from the goal in order to facilitate its achievement. It is easiest to conform to group norms if one is committed to the group's goals. Even if a member does not share the group goals, he must act as if he does, for if he does not conform to the norms, he will be punished by, or expelled from, the group. Conformity to norms is related to other group properties. It has been shown, for example, that the more cohesive a group is, the more members tend to conform to the group norms.

5 *Members are differentiated into a structure.* The members are not completely homogeneous. Members develop expectations of particular individuals. In other words, members come to perform different *roles* within the group. Moreover, as we shall examine in detail, some members are liked more than others and some members exert more influence than others. Some members become what we call 'leaders'.

These five properties or criteria certainly help to clarify what social psychologists mean by the small group. They also serve to introduce us to the ways in which social psychologists try to analyse groups. But at the same time it must be admitted that the five properties fail to give a clear and adequate specification of a group. Let us consider a class of children who have just been admitted into a secondary school. A few of them know one another and were friends at a previous school; many are strangers. They have been assigned to the class randomly by the teacher. As they are, they are probably not a group in the social psychologists' sense, for they do not meet the five properties. If we look at this same class of children a year later, we may find that they have become a group in that they now meet all the five properties. At which point did they cease to be an 'aggregate', that is, a collection of persons in common spatial location, and become a group?

If we wish to study the behaviour of people in groups, we have to begin our investigation at some particular point. We cannot look at the whole group life at the same moment, no more than we can understand the life of an organism such as a frog unless we reduce the complex whole into smaller parts. However, in dissecting the group into convenient 'bits' which can be analysed separately, we run the risk of losing sight of the significance of the whole. For preference, then, we would make as few basic 'bits' as possible. In the biological sciences the basic division is between anatomy and physiology. For social psychologists, one of the most simple means of analysing group behaviour is to consider the group as consisting of a *culture* and a *structure*. Although this is a very useful analytical distinction, the two interpenetrate in very important ways.

Group culture

When we consider the culture (or ideology) of a group, we are mainly concerned with the fact that groups have values, beliefs and norms. The focus is on the *homogeneity* of the members; we are stressing what they share in common. A group's *values* are the over-all guides to group behaviour, for it is the values which express what members regard as good, ideal and desirable. Group values are thus closely related to group goals. A religious group, for example, will have among its basic values the perfection and salvation of all its members and the conversion of non-members to these ideals. Among a group of teachers in school, basic values will be concerned with the intellectual, moral and social training of the pupils. These values will sometimes vary in different schools. Schools of a religious foundation, for example, tend to contain teachers with a higher valuation of religious and moral education than is the case in secular schools.

Values express themselves in the *beliefs* of members of the group. Beliefs are more specific than values. From the value 'religious education is desirable' flows a set of beliefs such as 'it is important for pupils to study the life of Christ', 'pupils should be taught the catechism' and 'prayers in school are an essential part of the educational experience'. When we remember that there are different religious groups, Christian versus Hindu, Roman Catholic versus Methodist, then it is clear that the same basic value—e.g. religious education is desirable—often leads to quite different sets of beliefs.

Many teachers share the value that 'more education is desirable' but it is a smaller number of teachers who on the basis of this value will share the belief that 'children should be given a longer period of compulsory education'. I have said that in examining the group culture, the accent is upon the homogeneity of members. With respect to values and beliefs, members of a group tend to share the same or very similar values and beliefs. This is not to say, of course, that there will be no disagreement amongst members, but rather that such disagreement will be in matters of detail about accepted values, or it will be disagreement about values which are irrelevant to the group. There are several reasons why group members tend to share common values. In the first place groups are selective in their membership. 'Birds of a feather flock together'; people want to join groups which are known to possess values congruent with their own values. An ardent atheist does not usually want to teach in a Church school, and even if he does, the school is unlikely to appoint him if there is a choice of candidates. Further, groups tend to be exposed to common information and ideas compatible with group values. In this sense the group acts as a filter on incoming information and rejects what is inconsistent. A Conservative Club does not usually subscribe to socialist periodicals. Even when information that is opposed to group values penetrates into the group, members interpret the information in the light of group values. A socialist pamphlet in a Conservative Club will be held up as an example of socialist 'errors' and 'lies'. It can be said, then, that there is a group interpretive scheme which is common to its members. When they are with the group or their membership in that group becomes salient, it is this interpretive scheme that will be activated. An individual's unique interpretive scheme is in part created and certainly supported by the (overlapping) interpretive schemes of the various groups to which he belongs. Once having developed a reasonably coherent set of interpretive schemes, the individual is then predisposed to favourable attitudes towards groups with compatible values and beliefs and interpretive schemes. The problems can become acute when involuntarily he is compelled to join a group that is incompatible in these respects.

Group *norms*, which flow from the group's values, are specifications of the beliefs, feelings, perceptions and conduct that are proper to group members. Norms are sets of shared expectations applied to the whole group and their purpose is to regulate conduct within the group so that the group goal may be achieved. Thus norms are a form of social control. Norms must be enforced, so they are backed by *sanctions*; rewards are given to members who conform to the norms and punishments to those who deviate from the norms. Sometimes the norms are formal, as when they are expressed in the rules and regulations of the group, but often they are informal. In the latter case the norms and sanctions play a subtle but important part in the life of the group and close observation is required before they can be specified.

Members of groups typically find it extremely difficult to explain to an outsider what the norms of the group are. This is partly because to members the norms are simply part of the taken-for-granted aspect of life in the group and partly because norms are often not stated explicitly. So if a teacher tries to 'observe' the norms of a group of pupils, a difficult and delicate task especially since the pupils may not behave normally if they sense they are being observed, then the teacher must take note of (i) how the norms are defined, what behaviours are expected or *not* expected, how the norms are expressed so that members become aware of them; (ii) how the members are constantly under surveillance by other members, how they monitor one another's behaviour to check on the conformity or non-conformity to the norms; and (iii) what the sanctions (rewards and punishments) are, how, when and by whom they are administered. This last point is particularly difficult for the observer, since the sanctions are very subtle. A smile or a nod from a leading member of the group can be most rewarding to other members, just as a slight frown or shrugging of the shoulders can be a signal of displeasure which warns the member concerned that he is departing from group norms. Extreme sanctions such as lavish praise, ridicule or ostracism are much rarer, though the observer can rejoice when he sees such reactions since they indicate that massive conformity or nonconformity are calling forth these sanctions. But in general it is much more difficult to observe and assess the significance of the smile, the frown and the mild teasing which are the constant feature of group life.

Most studies of life in groups do not give us a very extensive insight into the concealed intricacies of group norms. Rarely are we told of the extent to which members are aware of the norms; how much agreement among members there is about the norms; to whom and under what conditions and by whom the sanctions are applied; the degree to which the norms are rigorously enforced. However, one feature of norms which has received some attention is what has been called the 'latitude' of norms. Whilst norms prescribe the behaviour that is expected of members, they cannot specify in exact detail what is required. In other words norms can specify no more than what the Sherifs (1964) call 'the latitude of acceptable behaviour'. By this they draw attention to the fact that within a given norm there is a range of tolerable behaviour. There may be an ideal behaviour which is expected, but behaviours which fall short of the ideal may still lie within the acceptable range, though they will not result in as much reward or punishment as behaviour which falls nearer the upper or lower limits of the latitude of acceptable behaviour. A good example is based on work by Jackson (1960). Suppose some pupils are placed in a group to discuss a topic suggested by the teacher. A norm that members should contribute to the discussion will soon be evident, since if no-one contributes, there can be no discussion. The *amount* a particular individual speaks will be part of this norm. If the person says nothing, his behaviour may be disapproved. If he says little, the amount of disapproval shown to him will decrease, but in Figure 5.1

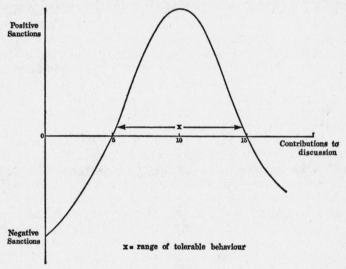

FIG. 5.1

—which is purely theoretical—the person who speaks for only 4 per cent of the discussion time is still not given any approval, on the grounds that he is not contributing a 'fair share' to the discussion. A person who speaks 5 per cent of the time has just entered the 'latitude of acceptable behaviour' and is treated with what can be called indifference, namely an absence of reward or punishment. From now on, the more he speaks, the more he is rewarded, until he reaches 10 per cent, which is the ideal behaviour and is the point of maximal reward. Speaking for more than 10 per cent receives less approval and such a person is seen by the members as taking more than his fair share in the discussion. Beyond 16 per cent, the speaker steps beyond the other limit on the range of tolerable behaviour and is likely to provoke various negative reactions from group members who see him as 'hogging' the discussion. Presumably most norms could be analysed in this way, though in practice it is very difficult to specify and measure the latitude of acceptable behaviour, though we do know that the more important an activity is to a group, the narrower will be the latitude of acceptable behaviour.

This last theoretical example of the group discussion also highlights the problem of observing sanctions. Just how do members react when a member talks too much in a discussion group? In my experience, the first negative reaction is to withdraw attention from the speaker, especially by declining to look at him. Later, members become more openly inattentive, by fidgeting or by looking elsewhere, such as through the window. If these sanctions are ineffective, members will make active attempts to draw the speaker's attention to his deviance, by making loud yawns or looking at one's watch. Finally, after attempted interruptions, the speaker will be told to shut up. In this way we can see that the longer the speaker goes on talking, the further he steps beyond the latitude of acceptable behaviour, and the more severe the group's sanctions become. Fortunately most of us are very sensitive to the mild sanctions and respond to them by making our behaviour fall into line with group norms long before extreme measures have to be taken.

A clever, and now classic, experiment by Stanley Schachter (1951) demonstrates what happens to the person who does refuse to fall into line. Schachter insinuated confederates into a discussion group. The *mode* was the confederate who followed the group's solution to the problem under discussion, the treatment recommendations for a juvenile delinquent. The *slider* disagreed with the position taken by most group members in the early stages of the discussion but later moved or slid with the majority view. The *deviate* confederate was instructed to take a consistently opposite view to the dominant one. When it was clear to the group members that the slider and deviate were failing to conform to majority opinion, they increased the amount of communication directed to them, presumably in an attempt to persuade them into accepting the dominant solution. When the slider accepted the persuasion, the amount of communication directed to him declined. The deviate, however, refused to slide. Still more communication was directed to him but after a certain point, when the members concluded that he was not to be persuaded, communication to him ceased. However, it was clear from questionnaires given to group members after the discussion, that the deviate was not liked by the group members and was not regarded as a desirable discussion group member for future occasions. He was, in short, rejected by the group.

It is significant, however, that this clear rejection of the deviate was more readily expressed on paper than in the overt behaviour. I have already suggested that in observing real life groups it is rare to see the application of extreme negative sanctions. This is partly because there is great pressure exerted on members to conform and refrain from giving open expression to their deviant views or behaviour, and partly because the members who are likely to receive such sanctions, the non-conformists, do not remain long in the group. Whyte's (1943) description of life in a neighbourhood gang provides an excellent description.

> In the spring of 1937 Nutsy was recognised informally as the superior of Frank, Joe, and Alec, but his relations with a girl had already begun to damage his standing. A corner boy is not expected to be chaste, but it is beneath him to marry a girl that is 'no good'. Nutsy was going so steadily with this girl that marriage seemed a distinct possibility, and, reacting to the criticism of his friends, he gradually withdrew from the gang.

In other words, expulsion of Nutsy from the gang was not necessary since the other members were able, by means of many less drastic sanctions, to make life sufficiently unpleasant for Nutsy that he voluntarily withdrew. Unfortunately Whyte does not tell us the specific content of the gang's 'criticism' of Nutsy.

There has been considerable research by social psychologists to examine the conditions under which people can be persuaded to yield to group pressure. Most of this research has been in rather artificial laboratory situations. The classic research on conformity is that of the American psychologist, Solomon Asch (1951). Nine students are seated in a semicircle as part of a psychological experiment. The experimenter presents two cards. On one card is a single vertical line, and on the other three vertical lines of different lengths, one of which is as long as the line on the first card. The task is to say which of the lines on the second card is of the same length as the line on the first card. The subjects announce their judgments in the order in which they have been seated. Since the judgments are very easy, all the students are unanimous. However, on the third trial one student near the end of the group disagrees with the other students. To this deviant the situation is very disturbing, for he does not know that the other eight students are confederates of the experimenter and that it has also been agreed beforehand that on certain trials the confederates will reach a unanimous but clearly incorrect judgment. The dramatic result of this experiment was that one-third of the 'naïve' subjects in this experiment followed the majority in making an obviously erroneous judgment in one-third of the trials.

Since one would expect the subjects to be aware of the gross discrepancy between their private judgment and the announced verdict, it is not surprising that in general they experienced considerable tension and anxiety. About one-quarter of the subjects remained independent throughout the experiment and refused to yield to group pressures.

At the other extreme is a group of subjects which yielded on most of the trials. Some of these were simply compliant; they followed the majority because of some overpowering need not to appear different from or inferior to others, but they still retained a discrepant private judgment. A few tried to rationalize their conformity by blaming one's own poor eyesight or by claiming that 'it looked different from where I was sitting'. In a few very extreme cases the subjects believed that they had made correct judgments and were unaware that their estimates had been distorted by majority opinion.

That intelligent university students should so frequently conform to majority opinion against the evidence of their own eyes has disturbing implications for the power of conformity in less dramatic situations in society at large. Further experiments were clearly needed. The most ingenious investigator to follow Solomon Asch has been Richard Crutchfield (1955) who ingeniously contrived an experimental situation in which all the subjects could be 'naïve' and thus avoided the expensive need for many confederates. Crutchfield's results confirm Asch's on perceptual judgments—about one-third of the judgments are conformist. However, Crutchfield also conducted some experiments with *opinions*. For example, when professionals and businessmen were led to believe that other subjects agreed with the statement *I believe we are made better by the trials and hardships of life*, 31 per cent followed the majority, whereas none of the control subjects—not under pressure to conform—agreed with the statement. Again, whilst only 19 per cent of students in a control situation agreed with the statement *Free speech, being a privilege rather than a right, it is proper for a society to suspend free speech whenever it feels itself threatened*, 58 per cent of those in a group pressure situation conformed. Army officers were presented with the statement *I doubt whether I would make a good leader*. Such a view is clearly incompatible with an army officer's position, so not surprisingly none of the control subjects agreed. Yet under group pressure where the officer was led to believe that other officers had agreed to the statement, 37 per cent yielded to group opinion.

The implications of the experiments of Asch and Crutchfield are highly disquieting, since they suggest that people can be persuaded to conform, even if in many cases this conformity is no more than an expedient compliance, to a surprising degree and against the evidence of their senses and on matters of opinion to which they do not individually subscribe. It is true that these experiments were not conducted in 'real' groups but in artificial laboratory conditions. It is difficult to experiment on conformity in real groups, but we have no reason to believe that degree of conformity indicated in these experiments would be reduced in a real group. Indeed, the evidence is to the contrary for it has been shown, though on less dramatic matters, that amongst highly cohesive groups (that is groups which are highly attractive to members) conformity tends to be much higher than in uncohesive groups. In the main, laboratory groups are uncohesive since they are formed simply for the experiment and have no real significance for their temporary members. In a cohesive group of friends the members have a great need to be accepted by their fellows, and the rewards for being allowed to remain in the group and the sanctions that can be brought to bear on deviating members are tremendously powerful. If this were not the case, the Nazi political and military machine would never have become a terrifying reality. More groups than we realize have greater powers over members than we imagine to pressure members in directions that go against individual opinions, judgment or conscience. Under skilful manipulation groups can always be used for evil purposes, or for political objectives as notably in China today. In the light of this the importance of 'education for independence' assumes an urgent significance.

Group structure

If the culture is one side of the coin in the study of groups then the structure is the other side. Whereas in group culture it is the homogeneity of group members that is emphasized, their common involvement in values, beliefs, norms and pressures to conformity, when we consider group structure it is the *heterogeneity* of members that is stressed. In other words it is the structure which differentiates the members from one another. The key notion in this process of differentiation is that members are ranked into a set of *hierarchies*, by which in certain respects some members are more valued by the group than are other members.

Before we can analyse this process in detail, it is essential to distinguish the formal structure from the informal structure. In many groups some members are assigned to formal positions. Clubs and societies frequently elect officers to execute special functions for the group, such as president, chairman and secretary. Sometimes the officers are appointed by an authority external to the group. In a few cases we have a mixed variety where members elect one officer who then has a right to appoint officers to serve under him. In many cases the roles of the officers are governed by a set of rules which expound their duties and rights. In large social organizations the formal structure is likely to be extremely complex. The rules and regulations controlling the behaviour of members will be minutely detailed. Patterns of authority, the chain of command, specialization of tasks and responsibilities, channels of communications, all these will be part of the rational plan or blueprint that is drawn up to determine the behaviour of members. Every social organization has its own version of Queen's Regulations.

Many small groups do not have a formal structure. But it is erroneous to conclude that such groups therefore do not have a structure. It is simply that the structure is *informal*. Some groups have a formal structure, others do not; but all groups have an informal structure. The distinction between the two types of structure is very important. Consider a class of pupils in a school. Not infrequently the school class has a formal structure. The officers, such as the class president or the form captain and various other prefects and monitors, may be elected by the pupils themselves or appointed by the teacher. When the officers are elected, it is likely that the formal and informal structures will overlap and interpenetrate, since in general the pupils will elect to the formal positions class members who are most valued by the group. If the officers are appointed by the teachers, then the two structures may no longer interpenetrate. The teacher will probably appoint pupils that he values, but these pupils may not be the ones who are valued by the pupils and who have a high rank in the informal structure. Indeed, the teacher may appoint pupils who are among the least valued by the class, in which case the formal and informal structures will be in conflict.

To recognize the important consequences of such relationships between the two structures, we must try to analyse in depth the dynamics of the informal structure. To the outsider—and in relation to the class the teacher is in many respects an outsider—the informal structure is concealed; its workings and often its very existence are shrouded in mystery. Yet its presence and its hidden processes are of crucial significance for the group members and thus cannot be ignored by the teacher.

The informal structure of a group is concerned with the differential ranking of group members according to the degree to which members are valued by the group. The product is what from now on I shall call a *status hierarchy*. Three main dimensions of the status hierarchy have been elaborated by social psychologists, though there is unfortunately no agreed terminology with which to describe them. In other words, there are three forms of status. The first is what is often called *sociometric status*. This dimension is concerned with the distribution of liking within the group, whereby some members are liked more than others. The members who receive most liking are popular; those who receive least are unpopular. This dimension is called sociometric status out of respect for Moreno, who invented a method of measuring the distribution of liking within a group which he called sociometry.

A sociometric test typically asks pupils to name three pupils with whom they would like to associate in three areas. For instance, pupils are asked whom they would like to sit next to in class, with whom they would like to work on a group project, and with whom they would like to share a holiday or play situation. Thus each child has nine votes at his disposal. When we consider the distribution of these nominations we find that some children receive many choices and others receive very few. The former, namely the popular pupils, are referred to by sociometrists as 'overchosen' or 'stars', and the latter are termed 'underchosen'. Children who cast votes to others but receive none are called 'neglectees' and pupils who neither give nor receive choices are called 'isolates'.

Sociometry has become a highly developed system with its own language and forms of analysis. Most teachers are now familiar with the most common form of representing the sociometric structure, namely the sociogram, but many more elaborate forms of measurement are readily available (Proctor & Loomis, 1951; Evans, 1962). One of the reasons why the sociogram has become popular is that it reveals the clique or sub-group structure within the larger group.

The sociometric structure arises out of the tendency of human beings to develop feelings of like and dislike towards others. It is because the evaluation of others in terms of liking is so basic to human interaction that it becomes one of the main dimensions by which group members can be differentiated. Whilst it is a relatively easy matter to measure the distribution of liking within the group, it is much more difficult to explain this distribution. Why is it that some members are popular but others are not? Social psychologists who have specialized in sociometry have conducted extensive researches into the correlates of high and low sociometric status within children's groups. In some school classes the popular children tend to be more intelligent (Bonney, 1944; Heber, 1956; Thorpe, 1955) but this is not always the case (Kelley, 1963). Sometimes popular children are disproportionately from the higher social classes (Bonney, 1944), sometimes they are not distinguishable from the rest in this regard (Dahlke, 1953). We shall examine the reasons for these inconsistent results later. Even where such factors as intelligence and social class are shown to be associated with popularity, it is not at all easy to explain why this should be the case. In other words, even where these factors are demonstrably *correlates* of popularity, it is difficult to explain for what reason they might be regarded as *determinants* of popularity. Attempts to relate popularity to personality characteristics have been more successful. Usually the more popular children are more cheerful, happy, considerate, fair-minded, sociable, extravert, socially sensitive and have a better sense of humour. Pupils of low sociometric status are often belligerent and quarrelsome. These findings confirm common-sense predictions. We can see very good reasons why one should be attracted to the former personality but be repelled by the latter variety.

The second dimension of status within groups is concerned with *social power* or influence. We may define social power as 'the potentiality for inducing forces in another person toward acting or changing in a given direction' (Lippitt, Polansky & Rosen, 1952). A person with high social power possesses the ability to exert influence over another so that the second person will behave in line with the intentions or desires of the first person. As the sociometric structure betrays the unequal distribution of liking within the group, so the social power structure reveals the unequal distribution of influence within the group. Group members at the top of the social power hierarchy influence more than they are influenced and have a high resistance to being influenced; low social power members have a low resistance to influence from others and are influenced more than they themselves influence.

The interpersonal nature of power relationships is made clear by Emerson's (1962) analysis. A person can have power over another to the degree to which the second person is dependent on the first. In other words, the power of one person is definable in terms of the dependence of the other. This power-dependence relationship between two persons A and B can be represented as

$$PAB = DBA$$

A's power over B is equal to B's dependence on A. Whilst A may have power over B is one respect, it is quite possible that in other areas B has power over A. Two types of relationships emerge. In the first the power *as a whole* is shared equally, though in particular situations the power is sometimes exerted by A and sometimes by B. This relationship of balanced power can be represented as

$$PAB = DBA$$
$$=\qquad=$$
$$PBA = DAB$$

If, however, A influences B to a greater extent than B influences A, then A can be said to be more powerful than B and B more dependent than A. This is clearly indicated in the diagram.

$$PAB = DBA$$
$$\vee\qquad\vee$$
$$PBA = DAB$$

One of the best experimental studies of social power among children is that of Lippitt, Polansky & Rosen (1952), whose subjects were boys at a summer camp. Measures were taken of *attributed* social power, how the children rated one another in terms of the ability to influence ('who is best at getting others to do what he wants them to do?'), and *manifest* social power, that is actual success in exerting influence as observed in the daily life of the camp by the researchers. There was a high level of agreement among the children about which members possessed high social power and the study shows that children who are high on attributed social power are also high on manifest social power. High-power children are more active, make more direct influence attempts and are more often successful in their influence attempts than are low-power children. Moreover high-power children are more often imitated, which is a form of unintended influence. Low-power children are deferential and approval-seeking in their behaviour towards high powerers, and if they do try to influence are more non-directive in their approach, that is, they are more likely to suggest 'Shall we . . . ?' than to state 'We shall . . .' In short this study shows that children are aware of the distribution of social power within their groups and that this distribution has a marked effect on social relationships in the groups.

The third element which differentiates group members into a status hierarchy is *prestige*. As we shall see, prestige is normally the least important of the three dimensions. Unfortunately the term prestige is used by different writers in so many different ways that it is a highly ambiguous concept. In this book I shall be using it in a specialized and restricted sense. Whereas liking and power status are acquired by particular group members in their relationships with one another in the interactions of the informal group, prestige arises only within a *formal* structure. This is because prestige is attached to positions, not persons. All occupations have varying degrees of prestige and can be arranged into a prestige hierarchy. Some professions, such as medicine and the law, have high prestige status. The point is that the prestige is attached to the position. Dr Smith has high prestige because he is a physician, not because as John Smith he has particular qualities or behaves in certain ways. Often these positions have prestige symbols—what are popularly called status symbols—which make the position highly visible to others. Teachers wear academic gowns, soldiers wear uniforms, and in the Civil Service you can gauge a man's position on the basis of the size of the carpet in his office.

In the small group, prestige can become an important dimension of status where there is a formal structure. The group president or secretary are positions that may carry considerable prestige and for this reason members may aspire to these positions. If there is no formal structure, there can be no prestige structure. The possession of high prestige status may help a person to acquire high status along other dimensions, but this is by no means always the case. A head-teacher has high prestige status, but if the teachers who serve under

101

him do not like him and are little influenced by him then his socio-metric and social power status will be low.

School prefects are a good example of the complex way in which prestige relates to other forms of status. The position of prefect carries great prestige. The prestige comes with the office and does not have to be earned. Thus one of the major problems of the prefect is to acquire sociometric and social power status that are congruent with the high prestige status. The situation is complicated by the fact that a prefect is delegated definite formal power by the teachers. Since he is expected to carry out supervisory tasks and enforce school rules and regulations he is given the power to punish pupils by means of detentions, impositions and sometimes even corporal punishment. However, a prefect may also influence the behaviour of pupils with-out resorting to his formal power and he is likely to elicit feelings of like and dislike from them. The interpenetration of formal status (prestige and formal power) with informal status (popularity and social power) can be clarified by considering different types of prefect. The 'hard' prefect believes in carrying out his duties to the letter. Whenever he discovers that the rules are being broken, he punishes the offender according to the book and does not easily listen to or accept excuses. He does not relish the task, but he does not shrink from it. He does what he considers to be his duty. In a more extreme form he becomes the 'tyrant' who fulfils his duties with ardour, actively seeking out offenders whom he punishes ruthlessly, even when the offence is minor or merely technical. He arrogantly abuses his power because he enjoys it. The 'hard' prefect and the 'tyrant' rely entirely on their formal power. They do not possess informal social power; they can influence people only under threat of punishment. Obviously they have low sociometric status. The 'soft' prefect is one who attempts to exercise his formal powers but finds that he cannot do so. His diffidence and lack of confidence prevent him from en-forcing the rules and the pupils do not obey him. In extreme cases his threats based on his formal power elicit scorn and laughter from pupils. He may try to exercise informal power by making personal pleas or similar influence attempts but in this he is equally unsuccess-ful. Whilst the 'soft' prefect is not disliked, he is not liked either. He is despised. The 'irresponsible' prefect avoids the problems of his office by declining to exercise any power at all, either formal or informal. He shirks his duties and whenever possible remains in the sanctity of the prefects' room. He accepts and enjoys the rights and privileges of his position, but rejects his duties and obligations. In some cases this may be because he enjoys high status in other respects, e.g. as a star footballer, which may be jeopardized if he tries to enforce school rules.

The 'ideal' prefect, who like the 'tyrant' is so vividly portrayed in schoolboy stories, prefers informal to formal power. Whilst he is willing to use his formal power and does so successfully on occasion, he is generally reluctant to do so. He is willing to listen to excuses and explanations and to give offenders a second chance. It is no pleasure for him to punish. Because he exercises his formal power so rarely, and never in an arbitrary or unfair manner, he is liked and admired and respected. Pupils obey him and are open to his influence. Through his greater use of informal power he is able to influence pupils voluntarily to conform rather than to punish them for non-conformity. He transforms his high prestige and formal power into high sociometric and social power status. He is what we call a 'natural leader'.

Within the informal group, prestige status and formal power are of course absent by definition. In the informal group it is the relationship between sociometric and social power status which is problematic. Do these two forms of status tend to hang together or are they alternatives that do not reside in the one person? Before we answer this question we must consider the more fundamental issue of why some persons acquire either type of status. To show that informal groups develop sociometric and social power hierarchies does not tell us why they emerge in the first place. In other words, we must examine the reasons for the unequal distribution of liking and influence in the group. To do this we must introduce some new concepts. All group members bring to the life of the group certain *properties*. These properties may be a possession (e.g. a car or a cricket bat), a skill (e.g. the ability to fight or to play a game well) or a characteristic (e.g. a personality trait or an interest). Because groups have distinctive values and goals some of the many properties of the group members are more relevant to the life of the group than others. A property such as the possession of a cricket bat is more relevant to a group that is interested in cricket than to one that is not. When a property is valued by a group, because it is likely to make a contribution to the achievement of the group's goal, it is called a *resource*. When a member possesses a resource (a property that is of value to group members) he is able to mediate rewards to the group, and this ability gives him power over the group members. The group member who possesses the cricket bat has power to determine whether or not the group plays cricket, at least to some degree.

The concept of resource is important because it emphasizes the interpersonal nature of power. In Emerson's analysis of power it was made clear that power is not an attribute of the single person but something which arises in a relationship between two or more persons. The concept of resource is interpersonal in that a property becomes a resource only when it is valued by another person. One gains power by having a property that is valued by others. It is also

103

an essentially economic concept in that the more scarce a resource is within a group the more it will be valued by the group members and thus the more power it will give to its owner. The possession of a cricket bat will give little power to its owner if all the members have a cricket bat—or if alternative sources of or substitutes for the cricket bat are available. The concept of resource clearly fits in with an exchange theory analysis of human behaviour.

The relationship between resources and social power has been demonstrated by Gold (1958) among children aged between five and twelve years. Gold gave the children two tests, one to find out which properties were valued by the children and which members possessed the resources, and the other to find out who exercised most influence. He confirmed that the group members who were attributed most social power also possessed more resources. In all the groups a helpful and friendly personality was regarded as a resource, but it was only in boys' groups that strength and fighting ability were resources. In the study of boys at a summer camp by Lippitt, Polansky & Rosen, discussed earlier, the boys who possessed the greatest social power were also superior in camp-craft skills, which would obviously be valued by the boys and thus contribute to status.

We can now return to the question of the relationship between sociometric and social power status. Several researchers have examined the problem and find that the two tend to correlate positively. The Sherifs (1964) found that in boys' groups the two forms of status correlate between 0·64 to 0·84 and Lippitt, Polansky & Rosen (1952) report almost exactly the same result, 0·63 to 0·82. In short, those who are more liked also exercise the most influence. The concept of resource helps us to understand this correlation, for the same resource may be the basis of both liking and power. In most groups a friendly personality is valued by the members since such behaviour makes life pleasant. Friendliness stimulates feelings of liking, leading to sociometric status, and also gives power as well. A similar situation arises with other resources, such as the ability to play a game well. In a football team the star's ability with the ball is highly valued by the members, who want to beat their opponents, and he thus acquires power. But his skill and expertise arouse admiration, which is a form of liking. It is because one resource can bring attraction *and* power to its owner that sociometric and social power status tend to go together.

We can now make sense of some of the earlier findings on the relation between popularity and group member characteristics. Some studies of children's groups revealed a correlation between popularity and intelligence, but others did not. This can now be explained in terms of the degree to which intelligence is a group resource. Where intelligence is valued by group members, then intelligent members will acquire informal status. In Hallworth's (1953) study of several classes in a mixed grammar school, popularity correlated with intelligence or attainment in some classes but not in others. We can explain this variation by considering the group's values. In one class the central value among the girls was academic success. From this fact we can predict that there will be a positive relationship between informal status and academic position. This is so, for there is a very high correlation between popularity and examination performance. Indeed, sociometric status gives a better prediction of academic success than does the intelligence test score! In short, if one wishes to examine the reasons behind the nature and the distribution of informal status within the group, one must consider the group's central values.

In our discussion of group structure we have been concerned with the unequal distribution of influence and liking among group members. It is not the case that one person does all the influencing and receives all the liking. It is a matter of degree. Some persons influence and are liked more than others and all members can be ranked into a hierarchy according to the extent to which they influence or are liked. How then does the concept of group *leader* fit into our conception of group structure and status hierarchies?

In earlier years leadership tended to be conceptualized as an all-or-none phenomenon. Either a person was a leader or he was not. When such a conception dominated in psychology—as it still dominates the popular view of leadership today—the main problem was to discover the characteristics or traits which distinguished leaders from non-leaders. After many years of investigation the result was a highly confused and inconsistent picture. For every study which appeared to demonstrate a clear relationship between leadership and a particular personality trait, another could be found which failed to confirm the first result.

The low levels of the correlations and the inconsistency of the experimental results marked the end of the trait approach. A different conceptualization of leadership was needed and began to emerge. Interest shifted from the study of individual personality towards a consideration of the leader's role relationship in interaction with other group members, the goals and activities of the group, and the current situation of the group. This is not to suggest that the leader's personality is irrelevant but rather to see personality in relation to other factors. As C. A. Gibb (1947) states: 'Leadership is both a function of the social situation and a function of personality, but it is a function of these two in interaction.'

Our analysis has conceptualized leadership in terms of the more general structural differentiation within the group. The term leader is applied to the member (or members) who emerges at the top of the social power and sociometric status hierarchies. This assumes that these hierarchies are fairly static, but it may be that one person may not exercise most social influence in *all* situations. If this is the case, then we shall have to say that the leadership shifts between different members in different situations according to which member is exercising most influence at a particular time. It is true that at times many groups may find themselves in situations where the person who normally exercises most influence loses his leadership role and gives place to another member who has more resources to cope with the novel situation and thus assumes the leadership. However, in real life groups such situations are likely to be rare. Most groups operate within a very limited variety of situations in which one person is in general likely to exercise more influence than other members. It is to such persons that we could apply the term leader. In Kelvin's (1970) words: 'The leader is not simply the particular individual who happens to influence the group at a particular moment; he is, rather, the individual who influences it most consistently over a more or less prolonged period.' At the same time we must remember that many groups, when asked, deny the existence of a leader. This may be because the group is unaware that one person is consistently exercising more influence than others or because they may resent the notion that one member is more powerful than others, even though such is the case. But it may also be true that among small groups of three or four friends it can justifiably be claimed that there is no leader. The differences in the amounts of influence exercised by individual members may be very small, or influence may be exercised by different members in different situations and on different occasions. Thus no one member may merit the title of leader. The exercise of influence is an inherent part of group life, but the existence of a leader is not.

Given that most groups do contain a general leader, we need to examine in further detail the behaviour of such persons that leads them to rise to the top of the status hierarchy. The most important element, as we have suggested, is the possession by the leader of resources that allow him *to make the greatest single contribution to the group goals*, be they 'instrumental' or 'expressive'. In this sense the structure of a group is closely linked with its culture. Structural differentiation is related to each member's ability to realize group values and goals. Hamblin (1958), in an ingenious laboratory experiment, showed that a person who is seen to be most skilled on the group task is perceived as the group leader, but when the task performance is manipulated so that the leader ceases to make the principal contribution to task achievement, he loses his position and is replaced. This phenomenon is readily observable in political life.

The relationship between task skill and leadership is complex. As Whyte (1943) has noted, the leader need not be the most outstanding footballer or fighter, but he must have some skill in the group's major pursuits. The leader also promotes activities in which he is skilful, so that his high level performance is both a consequence of his position and an important support of that position. Should the group's central activity change due to external factors, then a change in the group's structure and leadership is possible. The Sherifs (1964) quote a case where a tough, lower-class group of boys, with the help and encouragement of an adult, developed an interest in basketball. After a period of training and coaching the original leader began to lose status and was replaced by another boy who was both a better player and more effective in team decisions.

Sometimes a group member may be more skilled at a task than his position in the status structure would seem to warrant. In such cases the group may pressure the member to display a task performance that is congruent with his status. In Whyte's (1943) study, Alec was extremely skilled at bowling, but his status in Doc's gang was very low. A competition between members of the gang was arranged.

Alec let it be known that he intended to show the boys
something. . . . After the first four boxes [frames], Alec was
leading by several pins. He turned to Doc and said, 'I'm
out to get you boys tonight.' But, then he began to miss, and,
as mistake followed mistake, he stopped trying. Between
turns he went out for drinks, so that he became flushed and
unsteady on his feet. He threw the ball carelessly, pretending
that he was not interested in the competition. His collapse
was sudden and complete; in the space of a few boxes he
dropped from first to last place.

Alec's failure to produce a performance congruent with his ability seems to have two sources. Firstly, his knowledge of his low status in the group undermined his confidence in his ability to beat a high status member. Secondly, the others heckled him when he was performing too well. In fact Whyte himself won the contest.

Every corner boy expects to be heckled as he bowls, but the
heckling can take various forms. While I moved ahead as
early as the end of the second string, I was subjected only
to good-natured kidding. The leaders watched me with mingled
surprise and amusement; in a very real sense, I was permitted
to win.

Another good example of the way in which the group situation can influence the ability of certain members to contribute to the group goal is available in the N.F.E.R. report on streaming (Joan Barker Lunn, 1970). There was a greater tendency for boys of above average ability to emerge as sociometric leaders and for boys of below average ability to be neglectees in non-streamed schools than in streamed

107

schools. This finding can be explained in terms of the way in which school organization affects the resources in the children's groups. In the streamed school the pupils within any one class are very similar in ability and are less likely to be given group work. In the non-streamed school, children of all abilities are represented in each class and group work occurs more frequently. In the A stream of a streamed school the fact that a pupil is of above average ability cannot serve as a resource to aid the acquisition of status since *all* the pupils are of above average ability and ability does not differentiate the pupils. In the non-streamed school, however, the boys of above average ability are in a minority and are able to make a greater contribution to the achievement of academic goals, especially where pupils are working in mixed ability groups within the class. The bright boy's ability serves as a resource and grants him status. Significantly this greater sociometric status of above average boys is evident on the 'work with' criterion of sociometric status but not on the criteria of 'play with' or 'best friend'. This is in line with our explanation since greater ability is a resource when the goal is academic ('work with') but in other situations ('play with', 'best friend') the possession of greater ability is irrelevant to group goal achievement. A related finding which is of considerable interest to us is that in non-streamed schools this effect was more powerful when classes were taught by the more traditional (Type 2) teachers than by the more progressive (Type 1) teachers. This suggests that the greater valuation of academic ability and the lower interest in the slow learners characteristic of Type 2 teachers was conveyed to the pupils and influenced the ways in which they valued one another. This is one of the rare pieces of evidence which suggests that the teacher's attitude can affect the informal status structure of pupils.

A second way in which the group's culture and structure are inter-related is the area of conformity to group norms. The members of high status, the leaders, *are the most conformist to the group norms.* Members who conform least have the lowest status. That conformity to group norms is one of the dimensions of structural differentiation is easily explained by the fact that lack of conformity to group norms clearly threatens the stability and cohesion of the group and also the achievement of group goals. The member who conforms helps the group and is valued accordingly. The leader, then, tends to be an exemplar of the group norms.

The fundamental importance of conformity to norms in the acquisition of status is demonstrated in the work of Merei (1949) on nursery children in eastern Europe. Merei, from his observation of these children, was able to distinguish those who consistently exercised most influence (the leaders) from those who were influenced (followers). These latter children he assigned to a number of new groups. After a time each group had developed a distinctive culture and set of norms concerning such matters as the seating arrangements, the division of toys, ceremonies, special language usage and so on. Then one of the 'leaders' was added to the group. The leader immediately tried to give orders but his attempted influence was not automatically accepted by the rest of the group. On the contrary, he was ignored or rebuffed. The leader had to learn the norms and traditions of the group and he then began to exercise influence in these terms. In other words he had to adapt to the group culture before he could assume leadership. One type, whom Merei calls the diplomat, followed this pattern but also began to introduce small changes into the group culture and became the leader of these new games. Later he was able to effect more radical revisions in the group's traditional games.

There is also evidence that the leader can deviate from the group norms more than others. If the group meets a crisis the leader may well need to do so in order to save the group or to ensure that the group can continue to achieve its goal even though the circumstances of the group have changed. Hollander (1960) has shown that those who eventually emerge as leaders of a group tend to be more conformist than others early in the life of the group, but that once the leaders have achieved their high status, deviation from the norms incurs less disapproval than does deviation by lower status members. The Sherifs (1964) have suggested that in matters of great importance to the group the leader is allowed less room for deviation from the norm but that in more peripheral areas the leader is allowed greater latitude for non-conformity.

The leader of a group *tends to be central in the communication structure*. He must have access to information about what is happening in the group and he must also be able to disseminate his views to other members. Whyte (1943) talking about the Norton Street gang, shows that the leader is the focal point of group organization. When he is absent the group breaks up into small cliques. When he appears, the discussion is co-ordinated and focused on him. Members do not speak unless they know that the leader is listening. Although the members thus direct many of the communications to the leader, Whyte reports that the leader does not always communicate with the group as an undifferentiated mass. Often when mobilization of the group is required, the leader communicates his views to the lieutenants first. In other words, communications from the leader often pass down the channels of the status hierarchy.

Whilst the status differentiation of members within the group structure is a relatively easy group phenomenon to demonstrate, it is much more difficult to examine the *process* by which this differentiation occurs. The Sherifs (1964) have shown that it is the extreme positions which emerge first, a process which they call 'end-anchoring'. Group members first identify the leader, who acts as a primary anchor, and then the low status members emerge and act as a secondary anchor. Group members of intermediate status are the last to be differentiated and in practice these members cannot be assigned an exact rank order position. It may be that they are never clearly differentiated but it is also possible that there are frequent minor changes of rank order among middle status members.

Recommended reading

D. CARTWRIGHT & A. ZANDER, *Group Dynamics*, Tavistock, 1963 and subsequent editions.

J. KLEIN, *The Study of Groups*, Routledge & Kegan Paul, 1956.

M. OLMSTED, *The Small Group*, Random House, 1959.

M. & C. W. SHERIF, *Reference Groups*, Harper, 1964.

W. J. H. SPROTT, *Human Groups*, Penguin, 1958.

For a quite different approach to group life see:
W. R. BION, *Experiences in Groups*, Tavistock, 1961.

part two

Applications

6 Teacher–pupil relations: a basic analysis

In this chapter, and the remaining chapters of the book, we shall be making a more systematic application, to educational contexts and situations, of the theoretical ideas and concepts of social psychology which were outlined in Part One of the book. In so doing, I will not only make the assumptions of the symbolic interactionist, but I shall also necessarily make a number of important value-judgments about schools and classrooms, and about education in our contemporary society. At times, the writing is openly polemical. The reader has, I think, the right to know where I stand. At the same time I hope that my analysis is not so heavily clouded by my own value position that the reader will be prevented from dissenting from, or offering alternative interpretations to, my analysis and my prescriptions. What I have written is presented in the spirit of a dialogue. Because it is a book, the dialogue is one-sided. I trust that the reader will always seek to respond to what is written with his own analysis and views and avoid the danger of merely being persuaded by it. Practical applications are by their nature controversial, not least because they raise a variety of moral and ethical questions. But I hope, too, that they will be controversial in that they will lead the reader to question the adequacy of the theory and research from which the applications are drawn.

If we are to analyse the ways in which teachers and pupils define the situation and reach a working consensus, we must first of all consider those characteristics which are peculiar to interactions between teachers and pupils. Our model of interaction must, in other words, take account of the distinctive quality of teacher–pupil relations in classrooms. Perhaps the most striking feature of the world of the classroom is that the pupils are compelled by law to be present in school. Most interactions are entered freely by the participants. If, for whatever reason, the interaction is unattractive or unsatisfying, the participants can withdraw. Pupils at school have no choice: they are required to enter into interaction with the teacher. This feature is not unique to schools. In mental hospitals, in prisons, and in the armed services, the patients, prisoners and enlisted men are in a similar situation. In practice, of course, pupils are usually by no means reluctant participants, but this does not alter the involuntary basis to their presence in school, for there are times in the lives of all pupils when they would prefer not to be at school. If they do *want* to be present, so much the better. If they do not want to be present, they will be compelled to attend. A pupil who does not wish to go to school has two means of escape. He can play truant, which is at best a short-term measure, since the system employs agents who will seek him out and require him to return. Alternatively he can withdraw from school not physically but *psychologically*, for instance by day-dreaming, or by committing himself only minimally to the requirements imposed on him when he is present. (Psychological withdrawal is more frequent and a more complex reaction by the pupil to his involuntary presence in the classroom and we shall consider it in more detail later). Even 'normal' children, who presumably do not complain excessively about having to go to school, and who enjoy much of their lives in school, tend to associate absence from school, especially holidays, as a time of freedom and blessed release.

Teachers also recognize the involuntary nature of the child's presence in school in many subtle ways. For example, it is not uncommon for teachers to reward 'good' children by letting them out of school a little earlier than the rest of the pupils. As Philip Jackson has pointed out, this is reminiscent of the remission system in prisons —time off for good behaviour.

The second distinctive feature of teacher–pupil interaction is the enormous power differential between the two participants. This again is not unique to classrooms. Most men and women enter situations with a similar power differential when they interact with their superiors at work. What is notable about the teacher–pupil relationship is the fact that the pupil spends so much of his time directly in such a relationship and that the power differential between teacher and pupil is so great. In classrooms, teachers are permitted to and frequently do make almost all the decisions affecting the child's behaviour. What the teacher says goes. It is the duty of the pupil to accept and obey—preferably without question. The teacher's power derives from several sources: from his status as an adult; from his traditional authority as a teacher; from his legal authority; from his expertise in the subject matter he is teaching. The power differential shows itself in the asymmetrical rights possessed by the teacher, rights which extend far beyond the right to invoke formal sanctions. For example, the teacher has a generally accepted right to intrude into or interrupt the child's activities at will. A child in school can have no legitimate privacy and no legitimate secrets. 'Show me what you have in your desk' or 'Empty out your pockets onto the table' are permissible requests from teachers—even though they may be resented by the pupils. On the other hand, the child must learn to respect the teacher's privacy, for the teacher cannot be intruded upon at the child's whim. If he wishes to speak to the teacher, he must signal the teacher with a raised hand and wait patiently for the teacher to catch his attention and give permission to speak. A teacher's action to the pupil which is defined by the teacher as 'being helpful' could, if it were reciprocated by the child to the teacher, be easily defined as 'being rude'.

The outcome of these two distinctive characteristics of teacher–pupil interaction is the great inequality of the two participants in the process of defining the situation. The dice are loaded in the teacher's favour. He can take the initiative in defining the situation and possesses the power to enforce it on the pupils.

Since the teacher is in a position to determine and enforce his own definition of the situation on the pupils, then the behaviour of the pupils will be highly dependent on the teacher's behaviour. This is to be expected since, in terms introduced in Part One, teacher–pupil interactions are typically *asymmetrically contingent*: the pupils' behaviour is much more contingent on the teacher's behaviour than the teacher's behaviour is contingent on the pupils' behaviour. That is to say, pupils' classroom behaviour is a product of, and a response to, the teacher's interpretations of his role and his teaching style. Whilst it is true that the pupils' behaviour is influenced by many other factors than the teacher's behaviour, and whilst it may be that the teacher adapts his behaviour in response to the special characteristics of the pupils in his class, we would expect the pupils to adapt to the teacher to a much greater degree than the teacher to the pupils.

The studies of Anderson & Brewer (1945) are of direct relevance to us, because these were experimental investigations of the behaviour of teachers and pupils in classrooms. From their observations they suggest two basic extreme teacher types, the *dominative* and the *integrative*. The dominative teacher can be characterized as working *against* the pupils. He thinks he knows best; issues orders and imposes his decisions; wishes the pupils to obey and conform; dislikes discussion or criticism; tends to threaten and blame. The integrative teacher, in contrast, can be said to work *with* others. He requests rather than orders; consults the pupils and invites their co-operation; shares the control and responsibility; encourages the pupils' ideas and initiative. Under integrative teachers the pupils make greater contributions to the lesson; show great appreciation of others; are more friendly and co-operative; are less inattentive, aggressive and resistant to instruction.

It is this research which offers the greatest support for our contention that it is the pupils who adapt to the teacher rather than vice versa. The teachers remain consistent in their teaching style even with different classes of children. But the pupils change their behaviour as a function of the teaching style. When pupils move from an integrative to a dominative teacher (or vice versa) marked changes in their behaviour occur. It is the teacher, then, who is the principal creator of the climate that prevails in the classroom; the pupils' response is largely determined by the teacher's behaviour.

The teacher's classroom role

Given that the teacher has greater initiative and power in defining the situation, how does he indeed define it? Obviously his first step is to define the situation in such a way that he can perform his role as teacher in a way he regards as adequate. His definition of the situation must be congruent with his conception of his classroom role. Such a role conception will in the last analysis be unique to the individual teacher. Our present task is to consider the range of role conceptions that teachers might assume in the classrooms. Many writers have devised sets of teacher *sub-roles* that are relevant to classroom interaction. These sub-roles really refer to the *tasks* which fall upon the teacher in the performance of the teacher role in the classroom. Sorenson (1963) suggests six principal sub-roles for teachers.

Adviser—recommending courses of action for student.
Counsellor—helping the student to discover for himself.
Disciplinarian—adhering to rules and administering punishment.
Information giver—directing learning and lecturing.
Motivator—using rewards to stimulate conformist activity.
Referrer—securing help of outside agencies.

Another set of six sub-roles, with special reference to the Primary school, has been suggested by Blyth (1965). There seems to be relatively little overlap with those of Sorenson.

Instructor—direction of learning and lecturing.
Parent-substitute
Organizer—including discipline.
Value-bearer—transmission of society's dominant values.
Classifier—evaluation of academic and other behaviour.
Welfare-worker

Trow (1960) suggests eight classroom sub-roles under two headings.

Administrative and executive roles
  Disciplinarian (Policeman)
  Measurer and record keeper (Clerk)
  Learning-aids officer (Librarian)
  Programme director (Planner)

Instructional roles
  Motivator
  Resource Person
  Evaluator
  Adapter

Many other similar lists of sub-roles, of varying lengths, have been offered. Redl & Wattenburg (1951) suggest fifteen basic sub-roles for the teacher, including the roles of *referee* and *detective*. Unfortunately there seems to be no easy way of reconciling these different compilations of teacher sub-roles. Nor does there seem any logical limit to the number of sub-roles that we could postulate. A more serious difficulty is that almost none of these lists applies to *all* teachers. Indeed some lists, such as that of Blyth, are intended to apply to teachers of one particular sector of the teaching profession. In my own view it would be simpler to try to construct a set of sub-roles which apply to *all* teachers, i.e. a set of sub-roles which comprehends the teacher's tasks that are common to all teaching situations. The additional sub-roles suggested in the literature would then be subsumed under the more basic sub-roles.

All teachers have two basic sub-roles which they cannot escape. These are the roles of *instructor* and *disciplinarian*. The task of the teacher as disciplinarian is the establishment and maintenance of discipline and order in the classroom. It is the task of who shall do what, when and how. It is the creation of rules of conduct and rules of procedure. This includes the teacher's task in organizing the grouping of the pupils, the distribution of equipment, the timing, form and extent of movements by pupils within or in and out of the classroom. Many of these rules define how the pupil is expected to treat and respond to the teacher, as well as how the pupils must treat one another. Also included in the disciplinarian role are the means of maintaining the rules, including the fixing of rewards and punishments for adherence to or deviance from the rules.

This is a wider interpretation of the term 'discipline' than is usually the case. Moreover it is not a value-laden concept, for teachers resolve the discipline task in a wide variety of ways. For example, the teacher may interpret his role autocratically by making all the rules himself, imposing them on the pupils and requiring the pupils to show unquestioning obedience to the rules. Or he might take a much more democratic approach, by which the rules are established as a joint decision of teachers and pupils after a full and free discussion. How the task is resolved will be unique to each classroom. The point I wish to stress here is that any situation which requires teaching and learning between persons has a discipline problem, from the primary school to the universities, though there is an enormous variety in the extent to which this problem is problematic.

In schools most teachers are concerned to establish or maintain themselves as masters of the situation. The teacher feels that he must be *in control*. To be in control means that the teacher must be able to make the rules of conduct and obtain conformity to these rules by the pupils. When the teacher is either unable to impose rules and/or attain obedience to them, he is said to have failed in his disciplinarian role, for the pupils are out of control or undisciplined—masters of the situation.

How then do teachers ensure that they are in control? The root of being master of the situation is thought by most teachers to consist in the child's obedience to the teacher's orders, because if the pupils do not obey him the social order is threatened and the teacher's prerogative of rule making will be eroded. It is for this reason that discipline is in the popular mind linked with punishment, for punishments are one of the standard ways in which the teacher tries to enforce obedience. Another element in maintaining control is for the teacher to create a certain formality in his relations with the pupils. As Waller (1932) puts it: 'Formality arises in the teacher–pupil relationship as a means of maintaining social distance, which in its turn is a means to discipline.' This is the doctrine of 'non-involvement' with the pupils, which seeks to preserve the teacher's emotional independence and inhibit familiarity between teachers and pupils. To abandon formality is to risk loss of what teachers call 'respect' from the pupils.

Because the disciplinarian sub-role is so central a task in classrooms, behaviour on the part of pupils which threatens this role must be defined as 'bad', and be discouraged or punished. Thus impoliteness, insolence, impertinence and disobedience are among the cardinal sins of schoolchildren. Student teachers are often surprised at the apparent intolerance of teachers on such matters. In the students' eyes, a little insolence does not merit a major punishment. Such students have not accepted the not uncommon view among teachers that threats to the discipline role cannot be accepted and that the offenders must be punished *pour encourager les autres*.

The second basic sub-role that is common to all teachers is what we shall call the instructor role. As *instructor* the teacher must get the pupils to learn *and* show evidence of their learning. There are two basic aspects to the instructional task. The first concerns *what* shall be learned and refers to the content of the curriculum. The second concerns *how* this shall be learned and refers to the teacher's

118

teaching methods. As part of his instructor sub-role the teacher must exercise his expertise in his subject; he must evaluate the pupils' progress; he must motivate them to want to learn and persist in making efforts towards that goal.

As in the case of the disciplinarian role, we must insist on a distinction between the role itself and the way in which the role is interpreted and performed by a particular teacher. It would be quite erroneous to regard the term instructor as implying a particular means of getting the pupils to learn. Teachers differ about the content of the curriculum, though here some uniformity can be imposed by the requirements of the syllabus of an external examination, as in most secondary schools. In the primary schools, where such external constraints are more rare, much greater variability in curriculum content is to be found. It is in the area of teaching method that the greatest variability is to be found. Teachers may fulfil their instructional sub-role by lecturing and dictating notes, by organizing group projects, or by promoting learning by each pupil on an individual basis. They may examine frequently or hardly at all. They may motivate the pupils to work by threat of punishment or by praise and encouragement, or by a blend of both.

In performing the instructor role, most teachers make efforts towards keeping the interaction in classrooms highly *task-related*. Talk must be instrumental to the furtherance of learning. Most teachers succeed in this aim. Ned Flanders has shown that between 85 and 95 per cent of classroom talk is task-related. Teachers tend to be suspicious of talk between pupils during lessons, because they are aware the pupils are likely to engage in talk which is not instrumental to learning. When non-task-related talk arises, it must be on the teacher's initiative, with the teacher's consent and on the teacher's terms. Otherwise it will be seen as a threat to learning process (wasting time, a red herring, and so on). Thus it is only the teacher's jokes that are funny. Many of the crimes that pupils commit in classrooms are indicative of the pupils' failure to abide by the expectations which spring from the teacher's instructional task—laziness, copying, talking. The fact that the single word 'talking' can appear on a detention register or misbehaviour report is significant. Such 'talking' is by definition illegitimate, that is, either talking when silence has been called for or talking about matters that are not task-related. In their communications to one another teachers do not need to specify more than the single word 'talking'; the rest is part of the teacher's shared assumptions and perspectives.

The distinction between the disciplinarian and instructor sub-roles of the teacher is a useful analytical one, but in practice they tend to fuse. As *organizer* the teacher may group the pupils to serve disciplinary objectives ('You two boys come and sit at the front where I

119

can keep an eye on you'), or instructional objectives ('I will allow the bright children to work together so that they aren't held back by the slower ones'). Similarly the teacher's *moral* functions can be expressed within his instructional role, as in religious education, or within his disciplinary role, as when the teacher punishes a boy for being impolite. Frequently the two sub-roles blend together in the everyday behaviour of teachers. The value of the distinction between the two sub-roles rests on two points; that it represents a simpler and more comprehensive view of the teacher's classroom behaviour than lengthy lists of such roles; and that it is not possible to conceive of a teacher who does not *in some form* have to concern himself with the establishment of discipline and the promotion of learning.

It has already been suggested that there are great variations in the ways in which teachers interpret and perform the two basic sub-roles. What are these factors which influence how the teacher performs his role in the classroom? The most obvious factor is the uniqueness of any particular teacher—his background, training, attitudes, needs, personality. All these become major influences on the way in which the teacher perceives and performs his role. The second factor is a situational one, the role-set of 'significant others' with whom the teacher is in close contact in the performance of his duties. The pupils are the principal role partner of the teacher in his classroom role, and it is with them that the teacher must directly negotiate his role. We shall consider the teacher's relations with the pupils in more detail shortly. At this point it is useful to recall that the pupils are not the only important influence on the teacher's conception of his classroom role. Within the school the expectations of the headteacher and the other members of staff can be expected to exert considerable influence on the teacher's conception of his classroom role. Other persons, such as administrators, inspectors and parents may also be influential, but because they have much less contact with the teacher than do his colleagues, their influence is likely to be much weaker. The point is that in many respects it is the headteacher and colleagues, rather than the pupils themselves, who have the greater influence on the teacher's conception of his classroom role. As Waller (1932) put it:

> The significant people for a school teacher are other teachers, and by comparison with good standing in that fraternity the good opinion of students is a small thing and of little price. A landmark in one's assimilation to the profession is that moment when he decides that only teachers are important.

This means that the teacher enters into negotiation with the pupils with a predetermined intention of living up to the expectations of his colleagues.

The influence of headteacher and staff on the teacher's classroom roles is of special interest because usually such persons are not present during the performance of his *classroom* role. The teacher in the classroom is typically insulated from their observations of his behaviour. One main reason why they exert so much influence in spite of their inability to observe directly is that they are a major source of the teacher's self-evaluation. The teacher does not judge his abilities as a teacher on the sole basis of the pupils' response. (If he did, how could a teacher who fails to make much progress with a 'difficult' class retain any self-esteem?) The teacher tends to use the attitudes of his colleagues to him as a measure of his worth as a teacher. These colleagues estimate the teacher's abilities on the basis of the information they can glean about the teacher's classroom behaviour, which they cannot directly observe in detail. Sources of such information are what they see through the classroom windows as they pass by; what the pupils say about him; how they see the pupils acting towards him in the more 'public' places such as in the corridor, at lunch, on the games field, etc.

The teacher knows that he will be judged by his colleagues in terms of his ability to master the two basic sub-roles of maintaining discipline and promoting learning. A teacher must therefore make sure that the information which is available to colleagues is congruent with successful classroom performance. Thus the teacher will strive to be treated by pupils in 'public' places in a manner that implies he is in control in his own classroom. For example, if pupils are polite and not insolent to him on the corridor, his colleagues will infer that this is the way he is treated in his classroom. Should the pupils be rude and disobedient to the teacher in public, the teacher will be embarrassed by this loss of face which implies a lack of competence in the classroom. It is because teachers cannot avoid such encounters with pupils in public and in the presence of colleagues that it is difficult for the teacher to maintain a false 'front' that he is more competent than public evidence supports.

This concern by the teacher to produce evidence that he is succeeding and to suppress evidence to the contrary, greatly affects what the teacher does in the classroom. He will try, notably in secondary rather than in primary schools, to make sure that children are sitting in a neat and orderly way, rather than roaming in apparent chaos around the room, not only because he might think this is a personal test of his own discipline or in his view the best means of promoting hard work by the pupils, but also because he knows that if the head-teacher or a colleague observes this, either through the windows or by an entry into the classroom, this situation will be used as evidence for his success in maintaining discipline and promoting learning. Similarly, he will try to keep the noise level of his pupils to a minimum, not only because it might disturb the teacher in the next room,

121

but also because he feels that the teacher next door might infer from the noise that the class is inadequately disciplined and therefore not learning. Again, teachers in secondary schools must produce evidence that their children are learning, and the most 'objective' or 'concrete' form of such evidence consists of examination results. So the teacher is concerned that his children should achieve good results not only for the children's sake but also because he knows that the pass rate and grade levels of the pupils' examination performance will be taken by his colleagues as an index of his ability to promote learning.

Thus the expectations and evaluations of colleagues are a major influence on the way in which a teacher interprets and performs his classroom role. In my own view, this reliance of teachers on the estimations of their colleagues—which I might add, they are very anxious to deny—represents the greatest conservative force, the greatest inhibitor of educational change and experiment in our secondary schools. For a teacher to introduce innovations into his classroom, he has to take risks and live dangerously. Yet the teacher is unlikely to take such risks unless he is prepared to reduce, but not totally reject, his dependence on colleagues' evaluations, which are usually rooted in the traditional indices of discipline and learning, namely noise and examination results.

Role style

It has several times been stressed that every teacher interprets and performs his role in a unique way. Indeed every lesson a teacher conducts can never be precisely repeated. At the same time, every teacher behaves with some degree of consistency on different occasions and may thus be said to develop a *style* of performing his classroom role. It should be possible to distinguish different styles which are common to many teachers and construct a list of teacher types with recognizable role styles. One example we have already discussed is the distinction made by the 'interaction analysis' researchers between 'direct' or 'teacher-centred' and 'indirect' or 'student-centred' teachers. As in the case of classroom sub-roles, many writers have suggested long lists of different role styles (Waller, 1932; Redl, 1951; Bush, 1954; Thelen, 1954; Soles, 1964; Hoyle, 1969). We shall consider a selection of the suggested role styles, which clearly embody different interpretations of the classroom role, different conceptions of the teacher–pupil relationship, and different educational philosophies. Willard Waller, whose book written in 1932 was the pioneering study of interpersonal relations in schools, suggested the following list:

1   the parent substitute.
2   the cultural or social ideal.

3 the officer and gentleman.
4 the patriarch.
5 the kindly adult.
6 the love object.
7 the easy mark.
8 the nincompoop.
9 the tyrant.
10 the weakling.
11 the flirt.
12 the bully.

Waller's brilliant and insightful cameos of these teacher types, though now somewhat dated, remain unsurpassed. Take, for example, the case of the *patriarch*. Waller notes that this elderly teacher, who takes a fatherly interest in his pupils, is treated with great affection. His discipline is not firm and he rules by personal influence rather than by means of formal sanctions. In some respects he may appear to be incompetent in academic matters, but the pupils will happily defend him and insist that he has taught them a great deal. His idiosyncrasies, his readiness to fall for 'red herrings', his anecdotes, his absentmindedness, all these are fully approved by the pupils. Waller rightly notes that age alone does not make one into a patriarch and that there is rarely room in a school for more than one such teacher.

Clearly these different role styles described by Waller represent different definitions of the situation, different conceptions of teacher and pupil roles, different educational philosophies and goals. They are variations on a theme; many represent deviations from an implicit 'normal' or 'ideal' teacher. Whilst they are not treated in any systematic way, they all have the flavour of 'real' teachers and an experienced teacher, on reading Waller's descriptions, instantly and effortlessly finds that present or former colleagues spring to mind.

Herbert Thelen (1954) takes a different approach to teacher role styles, which are conceived in terms of *models*.

> It is as if the teacher had a model in mind and operated consistently to make the classroom conform to this model; it represents the teacher's idea of what the classroom should be like. When the classroom situation deviates from this image, the teacher then tries to rectify matters by taking action. . . . The teacher's model summarizes for him the principles of learning; his action is taken to maintain the model, using principles of educational method as his guide.

Thelen suggests seven basic models, which can be briefly summarized.
Model 1: Socratic Discussion: After the pupils have learned some

123

facts, the teacher introduces a challenging discussion to clarify concepts and values and to test conclusions.

Model 2: The Town Meeting: The teacher and pupils discuss, in an open, friendly and co-operative manner, how to organize and carry out specified learning activities.

Model 3: Apprenticeship: The pupil identifies with the teacher and learns many attitudes in imitation of the teacher, who actively nurtures the pupil in his own image.

Model 4: The Army Model: The teacher tells the pupils what to do and how to do it, sees that it gets done and finally evaluates how good a job he thinks it is.

Model 5: The Business Deal: The teacher makes the best deal he can with individual pupils, discussing specifications for each piece of work and being available for consultation as the work progresses.

Model 6: The Good Old Team: The teacher's objective is to achieve a high standard of learning and almost any device of persuasion, cajolery, promises and threats that will produce high-level performance are regarded as legitimate.

Model 7: The Guided Tour: The teacher conducts the children through the field of study, giving information, stories and opinions, calling attention to objects of special interest, and answering questions.

In many respects these models are an advance on Waller's teacher types. They are more directly related to the teacher's instructional role and in addition they are less concerned with the teacher's personality and more truly interactional in specifying roles for both teachers and pupils.

The teacher's definition of the situation

Up to this point we have considered how, in defining the situation in the classroom, the teacher makes clear to the pupils his own conception of his classroom role and the specific ways or style in which he intends to perform his role. Implicit in the teacher's definition of his own role is a definition of the pupil role. The teacher cannot specify how he intends to behave without at the same time specifying how he intends the pupils to behave. Certainly he cannot succeed in realizing his own role conception unless the pupils' response is in accord with that conception. Thus the teacher's definition of his own role and his definition of the pupil role are opposite sides of the same coin. The teacher's expectations of the pupils will derive from, and be congruent with, his conception of his own role. So when the teacher explains to the pupils how he is going to behave towards them, he is simultaneously clarifying his expectations of them in their pupil role; and when he prescribes behaviour for the pupils, he is simultaneously disclosing his conception of his teacher role.

If the teacher's two basic-roles in the classroom are those of disciplinarian and instructor, then the teacher's expectations of the pupils will hinge upon the way in which the teacher interprets these two sub-roles. This means that it is as difficult to specify teachers' expectations of pupils as it is to specify how teachers conceive their own role. There will be as much variation in the one as in the other. So the teacher's expectations of his pupils cannot be characterized except in the most general terms, subject to modification in the case of a particular teacher. I shall take the case of the teacher with a fairly traditional conception of his role. As disciplinarian, the teacher tends to expect the pupils to be obedient, respectful, polite, formal and quiet. As instructor, he will expect the pupils to pay attention, work hard, not copy, and show interest and enthusiasm. It is such behaviour on the part of the pupils which is complementary to, and congruent with, the teacher's conception of his own classroom role. If the pupils do not behave in such ways, he cannot live up to his self-conception as disciplinarian or instructor—except, of course, by altering his view of the nature of the sub-roles.

The pupils will be evaluated by the teacher on the basis of the degree to which they conform to his expectations. In conforming, the pupils offer support to the teacher's role, and thus make the teacher's role performance highly satisfying. Hence he approves of such pupils and regards them as 'good'. If the pupils deviate from the teacher's expectations, they are withdrawing support, showing antagonism, and making it difficult for the teacher to perform his role. In consequence, the teacher's interactions with the pupils involve a loss and are experienced as dissatisfying; he disapproves of such pupils and regards them as 'bad'. Because teachers can have very different definitions of the situations, including very different conceptions of teacher and pupil roles, the same pupil behaviour can be perceived and evaluated very differently. A pupil can be seen as 'well-behaved' by one teacher but as 'lacking in life and initiative' by another teacher.

The teacher perceives and evaluates his pupils on the basis of the two aspects or dimensions of his own classroom role (cf. Parsons, 1959). The first dimension concerns the instructional role. The pupil is judged traditionally on the degree to which he pays attention, works hard, and shows enthusiasm and interest. The second dimension consists of discipline. The pupil is perceived and judged on the extent to which he conforms to the teacher's expectations as disciplinarian— traditionally the extent to which he accepts the teacher's authority, is obedient, polite and quiet. The pupil who conforms to the teacher's expectations on both dimensions is evaluated as a 'good' pupil; the pupil who deviates from the teacher's expectations on both is a 'bad' pupil.

There is considerable evidence which supports this analysis of the teacher's perception and evaluation of his pupils. Wickman (1928) has shown that teachers regard pupil moral offences, threats to the teacher's authority and violations of classroom order as more serious than shyness or unsociability

> Those problems which transgress the teachers' moral sensitiveness and authority or which frustrate their immediate teaching purposes are regarded as relatively more serious than problems which for the most part affect only the welfare of the individual pupil.

Hollins (1955), in an improved design, substantially confirmed this work on a British sample and found no differences between men and women teachers or the types of school in which they taught.

From our analysis we would predict that teacher would show greater liking for 'good' pupils than for 'bad' pupils. Williams & Knecht (1962) have demonstrated that the pupils who are most liked by the teachers tend to be the high achievers, that is those who conform to the instructional expectations. Instruction is a more intricate dimension than discipline since its central element—hard work—is confounded with attainment and ability. It is understandable that teachers should in practice experience certain difficulties in disentangling the complex of hard work, ability and attainment. Teachers tend to use the work the child produces, his attainments, as a measure of his hard work, for effort independent of attainment is not easy to observe and measure. I know of only one case where a teacher wrote on a boy's report, 'He has worked hard, but made no progress.' Yet where the attainment is high, it may be a product of high ability rather than high effort. Teachers are aware of this, as when they write on the report of a pupil with low attainment, 'She has ability, but makes little effort.' However, I suspect that although teachers can distinguish effort, ability and attainment from one another where the disparities are reasonably great, they cannot do so either as a matter of course or as much as they think they can. There are two reasons for this. Firstly the teacher is unlikely to have in his possession a full picture of a child's abilities. Secondly both attainment and effort are more open to regular inspection by the teacher in the everyday life of the classroom. Thus we would expect the teacher to give a more favourable evaluation to the pupil with high attainment, which implies that high effort has been expended, than to the pupil with high ability, which has no implication with respect to effort. This is indeed what is suggested by the findings of Williams & Knecht, who report that the correlation between teacher liking and attainment is 0·668, whereas the correlation between teacher liking and ability is 0·478.

Other researches support the view that the pupils who give the teacher role support are perceived more favourably. Lambert (1963) has shown that pupils who are rated by the teachers as *successful* are also rated as more able, curious, imaginative, clear thinking, capable, alert, friendly, enthusiastic and cheerful. It seems that teachers fall for the *halo effect* in perceiving and evaluating their pupils. Those who conform to teacher expectations are seen to possess a wide range of characteristics whilst those who deviate possess all the vices. The best demonstration of this is the work of Bush (1954) who found that teacher liking is related to every single characteristic on which he asked the teachers to rate the pupils—intelligence, attainment, class conduct, quality of thinking, emotional balance, and probable college success.

These more favourable perceptions and evaluations of the con-formist pupils are expressed in the teacher's treatment of such pupils. We all tend to give preferential treatment, perhaps unconsciously, to those we like and of whom we approve. Thus in the Lumley study (Hargreaves, 1967) the teachers favoured the pupils of the higher streams who were more conformist to teacher expectations than low stream pupils. High stream pupils were more likely to be taken by teachers on visits to local places of interest during school time, and were most likely to obtain places on the oversubscribed holidays abroad which were organized by the school. It has been shown by Toogood (1967) that the children who are given responsibility by teachers (e.g. made monitors and prefects, given supervisory jobs) are the pupils who are also perceived by the teacher as being more likeable, more co-operative, better behaved, higher attainers. Clearly all this work on the teacher's evaluation and perception of pupils is closely connected with the concept of the self-fulfilling prophecy discussed in an earlier chapter. If the teacher's behaviour towards a pupil is conditioned by his perception and evaluation of the pupil, then we need to know very much more than we do at present about the basis on which the teacher makes his perceptions, evaluations and categorizations.

Whilst it is true that conformity to his expectations of discipline and instruction is the principal basis on which the teacher perceives and evaluates the pupil, it is not the only basis. Hallworth (1961, 1962) had teachers rate the personality of their pupils. The results show that teachers tend to perceive pupils in roughly the same way. In the factor analysis of the ratings, two main factors emerged. The first factor, which is based on the teacher's implicit question 'How does this child get on with me?', is called by Hallworth the factor of conscientiousness and reliability. It involves such traits as emotional stability, trustworthiness, persistence, co-operation with the teacher, and maturity. This suggests that the first factor represents the teacher's estimate of the pupil's conformity to his instructional and disciplinary expectations. (That these combine into a single factor confirms our earlier suggestion that the disciplinary and instructional sub-roles are distinct only in analysis but not in real life.) The second factor seems to arise from the teacher's implicit question, 'How does this pupil get on with other pupils?' This factor involves such traits as cheerfulness, sense of humour, spontaneity, sociability; it is called by Hallworth the factor of extraversion. Now these factors are independent of each other; there is relatively little overlap between the first factor—the teacher's pupil—and the second factor—the pupil's pupil. The research showed that there was more overlap between the two factors in secondary modern than in grammar schools. The reader might like to guess at the reasons for this: several clues to the answer have been laid earlier in the book. But this research does show quite clearly that the teacher perceives the pupil not only in terms of his relationship with the pupil, but also in terms of the pupil's relationship with his peers. Similar findings come from Nash's (1973) use of the repertory grid technique. In the secondary school, teachers use the dimensions *bright–dull, lively–lumpish, likeable–less likeable, well behaved–less well behaved* and *sociable–less sociable* as the central constructs in the typing of pupils. Clearly these dimensions reflect both instructional and disciplinary concerns as well as the quality of relationship between teacher and pupil, and pupil and pupil.

The teacher's perceptions, interpretations and evaluations of pupil behaviours are made evident in the common terms and labels which teachers use to describe particular pupil types or pupil characteristics. Some of these labels may be used in public (for example to parents) whilst others are restricted to communications, oral or written, between teachers. Almost all are used regularly by teachers in their verbal interactions with pupils.

	Positive label	*Negative label*
General	Good lad	Nuisance
	Sound	Pain-in-the-neck
	Promising	Fool
	Nice	Trouble-maker
	Making progress	Going to the dogs
Instructional	Hard worker	Idler
	Bright	Thickhead
	Neat	Untidy
Disciplinary	Quiet	Chatterbox
	Polite	Cheeky
Peer	Leader	Ring-leader
	Friendly	Bully
	Popular	Lone-wolf

Many other factors can be expected to affect the teacher's perception and evaluation of his pupils. For example, we might expect teachers to perceive children from different social backgrounds in different ways.

The impact of the pupil's social class and the teacher's perception and treatment of him have been of particular interest to researchers in recent years, especially in relation to streaming. Jackson (1964), Douglas (1964) and Barker Lunn (1970) have all shown that in the primary school the working-class pupils are disproportionately represented in the lower streams and the middle-class pupils in the upper streams. This in itself may simply indicate that middle-class pupils are on average of higher intelligence or have higher attainment levels than working-class pupils. However, the data cannot be fully explained in this way. Jackson has shown that the most common criterion for the allocation of pupils to different streams is the attainment test. Clearly such subjective estimates may be open to considerable bias. This seems to be confirmed by Douglas, who noted the overlap in test scores of pupils in adjacent streams. If we consider the pupils of the *same* measured ability, it is the middle-class child who tends to be assigned to the higher stream and the working-class child to the lower stream. Barker Lunn made a direct comparison between the teacher's ratings of a pupil's ability and his actual performance on an English test. In most cases the two measures agreed. But where they did not agree, working-class children were more likely to be underestimated and middle-class children to be overestimated.

We do not know how such perceptual bias, and its consequent discrimination, with respect to the pupil's social class operates. I am inclined to think that it is unintentional on the teacher's part, though some writers seem to suggest otherwise. It seems likely that the differences between middle-class and working-class pupils in speech, appearance, values, attitudes and behaviour, which can soon become very apparent in the classroom, are used by the teacher as part of the basis for estimating the pupil's intelligence, ability and future potential. It is clear that teachers need to be warned of the potential bias in their perception of pupils' abilities and of the way in which the perception can affect their treatment, including their expectations, of the pupils.

In summary, we can say that the teacher defines the situation in terms of his own roles and goals, especially as they relate to his instructional and disciplinary objectives, and assigns to the pupils roles and goals that are congruent with his own. He selectively perceives and interprets pupil behaviour in the light of his definition of the situation. On the basis of further interaction with the pupils and repeated perceptions of them, he develops a conception of individual pupils (and classes) who are evaluated, categorized and labelled according to the degree to which they support his definition of the situation. He then responds to pupils in the light of these evaluative labels.

The pupil's definition of the situation

We have considered in great detail the ways in which teachers seek to define the situation in the classroom. But what of the pupils? How do they wish to define the situation? In fact it is very difficult to discover how pupils in school wish to define the situation. We have to bear in mind that generally speaking, in their interactions with adults, children are used to having the situation defined for them. Indeed adults, especially parents, actively train their children to accept the situation as they, the parents, define it. The result is that most children in most of their interactions with adults assume a passive position of acceptance. They know who is boss. Life in school seems to be no exception. Children first go to school when they are very young—by the age of six at the latest. As the children are immature and typically somewhat bewildered in this new and strange world of school, they see their task largely in terms of discovering what is expected of them by the teachers. Should the six-year-old try to define the situation in ways that conflict with the teacher's, then the teacher will try to persuade the child into changing his notions of what school and being a pupil are about, and if necessary the teacher can strengthen his argument with formal sanctions. On the whole parents encourage the child to accept the teacher's definition of the situation —at school the child must do as he is told. By the age of ten the vast majority of pupils seem to have accepted the teacher's definition of the situation. School is an inevitable and inescapable and natural part of their lives. It is there and they accept it.

Researches show that most pupils seem to do more than accept the teacher's definition of the situation in school: they *like* it. This is so presumably because we as adults, parents and teachers, have succeeded in persuading children that school is a pleasant experience ('You're going to start school next week, Wendy? Won't that be lovely!' 'You don't want to go to school, Peter? Don't be silly. Schooldays are the best time in your life.') and also because what happens to children in school is indeed pleasant for the most part. All the studies of pupils' attitudes to school suggest that the vast majority like school. Even in a down-town seconday modern school like Lumley, 74 per cent of the boys in their final year say that they like school on the whole. The qualification of *on the whole* is an important one. As Jackson (1968) has reminded us, the pupils' feelings about life in school are probably very complex and somewhat ambivalent. Probably very few pupils are ecstatically happy in school and probably very few experience their schooldays in perpetual abject misery. For the average pupil, school is a mixture of good and bad, pleasant and unpleasant. When pressed to a simple choice between like and dislike in general, with no regard to specific aspects, he will usually choose the favourable rather than the unfavourable response.

Perhaps a more fruitful approach in discovering how pupils feel about their lot would be to study the pupil's reactions to the teacher himself. It is the teacher who defines the situation, who defines the roles of both teacher and pupil in the classroom. If we can find out the sort of teacher that pupils like, from this we might infer those definitions of the situation of which pupils approve and also the roles they prefer to perform, since both of these are strongly dependent on the way the teacher conceives his own role.

Studies of pupils' attitudes to teachers, both in Great Britain and in the United States, have produced a remarkably unified and consistent picture. It seems that Western school children, of all ages and in different types of school, are in very high agreement about the teacher behaviours which they like and dislike. From the researches (e.g. Bush, 1942; Tiedeman, 1942; Michael, 1951; Allen, 1961; Taylor, 1962) we can draw this picture of pupil attitudes to teachers.

Like A teacher who . . .	*Dislike* A teacher who . . .
(a) Discipline	
—keeps good control.	—is too strict; is too lax.
—is fair; has no favourites.	—has favourites; 'picks on' pupils.
—gives no extreme or immoderate punishments.	—punishes and threatens excessively/arbitrarily.
(b) Instruction	
—explains and helps.	—does not explain; gives little help.
—gives interesting lessons.	—does not know subject well; gives dull or boring lessons.
(c) Personality	
—is cheerful, friendly, patient, understanding, etc.	—nags, ridicules, is sarcastic, bad tempered, unkind, etc.
—has a good sense of humour.	—has no sense of humour.
—takes an interest in pupils as individuals.	—ignores individual differences.

131

Each area of the three listed is not given the same weight of importance by the children. In Taylor's (1962) study of British children of different ages and in different kinds of school, the instructional area was perceived as the most important, bearing about 40 per cent of the weight, with discipline next (33 per cent) and personality last (25 per cent). The pupils, like their teachers, see the instructional area, the process of learning, as the primary task of their life in the classroom. They approve of the teacher who can 'put over' his subject in an interesting way. They agree with the teachers that discipline is important as a prerequisite to adequate learning, a necessary means to the end of learning. Finally, they approve of teachers whose pleasant disposition creates a warm, relaxed friendly climate of personal relationships within which the learning process can proceed.

At the same time we should perhaps be a little cautious in accepting these findings at their face value. The picture which emerges is basically a stereotype of the good teacher. It may be that the questionnaires, by conceiving the ideal teacher in abstract terms or as a bundle of discrete characteristics that make satisfactory test items, tend to elicit such a stereotype. In real life the teachers that the pupils like or perceive as good may not have a close resemblance to the 'identikit' good teacher of the researchers. Perhaps if they had asked pupils to nominate their favourite teacher and then investigated the characteristics and behaviours of such teachers, a somewhat different picture would have emerged. Perhaps, too, if we took into account the pupils' own views, and examined the terms they use to describe and differentiate teachers (including their labels for teachers), then other dimensions of teacher behaviours would be brought to light.

The working consensus

The implication of our review of researches on pupils' attitudes to teachers is that the majority of pupils accept the teacher's definition of the situation and are relatively content to conform to the teacher's role expectations of them, providing that the teacher does not behave in ways which meet with their disapproval. Only teachers who maintain an excessively strict or lax discipline, who are boring and unhelpful in their teaching, and who have cold, humourless and unpleasant personalities should experience any difficulty in reaching a consensus with the pupils. Assuming that such teachers are in a minority, or behave in such ways for only a small proportion of the time, the definition of the situation in the classroom is readily agreed between teachers and pupils.

Three kinds of outcome in reaching a consensus about the definition of the situation are possible. The first can be called *concord*, which arises when consensus is high. Here the definitions of the situation by teacher and by pupils are congruent and compatible. The situation is pleasant for both participants; both can make profits. The second type of outcome is *discord*. In this case the definitions of the situations are incompatible, and consensus is low. The situation is unpleasant for the participants; each makes a loss. Between these two forms stands a third type, *pseudo-concord*. Here the definitions of the situation are congruent and compatible only in part. The situation is partly pleasant, partly unpleasant. It represents a doubtful bargain: sometimes the participants make profits and at other times losses.

It seems to me that the extreme types of concord and discord are relatively rare. Much more typical is pseudo-concord, or an outcome that lies between concord and pseudo-concord, where the consensus is far from perfect. Only in exceptional circumstances do teachers and pupils in classrooms reach concord or discord. In other words, it is rare for the definitions of the situation between teacher and pupils to be so incongruent that negotiation of a working consensus becomes virtually impossible, just as it is rare for the two definitions to be so compatible that negotiation of a working consensus becomes unnecessary. With respect to the instructional and disciplinary roles the pupils do not seem to be entirely content with the teacher's definition of the situation in the classroom. In the event most of the pupils do conform to a fair degree to the teacher's definition of the situation (which is why pseudo-concord often *looks* very much like concord), partly because the teacher is in a position to impose his definition of the situation with his much greater power. Negotiation becomes, at least in theory, unnecessary where one participant has the power to enforce his definition on the other. But the pupils do have some power, so when the teacher tries to replace negotiation with imposition he finds that he activates resistance, subversion and interpersonal antagonism that effectively promote discord. The absolute imposition of the teacher's definition of the situation is really impossible and the side effects of attempts to do so make such a course of action inadvisable. The teacher has to balance his own personal satisfactions with the need to impose a definition of the situation that is expected by the headteacher, colleagues and other role partners. So in practice the teacher does not always enforce his definition of the situation where he has the power to do so and where it seems to be demanded by his role partners. He aims instead at a negotiated settlement whereby teacher and pupils each go half way with respect to some demands and whereby in other areas the teacher withdraws or moderates his demands on the pupils in return for conformity to other teacher demands. This negotiated settlement may fall short of the teacher's ideal definition of the situation but it is realistic in that it averts discord and ensures that a fair number of his demands are met and that teacher–pupil relationships are generally good. The pupils, realizing that their position is not a strong one from which to bargain, are usually content with the concessions made by the teacher. Fortunately for most teachers the pupils underestimate the strength of their position especially in its collective form. The fears of teachers and headteachers with respect to 'pupil power' groups such as the Schools Action Union stem from the recognition that once pupil power is collectively mobilized it may be used effectively against the teachers' wishes. These teacher fears also indicate that teachers are aware that many school policies and classroom definitions of the situation are not entirely acceptable to the pupils. Like employers in an earlier age, the teachers are unwilling to concede to the pupils the rights which they demand. Since most of the pupil power leaders have been among the older pupils in grammar and comprehensive schools, headteachers can cope with such problems in the short term simply by expelling the leaders. The pupils, like the early trade unionists, are producing their martyrs and sending their organization underground.

It can be said that the state of pseudo-concord is the most typical expression of the working consensus in classrooms. It is pseudo-concord which most accurately conveys the flavour of classroom life, with its ups-and-downs, its good days and bad days, its moments of joy and delight alternating with boredom, frustration and depression. As R. F. Mackenzie (1967) puts it:

> [Difficult children] are still in the minority. The majority we can cope with; or rather, they are nice children and suffer their education patiently. They become moderately interested, like a group on a seaside holiday who are prepared to put up with charades until the rain stops. It's not what they would choose to do, but it's all right. But behind the half-hearted play-acting there is already the murmur of mutiny. . . .

The process by which pseudo-concord is stabilized into a generalized working consensus is exceedingly complex. One way in which we can analyse the situation is to clarify the *negotiative techniques* used by teachers and pupils through which each attempts to foster his own definition of the situation or to modify the other's definition of the situation. Let us consider the teacher's techniques first.

1. *Promises and threats*

Perhaps the most common of all techniques, promises and threats have the same basic structure. In a promise, the teacher says 'If you will do (or not do) *x*, then I shall reward you,' whereas in a threat the teacher says, 'If you do (or do not do) *x*, then I shall punish you.' Frequently, of course, promises and threats are not stated quite so bluntly as in these formulae; the teacher merely says what he wants, the consequent punishment or reward being merely implied.

2. *Excessive demands* (*or pseudo-compromise*)

This is a well-known negotiative technique which is used in a wide variety of bargaining situations. It is especially favoured by trade unions in pay negotiations. The union puts in a claim for a very high increase which it knows the employers cannot meet, but then 'compromises' at half this figure, which is in fact the amount they expected in the first place. Yet to put this figure forward originally would have been to place themselves in a disadvantageous bargaining position. In other words, the excessive demands technique is a way of anticipating the probability of an ultimate compromise that can be treated by both sides as an honourable settlement. By *appearing* to have compromised one is able to present oneself as 'reasonable'—and one warns the opposition that further demands are likely to be made in the future. A teacher can use this technique when, for instance, he demands that the pupils do a certain amount of homework knowing that the pupils will protest. He then apparently concedes by reducing the amount. Yet in effect he has exacted a higher amount of homework than the pupils would otherwise have been willing to do.

3. *Cautionary tales*

These are really veiled threats. The teacher has a fund of stories about what happens to pupils who follow certain courses of action. Instead of issuing a direct threat, the teacher simply describes what happened to persons who did this in the past, emphasizing that the outcome was not a happy one for the pupil. The teacher makes no direct show of his power, as in a promise or threat. Here the teacher apparently gives the pupil freedom of choice, but does this in the confidence (or hope) that the pupil will decide to refrain because he recognizes that the outcome will in some way be unpleasant for him.

4. *Appeal to higher authority*

This is another example of a subtle threat by invoking some agent other than himself as the source of the threat. Thus the teacher can say, 'I personally have no objection to your doing that, but what will the Head (or your parents, etc.) say?' The threatening agent need not be a person, as when the teacher claims that he is willing not to do a particular piece of work, but what about the 'O' level examination? The strength of this technique is that it implies that the teacher is really on the side of the pupils; the situation is redefined from one

135

in which teacher and pupils are in conflict to one in which teacher and pupils are both aligned against a common enemy.

5. *Bluff*

To bluff a pupil is to threaten the use of a sanction that the teacher knows he cannot, dare not, or would not in fact use. It is a show of pretended but unreal power. Typically the aim is to frighten the pupil into compliance or submission, so it is particularly effective when the teacher *appears* to the pupil to be in a state where he might use extreme measures—for example, a mock rage. Nevertheless this is a risky technique, for unless the pupils believe that the teacher will invoke these sanctions, they can make the counter-move of 'calling his bluff' and if they do this successfully the teacher's power is eroded and he suffers a severe loss of face.

6. *Personal appeal*

Once a teacher has an established relationship with a class or pupil, he can use that relationship as the basis for an appeal. Thus when the pupils commit actions of which he disapproves, he can say 'You've let me down' and induce feelings of embarrassment, shame or regret among the pupils. The technique often fails when used by student teachers, because they are appealing to a relationship which does not exist. A few teachers, with a high degree of charisma, can employ this technique with ease; they can even use the de Gaulle variant (from his famous *Aidez-moi, français* spoken on television) which if employed by most teachers would merely arouse the derision of the pupils.

7. *Appeal to tradition*

A teacher can sometimes dismiss a pupil request simply on the grounds that it is in conflict with tradition. For example, the teacher can say 'We've never done that before here,' or 'We never do that sort of thing in this school.' No rational argument is brought forward, but the implication is that the tradition represents the wisdom of the past both in terms of efficiency ('it works best this way') as well as morality ('this is the right way').

8. *Mystification*

A more extreme form of refusing rational discussion is the mystificatory technique, where the teacher justifies his own definition of the situation on the grounds that there are good reasons for this, but asserts that he is unable to reveal these to the pupils or that the pupils would not understand the reasons if they were revealed.

9. *Appeal to generalizability*

The teacher can sometimes concede that a pupil demand is not inherently unreasonable, but also claim that if the demand were granted then the consequences of so doing would be unreasonable. So the typical form is, 'If I let you do that, then everyone else will want to, and then where shall we be?' This was essentially the line taken by Edward Heath towards the miners in 1973–4 in their pay claim that would have breached Stage Three of his incomes policy. The pupil counter-move—which the miners took—is to argue that one is in some sense an exception deserving special treatment.

10. *Divide and rule*

A similar technique avoids the pressure to meet the request by inducing conflict or competition among the pupils. The teacher, noting the lack of total consensus among the pupils, can say, 'I'll consider the matter if you can all agree on what you want,' which effectively deflects the problem back onto the pupils.

11. *Stalling*

Once again the request is treated as reasonable, but the teacher claims that he cannot deal with it now but must postpone a decision until later—'I'll have to think about that one.' This is sometimes effective in that if the pupil is required to wait or to represent his case again at some unspecified date in the future, then he may simply forget about it in time. Or, at its second presentation, the teacher can decline to honour the request on the grounds that circumstances have changed.

12. *Converting rights to privileges*

In situations where the pupils have so much power that the teacher has little choice but to yield, the teacher can save face by responding as if he were granting privileges rather than rights. If the teacher, in submitting, can persuade the pupils that he is graciously declining to exert his own power to impose his own definition of the situation, he will stimulate the pupils' gratitude and successfully distract them from their own power which need not now be exerted.

137

13. *The crackdown*

This is essentially a counter-move to the pupil's technique of attrition (see below). When the teacher has yielded to the pupils in a number of ways, he may begin to feel that the pupils are taking advantage of his leniency and making inroads into his control of the definition of the situation. The situation is best described by Roth (1962) in his analysis of bargaining in a tuberculosis hospital.

> The doctor may wipe out earlier . . . privileges altogether, or at least firmly refuse to grant any more. The patients call such action a 'crackdown.' There will be periods of ill-feeling while the patients accuse the doctor of reneging on his bargain and the doctor accuses the patients of having tried to put a fast deal over on him. . . . For a time the patients will let up on their demands and their pressure against the limits in all directions because they believe the doctor is 'not in the mood' to tolerate or give in to pressure for more freedom of action. They 'lie low' in the same way as does a whorehouse operator who suspends activities temporarily when the district attorney announces a drive to 'wipe out vice.' The doctor in the meantime, is keeping a sharp eye open to see that he is not 'tricked' again. However, in hospitals, as in politics, such campaigns blow over. The patients dissect the doctor's words and actions, as well as pick up any information from ward personnel and others, to find out when the doctor has 'cooled off.' Finally, a few of the more venturesome patients will tentatively renew their demands.

Some of the negotiative techniques used by teachers can also be used by pupils—excessive demands, bluffing and promises being obvious examples. Let us now examine some of the more common techniques used by pupils.

1. *Attrition*

Pupils can sometimes assert their own definition of the situation simply by persisting in their demands until the teacher gives in. This can be achieved in various ways; by frequency of asking; by sulking when the teacher refuses the request; by declining to co-operate with the teacher in other ways. If the teacher finally yields, this sets the stage for a second move, namely the appeal to justice.

2. *Appeal to justice*

Pupils know that teachers like to be thought of as just and that pupils despise them if they have 'pets' or favourites. If the teacher has

138

granted a request to one individual or group, then pupils can use this as a basis for an appeal to justice. For instance, a pupil can claim, 'You let Jones go to the toilet, so why can't I go too?' or a class can claim, 'You let 3B off their homework, why not us?' Waller (1932) describes the situation neatly.

> Rules may be emasculated . . . through setting up exceptions
> which at first seem harmless to the established order but
> when translated into precedent are found to destroy some parts
> of it altogether. One value of experience in teaching is that it
> gives the teacher an understanding of precedents. A trivial
> favour to Johnny Jones becomes a ruinous social principle when
> it is made a precedent.

The teacher's counter-move here is to argue that the first case is in some way a special case, or to make an appeal to generalizability (see above).

3. *Divide and rule*

The pupil version of this technique hinges on making comparisons between teachers and demonstrating dissensus among the staff. Thus the pupils can assert that another teacher allows them to do something, for example do homework during 'private study' periods in the library, so why doesn't this teacher also?

4. *Selective use of teachers*

Pupils learn that some teachers are more likely to yield to requests than others and thus concentrate on those teachers. Student teachers and teachers who are new to the school are especially vulnerable here because they often do not know the traditional practices and customs of the school and are thus unable to make the appeal to tradition. Once the pupils have made sufficient inroads into one teacher's definition of the situation, they can use this as a basis for a divide and rule approach.

5. *Appeal to higher authority*

Pupils can sometimes challenge a teacher demand by invoking an authority which the teacher will regard as legitimate and therefore be reluctant to dismiss. Thus a pupil may claim 'My mum says I haven't to have showers' which invokes parental and perhaps also medical authority. The teacher's counter-move is typically to demand that this authorization should be available in a written form—a 'note'.

139

6. *Group co-operation*

Whilst it is a hazardous and formidable task for the single pupil to persist in rejecting the teacher's classroom definition of the situation, it is much easier for the pupils as a group to succeed in such a challenge. For when the pupils unite and make a concerted attack on the teacher's definition, the situation becomes much more threatening and it is much more difficult for the teacher to exert sanctions against them. The teacher is highly vulnerable to a united opposition. It is for this reason that many teachers, faced with a difficult class, follow the principle of 'divide and rule'—single out the main troublemaker and 'make an example of him'. A good illustration of a class where the pupils unite against the teacher is given in *The Blackboard Jungle* (Hunter, 1955).

'All right,' Rick said, 'will you take the first one, Miller?' He had chosen Miller purposely, hoping the boy would start things off right, especially after his chat with him the other day. . . .

Miller made himself comfortable in his seat again, and then studied the first sentence. Rick wasn't really anticipating much difficulty with the test. This was a fifth-term class, and they'd had most of this material pounded into their heads since they were freshmen. The first sentence read: *Henry hasn't written (no, any) answer to my letter.*

Rick read the sentence, and then looked at Miller, 'Well, Miller, what do you say?'

Miller hesitated for just a moment, 'Henry hasn't written no answer to my letter,' he said.

Rick stared at Miller and then looked out at the class. Something had come alive in their eyes, but there was still no sound. The silence was intense, pressurized almost.

'No', Rick said, 'It should be "Henry hasn't written any answer." Well, that's all right. I want to learn your mistakes. Will you take the next one, Carter?'

Carter, a big red-headed boy, looked at the second sentence in the test.

If I were (he, him), I wouldn't say that.

'If I were him,' he said rapidly, 'I wouldn't say that.'

Rick smiled. 'Well,' he said, 'if I were you, I wouldn't say that, either. "He" is correct.'

Something was happening out there in the class, but Rick didn't know what it was yet. There was excitement showing in the eyes of the boys, an excitement they could hardly contain. Miller's face was impassive, expressionless.

'Antoro, will you take the next one, please?' Rick said. He had been making notes in his own book as he went along, truly intending to use this test as a guide for future grammar lessons. He looked at the third sentence now. *It was none other than* (*her, she*).

'It was none other than her,' Antoro said quickly.

'No,' Rick said. 'The answer is "she". Take the next one, Levy.' Levy spoke almost as soon as his name was called.

'George throwed the ball fast,' he said.

'Throwed the ball?' Rick said, lifting his eyebrows. '*Throwed*? Come now, Levy. Surely you knew "threw" is correct.'

Levy said nothing. He studied Rick with cold eyes.

'Belazi,' Rick spoke tightly, 'take the next one.'

'It is them who spoke,' he said.

He knew the game now. He knew the game and he was powerless to combat it. Miller had started it, of course, and the other kids had picked it up with an uncanny instinct for following his improvisation.

Situations such as this are exceptional, for it is usually only under the guiding hand of a talented leader, such as Miller in the above example, that the pupils are able to mobilize themselves against the teacher. More typically the pupil is, with respect to the teacher, very much on his own.

The experienced teacher learns when to resist pupil attempts to assert their definition of the situation, when to compromise and when to insist on his own definition of the situation. Normally, he will insist on his own definition of the situation; when yielding or compromise would involve a fundamental neglect of his duties; when he knows that the pupils recognize that it is legitimate for him to impose his own definition of the situation. When the opposite of these conditions applies—when he feels relatively powerless, when the topic for negotiation is of no real significance, when to impose his own definition would be seen as illegitimate by the pupils—then the teacher is more open to negotiation, though if he is skilled in negotiative techniques he may still manage to achieve his own definition of the situation.

The dissatisfactions experienced in the classroom are not shared by teachers and pupils. It is the pupils who bear the greater burden. This must be so for several reasons. Among the most important is the fact of the plurality of pupils, to which we have already referred. Each individual pupil must subordinate his needs to the needs of the majority. Even under the supervision of the 'child-centred' and 'democratic' teacher, the individual will be regularly sacrificed to the needs and desires of the majority of the class. The principal reason why the teacher should experience fewer dissatisfactions than the pupils

141

consists in the teacher's great power. It is the teacher who can and does take the initiative in defining the situation and he has the power to enforce it on those pupils, whether large or small in number, who are reluctant to accept it. If the teacher feels that the prevailing definition of the situation, whether it is initiated by him or by the pupils, is too costly, then he is at liberty to change it—though it may not always be too easy to do so. The pupil, on the other hand, possesses no right to change the definition of the situation. If he tries to do so, it will be by subtle means, as we shall see. Often the children are probably content to accept the teacher's definition of the situation. In those cases where they are not, the pupils may win the occasional battle, but it is almost always the teacher who wins the war. There is relatively little the pupil can do about it, for the more he resists the teacher's definition, the more heavily the teacher will bring to bear the sanctions at his disposal.

In making such extensive use of the concepts of definition of the situation, pseudo-concord, working consensus, negotiative techniques, etc., it is clear that I am making the concept of power a central one in the analysis of teacher–pupil relations. Essentially a conflict model of the classroom is being offered. The analysis is in the tradition of Waller (1932) who, in a celebrated phrase, described the school as 'a despotism in a perilous state of equilibrium'. Over forty years later, in an age when power and authority are being questioned in many areas of society, including educational establishments, this phrase has a prophetic ring of truth. It may be that this power is today being exercised more benevolently; and it may be that the learners, especially in higher education, have made dramatic inroads into the power of teachers. Yet the power differential remains nevertheless. To the social psychologist, the problem is that of how the learners respond and adapt to the power differential. How in fact do they do this? To answer this question we shall have to take a somewhat different approach to the study of classroom interaction. We require a deeper and more subtle appreciation of the pupil's perspective and definition of the situation.

We need a more phenomenological approach in which we attempt to understand the meaning of classroom events as apprehended by the pupil. The distinctive nature of this approach has been well expressed by David Matza (1969). Although he is writing in the context of deviance, his words have a more general relevance.

> The decision to appreciate . . . delivers the analyst into the arms of the subject who renders the phenomenon, and commits him, though not without regrets or qualifications, to the subject's definition of the situation. This does not mean the analyst always concurs with the subject's definition of the situation;

rather, that his aim is to comprehend and to illuminate the subject's view and to interpret the world *as it appears to him*. The view of the phenomena yielded by this perspective is *interior*, in contrast to the external view yielded by a more objective perspective. The . . . phenomenon is seen from the inside. Consequently, many of the categories having their origin in evaluations made from the outside become difficult to maintain since they achieve little prominence in the interpretations and definitions of . . . subjects.

A switch to the pupils' perspective will prove to be very difficult since it is our natural tendency to look at problems of teaching and learning from the teacher's perspective and on the basis of teacher assumptions. Let me illustrate the difficulty with reference to an almost universal teacher practice, that of filling in pupils' reports. When the teacher writes, 'This pupil has shown very little interest this term', this seems a relatively uncomplicated matter. In effect the teacher is criticizing the pupil for showing little interest in the lessons as taught by the teacher. The fault is assigned to the pupil. If only the pupil would develop an interest in the subject and in the lessons, the pupil would make the desired progress. The teacher is perceiving and evaluating the problem on the basis of his own definition of the situation. But the alternative perspective is at least equally important, even though we do not normally look for it. The pupil might fill in his report with 'I have not made much progress this term because I am bored to death with the teacher's lessons in this subject. With different lessons or a different teacher next term I might make more progress.' Here the fault is assigned to the teacher. Neither perspective will in itself be sufficient to bring about a change in the pupil's interest. Although the pupil might say what he thinks to his parents, he cannot tell the teacher for to do so would be to cause offence and to displease the teacher. Thus there is no pressure on the teacher to take the pupil perspective.

In the above example the teacher may be unaware of the pupil perspective partly because the pupil cannot afford to make his perspective explicit and partly because the teacher would regard such a perspective as illegitimate. In other situations the teacher is more likely to be aware of the pupil perspective—though no less likely to regard it as illegitimate. Suppose the form 'clown' is giving one of his typical performances to the glee of his classmates. The teacher's interpretation and reaction will be related to such problems as: is this going to prevent work continuing? is he going to threaten the class discipline? is he going to make me look a fool? The pupil's interpretation and reaction is governed by such problems as: will he make us laugh? will he help us to escape any work? how can we help to

143

prolong his clowning? The perspective of the pupil may or may not be evident to the teacher. If it is, then it will give more rather than less weight to the problems deriving from his own perspective, since his awareness of the pupil perspective will be interpreted in terms of the support it offers to the clown's behaviour in opposition to his own definition of the situation.

My argument will be that teacher and pupil definitions of the situation appear to be more congruent than they are and that in reality they are more divergent than appearances would suggest. The evidence is based mainly on those writers and researchers who have taken a more phenomenological approach to classroom interaction. However, it must be admitted that at this stage our knowledge of the pupils' perspective is extremely primitive. There are very few works like *Letter to a Teacher* (1970) where the pupils make their own perspective disturbingly explicit. Here we are faced with evidence that does not stem from questionnaires designed and administered by teachers or researchers.

I am not, in the rest of this chapter, undertaking to make a phenomenological analysis of teacher–pupil interaction, much as such an analysis is needed. Rather, I have the more limited objective of emphasizing the need for such an analysis by demonstrating how little we have been concerned hitherto with the pupil perspective and by indicating the rich stores that await future investigations and analyses.

The pupil's definition of the situation: a different perspective

In maintaining a symbolic interactionist approach and simultaneously trying to capture the pupil's classroom perspective, then, the pupil's principal task is *to please teacher*. This recognizes the power differential between teacher and pupil and the contingent nature of classroom interaction, since it is from the teacher that the majority of classroom rewards and punishments flow. It is the teacher's rewards and punishments, mainly in the form of approval and disapproval, that form the pupil's principal rewards and costs. The centrality of this phenomenon from the pupil perspective has been noted by several writers. Miles (1964) suggests: 'The student's here-and-now task, as classroom learning goes forward, is, in effect, to please—or at least not to displease—the teacher.' The American anthropologist Jules Henry wrote an article in 1955 entitled 'Docility, or giving teacher what she wants', in which he suggests that in school, pupils must learn to find out what the teacher wants and then satisfy her. This is not always easy, since the teacher does not always make it clear what she wants. The pupils must hunt for signals from the teacher and then direct their behaviour accordingly. They must 'gropingly find a way to gratify the teacher' in order to 'bask in the sun of the teacher's acceptance'. Jerome Bruner (1966) has made the same point. 'Young children in school expend extraordinary time and effort figuring out what it is that the teacher wants.' The matter has been put most succinctly by Jackson (1968), when he points out that the pupil

> must learn how the reward system of the classroom operates and then use that knowledge to increase the flow of rewards to himself. A second job . . . consists in trying to publicize positive evaluations and conceal negative ones.

We are all familiar with the pupil reaction to having pleased teacher, with the pupil who joyfully and boastfully tells his neighbour, 'Look, sir has given me a silver star!' with the pupil who wallows in the admiration of his fellows when it is announced that he is top of the class. We are also familiar with the pupil reaction to having displeased teacher. A good example is available from Barker & Wright's (1951) study, *One Boy's Day*.

> [A second pupil] came back and asked him brightly and eagerly. 'What did you get in your spelling?' Raymond blushed and looked down at his desk. He fidgeted with his hands a moment before he answered. In a swift hoarse whisper he said crossly, 'None of your business.' He seemed quite embarrassed as he spoke. . . .
> Mrs Logan, who was recording the grades, said, 'Let's see the hands of those who didn't get 100.'
> Raymond sat there for a moment.
> He then very slowly and reluctantly raised his hand.
> The teacher called out the name of each child whose hand was raised, asking in each case for the number missed.
> After hearing the first child, she said pleasantly, 'Raymond, you missed two didn't you?'
> Raymond mumbled in embarrassment, 'Yes.' He looked very unhappy and blushed again.
> He looked blankly at his desk for a moment. While Mrs. Logan went through the rest of the names, Raymond continued to appear crestfallen at his failure to get 100.

The concept of pleasing teacher can readily draw on the language of exchange theory since it assumes that a significant part of life in school is concerned with the ways in which the pupil maximizes profits and minimizes losses in his relationship with the teacher. In other words, he must develop techniques whereby he can maximize the possibilities of receiving a favourable evaluation and minimize the chances of being evaluated negatively. Thus the most obvious way in which the pupil can maximize the rewards he receives from the

145

teacher is by learning what sort of behaviours in fact please the teacher, i.e. *by learning the system* then by behaving accordingly and making it evident to the teacher that he is indeed behaving in the approved manner, i.e. *by playing the system.* For unless the teacher is aware that the pupil is conforming to the expected pattern, there can be no reward—except insofar as by conforming he cannot receive a punishment for not conforming. Similarly, he can succeed in avoiding negative evaluations if he learns what displeases the teacher and then either declines to indulge in such behaviour or takes steps to hide such behaviour from the teacher. There are, then, three laws to guide the pupil in learning the skill of pleasing teacher.

First law: *find out what pleases and displeases the teacher.*

Second law: *bring to the teacher's attention those things which please the teacher and conceal from him those behaviours which will displease him.*

Third law: *remember that it is a* competitive *situation. The pupil must try to please the teacher and avoid displeasing him more than other pupils.*

The importance of the third law reveals itself in the well-known fact that pupils disapprove of the person who too openly conforms to the second law. The pupil who persistently and openly brings his own merits and efforts to the teacher's attention is dubbed a 'show-off' or an 'apple-polisher' or other less polite tags. Similarly, the pupil who brings the hitherto concealed misbehaviours of other pupils to the teacher's attention ('Sir, look what Smith's doing!') is rejected as a 'tell-tale' and a traitor. The existence of the third law creates difficulties in abiding by the second law because informal norms develop among the pupils to inhibit pleasing teacher at the expense of other pupils. Only the pupil who has learnt the third law can develop the requisite subtle skills to fulfil the second law without endangering his relationship with his peers.

In effect the pupil has to be highly competitive not only because competition is inherent in the pleasing teacher process, but also because the teacher will actively stimulate competition towards good work and exemplary behaviour, towards the marks and prizes that are given for outstanding achievements in the disciplinary and instructional areas. Yet the pupil must not involve himself too openly in the competition; it must not take on 'cut-throat' characteristics. If the competition is espoused with too much enthusiasm, with too overt an individualism, it will meet with teacher disapproval for it threatens the teacher's desire to create a spirit of harmony and co-operation within the class. Because pleasing teacher is competitive, every time one pupil succeeds, by implication all the other pupils fail. In short, he must learn to compete but to avoid the teacher disapproval given to those who appear to be too little or too much involved in the competition. At the same time he must learn to accept and control his disappointment at his failures in the competition, avoiding giving the impression that his failure is of no consequence to him or is profoundly distressing to him. It requires elaborate learning and the acquisition of subtle self-presentation skills.

The teacher's desire simultaneously to create a spirit of competition and co-operation expresses itself in a variety of classroom practices. An obvious example is the classroom quiz, where the class is divided into two teams. From the teacher's point of view such a device increases motivation; the pupils always enjoy a quiz. It encourages competition between the teams but co-operation within the team. As Henry (1966) has noted, this situation has two consequences which are not always noticed. We have the tragedy of the left-overs, the pupils that each team picks last and often reluctantly; their self-esteem is hardly improved by the situation. Further, when a pupil fails to answer his question correctly, the failure is a double one since he lets down not only himself but also all the other members of his team.

When a teacher asks questions of his pupils, he is sometimes amazed by the quite absurd wild guesses made by the children in the answers they offer. He should not be surprised, for the child is giving evidence that he has learned what the teacher expects of the 'good' pupil. If his guess is right, he will be rewarded with praise. If he is wrong, he will at least have tried and the teacher is often reluctant to condemn the pupil who tries. But if he sits in silence he cannot but receive disapproval from the teacher, for it is only 'bad' pupils who neither know the answer nor exhibit the spirit of enthusiasm. The 'wild guess' is a very reasonable response of the pupil, since such behaviour avoids certain punishment and carries a potentiality for high reward.

Probably the most notorious strategy for pleasing teacher is that of cheating. In cheating, the pupil is trying to give the teacher the impression that he has performed the desired behaviour when he has not in a situation such as an examination. Teachers usually exhibit anger and moral indignation towards the pupil who cheats because he has used what, in the teacher's view, are quite illegitimate methods of meeting the requirements imposed by the teacher. But to the pupil who has not done his homework and who in consequence is certain to fail in the test, cheating is a means of gaining a possible reward and avoiding a certain punishment. The only risk in cheating is that of being found out.

All practising teachers soon become aware of these strategies used by pupils. They learn to spot the pupil who appears to be poring over his Latin grammar book but is actually reading his comic hidden

under the desk. Nor are they always taken in by the professional syco-
phant or 'greaser' who so ostentatiously displays his conformity, who
always says the right thing, and who so anxiously offers his help
when it is not needed. Yet sometimes the strategies are more subtle
and succeed. After all, what use is a strategy if it does not pay off?
In one school I know the pupils would write the date in pencil in their
mathematics exercise books. If the teacher did not mark the work in
that particular lesson, then on the next occasion the pupil could
rub out the old date, substitute the new one, and spend the rest of the
lesson on matters more important than mathematics, secure in the
certainty that if called to account by the teacher, he could produce
incontrovertible evidence of having worked that day. Sometimes even
the common strategies pay off, not because the teacher is unfamiliar
with them, but rather because the teacher is so engrossed in his own
task that he forgets about the strategy. For example, the teacher
wishes each pupil to answer one question from those set in the textbook. To make sure that no child is accidentally left out, he assigns
the questions in a systematic way according to the pupil's seating
position. However, this gives the pupil the opportunity to use the
strategy of 'looking ahead'. He counts up the pupils who will have to
respond before him, calculates which question—all being well—
will be his, and then prepares his answer in advance. With such preparation his chances of giving a right answer are substantially improved. He succeeds in pleasing the teacher, but in so doing he defeats
the teacher's wider purpose of giving him practice at a whole set of
questions rather than at a single one. Ironically, the teacher, in approving the correct answer, reinforces the use of the strategy and
sabotages his own goals.

One of the most insightful exponents of children's classroom
strategies is the American John Holt (1964). From his own experience
as a teacher he illustrates the techniques that children adopt to mask
their ignorance. Let us take the case of one pupil. She knows the
teacher's attention is divided between all the pupils. She knows the
teacher tends to ask questions of those pupils who are not paying
attention or who seem confused and uncertain. Therefore she feels
fairly safe in putting up her hand, waving it excitedly as if she is
bursting to give the answer, even when she does *not* know the answer.
Yet she does this only when other hands are raised. To be the only
person with a raised hand, or to be the only person without a raised
hand, greatly increases the probability of being the target of the
teacher's question. The best means of avoiding the teacher's attention
is to follow the majority. One might add, as a gloss on Holt, that
pupils quickly learn that teachers very rarely ask a pupil two or more
questions in succession. When the teacher does so, especially when
the first answer was correct, it is a cause for surprise because it is

unusual. Sometimes it is a source of complaint—'But I've just done one, sir!' In being given the privilege or the chore of answering, pupils feel there should be fair shares for all. Thus after having answered one question, the pupil can afford to relax his attention.

A second strategy noted by Holt is that of 'hedging one's bet'. If a pupil who is unsure of the answer finds himself called upon by the teacher, he has a chance of gaining approval by giving an ambiguous answer which the teacher might take to be right. In a French lesson, ignorance of the gender of a word can at times be overcome by pronouncing a word which is somewhere between *le* and *la*. Similarly if the pupil is not sure whether a word is spelled with an *a* or an *o* he can write a letter which could be either of them. I remember as a child writing the word *receive* with two letters somewhere between *e* and *i* and with the dot exactly between the two. Other forms of this strategy are the mumbled answer and the addition of 'sort of' to an answer, which allows one to say, 'Yes that's what I meant', when the correct answer is supplied.

The strategies we have examined so far are examples of particular techniques for dealing with specific situations. If the pupil is to succeed in pleasing the teacher he must have at his disposal a whole range of self-presentation techniques which are readily available and adaptable to all eventualities. Some indication of the depth of the self-presentation skills acquired by pupils is given in this entertaining account by a pupil (Willans & Searle, 1958).

The only way with a maths master is to hav a very worried xpression. Stare at the book intently with a deep frown as if furious that you cannot see the answer. at the same time scratch the head with the end of the pen. After 5 minits it is not safe to do nothing any longer. Brush away all the objects which hav fallen out of the hair and put up hand.

'Sir?' (*whisper*)

'Please sir?' (*louder*)

'Yes, molesworth?' sa maths master. (*Thinks: it is that uter worm agane*)

'Sir i don't quite *see* this.'

nb it is essential to sa you don't quite '*see*' sum as this means you are only temporarily bafled by unruly equation and not that you don't kno the fanetest about any of it. (Dialog continue:)

'What do you not see molesworth?' sa maths master (*Thinks: a worthy dolt who is making an honest efort*)

'number six sir i can't make it out sir.'

'What can you not make out molesworth?'

'number six sir.'

'it is all very simple molesworth if you had been paing atention to what i was saing at the beginning of the lesson. Go back to your desk and *think*.'

This gets a boy nowhere but it shows he is KEEN which is important with maths masters.

Maths masters do not like neck of any kind and canot stand the casual approach.

HOW NOT TO APPROACH A MATHS MASTER

'Sir?'

'Sir Sir please?'

'Sir sir pleas sir?'

'Sir sir please sir sir please?'

'Yes molesworth?'

'I simply haven't the fogiest about number six sir'

'Indeed, molesworth?'

'It's just a jumble of letters sir i mean i kno i couldn't care less whether i get it right or not but what sort of an ass sir can hav written this book.'

(*Maths master give below of rage and tear across room with dividers. He hurl me three times round head and then out of window*)

It is no exaggeration to suggest that the art of pleasing teacher forms an important part of schooling which the pupil must learn. It can be said, in Jackson's (1968) words, to constitute

a hidden curriculum which each student (and teacher) must master if he is to make his way satisfactorily through the school. The demands created by these features of classroom life may be contrasted with the academic demands—the 'official' curriculum, so to speak,—to which educators have traditionally paid most attention. As might be expected, the two curriculums are related to each other in several important ways . . . Indeed, many of the rewards and punishments that sound as if they are being dispensed on the basis of academic success and failure are really more closely related to the mastery of the hidden curriculum.

This interpenetration has been neatly exemplified by Jules Henry (1966).

A child writing the word 'August' on the board, for example, is not only learning the word 'August' but also how to hold the chalk without making it squeak, how to write clearly, how to keep going even though the class is tittering at his slowness, how to appraise the glances of the children in order to know whether he is doing it right or wrong, et cetera. If the spelling, arithmetic or music lesson were only what it appeared to be, the education of the American child would be much simpler: but it is all the things that the child learns *along with* his subject matter that really constitute the drag on the educational process as it applies to the curriculum . . . School matamorphoses the child, giving it the kind of Self the school can manage, and then proceeds to minister to the Self it has made . . . It is simply that the child must react in terms of the institutional definitions or he fails. The first two years of school are spent not so much in learning the rudiments of the three R's as in learning definitions.

Pleasing teacher is a useful concept for bringing together both the 'formal' and the 'hidden' curricula and their collective impact on the pupil. It is a useful device for throwing light on the pupil role, not merely in its formal definition of what is expected of the pupil by the teacher, but in its wider sense of the total demands of the class-room situation with which the pupil must come to terms. Most of the previous work on the pupil role has been concerned with teacher expectations. In turning to the pupil perspective we must make a shift in emphasis towards the pervasive features of classroom life as they are experienced by the pupil. As Jackson has shown, the pupil has to cope with the problems of *delay* (e.g. waiting one's turn), *denial* (e.g. being refused permission), *interruption* (e.g. being called to the teacher's desk), and *social distraction* (e.g. not being free to talk to one's peers)—and these problems must be solved in such a way that teacher will be pleased.

Whilst there is a general pupil role common to most classrooms at any given age level within most schools, each teacher has his own unique set of expectations and demands, his own hierarchy of ap-proved behaviours and of misbehaviours, and his own system of reward and punishment. By the time a pupil has reached the second-ary stage of his education, he must, if he is to succeed in pleasing teacher, be able to learn the pupil role that is peculiar to each teacher as well as the general pupil role that is common to most teachers. To learn the pupil role and to succeed in pleasing teacher, the pupil needs the ability to recognize what is expected of him, a set of skills to meet these expectations, and a set of strategies that will allow him to depart from these expectations without incurring disapproval or to give the impression that he is meeting the expectations when he is unable or unwilling to do so.

As an illustration, one of the central elements in the pupil role requires that he absorb himself in academic tasks. Once the pupil has recognized the centrality of task-absorption, he must bring to bear or acquire the art of concentration and perseverance. Task-absorption also requires the pupil to eschew various distractions, both auto-involvements (Goffman, 1963) such as day-dreaming and gazing through the window, and the social distractions afforded by other pupils. Yet frequently these distractions are more attractive to the pupil than the academic tasks on hand, so he must learn how to indulge in them without the teacher being aware of it. He must acquire the skills of looking as if he is listening or reading or writing when he is not, of talking to or passing notes to his friends without drawing the teacher's attention. He must also be armed with appropriate escape routes in case his deception is unmasked—'Please miss, I was only asking him if I could borrow his rubber.'

We will not understand the reasons why children develop and use these self-limiting and self-defeating strategies unless we see life in the classroom from the pupil's perspective. As Holt puts it:

> Children see school almost entirely in terms of the day-to-day and hour-to-hour tasks that we impose on them. . . . For children, the central business of school is not learning, whatever this vague term means; it is getting these daily tasks done, or at least out of the way, with a minimum of effort and unpleasantness. Each task is an end in itself. The children don't care how they dispose of it. If they can get it out of the way by doing it, they will do it; if experience has taught them that this does not work very well, they will turn to other means, illegitimate means, that wholly defeats whatever purpose the task-giver had in mind.

We, the teachers, set them tasks and ask them questions and mark their exercise books to get them to learn and develop an interest in the subject. This is our objective and our definition of the situation. But it is not the pupils' objective; it is not their definition of the situation. Their problem is to 'make the best of a bad job'. To survive, to adapt to that from which they cannot escape, they develop strategies to keep us happy, to please us. For in pleasing the teacher the pupil protects himself and maintains his self-esteem. He keeps the stream of approval flowing towards him, and avoids the embarrassment, shame, disapproval, trouble and punishment which follow when he does or says the wrong thing.

The fundamental difference between the pupil perspective and the teacher perspective becomes clearer when we remember the teacher's view of the curriculum. The teacher thinks in terms of the course of study as a whole, extending over weeks, terms and years. He imagines a cumulative development of knowledge and understanding by the pupil, each lesson or step adding to the total building which he calls his subject syllabus. Every lesson is one more brick, cemented onto earlier bricks and serving as the solid foundation for the next brick. The pupil's perspective is often of a very different nature. As each child receives a brick, he simply pushes it to one side once it has been dealt with. There is never a foundation for the next brick and instead of the child ending up with a secure edifice he merely stands in the middle of a bomb site.

The pupil, especially if he is middle class in origin, is willing to accept these discrete 'bricks' dispensed by the teacher. He is essentially passive, respecting the teacher's authority and responsive to the teacher's rewards that are offered for so doing. His obedience, patience and deference inhibit rebellion against the disjointedness, lack of coherence and even meaninglessness that tend to characterize a surprising amount of what he does in school. Any signs of rebellion (e.g. careless work, lack of concentration, a failing interest) are soon quelled by an appeal to the future examinations, to which he is also highly responsive—and which can be used to persuade him to cement together some of the loose bricks that have collected in his mind. The lower working-class child is less responsive to the reward system of the teacher, less responsive to the examinations, (if he is in a position to take them), and more ready to rebel against the meaninglessness of the loose bricks that make up the lessons.

All pupils at times indulge in those attractive alternatives to what the teacher wants. Because the teacher finds it difficult to take the perspective of the pupil (whatever his social class), much pupil behaviour is perceived by the teacher as 'irrational' or 'stupid'. Because the teacher cannot see its purpose, he wrongly infers that there is no purpose to it. The power and age differentials between teacher and pupil conspire against the dissolution of such misinterpretations. The pupil, being anxious to please and not to displease and being relatively inarticulate, is unlikely to volunteer information that will make the rationality of his conduct apparent to the teacher. Even when the pupil does attempt to do so, the teacher's inability to change perspective leads him to perceive the proffered explanation as a mere excuse. In addition, because the pupil is a child, the teacher can put down the child's 'irrational' behaviour to 'childishness' or 'immaturity'.

In Holt's view these strategies are dictated above all by *fear*—fear of not pleasing, of saying something foolish or stupid, of being laughed at, of being the object of sarcasm, disapproval and punishment. Most teachers react to such a claim by thinking of other teachers—it is never our own pupils who are afraid. But the point is that we as teachers do not recognize the fear in our own pupils. We can recognize only the grossest symptoms of fear, but not the fear which pervades the classroom. For the fear is controlled by the children. To superficial observation they do not *look* as if they are afraid. Are we, the teachers, really aware of this? John Holt, typically forcing us to face the brutal truth, claims that we like children who are a little afraid of us, for it is this which makes them docile and deferential. The ideal pupil is one who is sufficiently afraid of the teacher to do as he is bidden, but without making the teacher feel that it is fear which is the motivating force, for that would threaten the teacher's image of himself as kind and lovable.

Holt goes much further than this, suggesting that a teacher is like a man in a wood at night with a powerful torch. He turns on the light in order to see, but in the beam of the torch the creatures do not behave as they would in the dark. Teachers cannot learn very much about children in classrooms if they look at them only as part of the teaching process when the children are aware that they are being looked at. Teachers will discover how the pupils feel and think and 'tick' only when the observation takes place when the pupils are not aware that they are being observed. This is a hard saying. Teachers always like to feel that they know how the pupils feel, that they understand them, and that they are sensitive to the nuances of their classroom behaviours. For what teacher finds it easy to confess that he has but a limited understanding of his pupils and at the same time retain his self-esteem and sense of competence? But it seems to me that Holt's observation is correct—at least as far as the vast majority of teachers is concerned. We believe we understand our pupils because we want to, but in truth we greatly over-estimate the extent of our understanding.

In my discussion of the pleasing teacher phenomenon with various groups of teachers and students during the past year or two, some critical members of the audience have suggested that I am over-estimating the degree to which pupils have to acquire an appropriate front, their ability to deceive the teacher and the teacher's naïvety in being deceived. This view fails to recognize the implications of Holt's statement. The teacher is indeed very sensitive to certain forms of pupil concealment, namely those which from the teacher perspective have been defined as illegitimate. A good example is cheating. The teacher will be on the look-out for cheating since he regards this as a moral offence and a threat to his instructional role. The pupil's lack of skill in this area of deception can soon become obvious as in the self-evident lie of the pupil who protests, 'I did the homework myself, honestly, sir.' The point is the teacher is insensitive to a much larger area of pupil deception because he is not motivated to recognize it as such. In their attempt to please teacher the pupils feign enthusiasm and interest, which the teacher does not recognize as such because he *wants* the pupils to be enthusiastic and interested. Were he to look behind the mask, the boredom he would see would threaten his self-esteem and sense of professional competence. The pupil does not need to be very skilled in his deception because in effect the teacher is in collusion with the deception. The pupil need only avoid showing his real feelings whilst he is being directly observed by the teacher.

The teacher himself teaches the pupil that he must hide his real feelings. The pupil learns that when he yawns with boredom he is rebuked by the teacher for being inattentive. I remember that in my first week of teaching I was very cross with a first-year pupil for handing in a very poor piece of work. At the end of my sermon the boy burst into tears. Inevitably my heart melted and I tried to comfort him, though telling him at the same time that he was too old to cry. Unintentionally I was teaching him to avoid revealing his true feelings of acute distress. He must, I was saying by implication, not distress me by showing that he was distressed, otherwise I would be unable to be the sort of teacher I wanted to be. It was easier to require him to change than to change myself. He did not cry again.

The teacher, in performing his teacher role, inevitably finds it difficult to perceive the situation from the pupils' perspective. Because the teacher is not fully aware of the effects of his own behaviour on the pupils, he persists in certain forms of conduct which, from his own point of view, seem likely to promote his instructional objectives, but which have the effect of driving the pupil into defensive strategies that actually inhibit learning. The teacher frequently fails to realize what the pupils are doing, and even when he does, he tends not to recognize the pupils' reactions as a response to his own behaviour.

The best exemplification of this, given by John Holt, is the teacher's addiction to the *right answer*. It will be recalled that earlier the teacher's instructional role was defined as the task of getting the pupils to learn and to *show evidence of that learning*. This rider is very important because much of the teacher's behaviour in his instructional role consists in looking for the evidence of the effect of his teaching on the child's learning. He must check that he is indeed promoting the pupil's learning. This is a surprisingly difficult task, for the teacher has to rely on what are essentially indirect indices of the learner's restructured mental faculties. Examination results can provide such a measure, but examinations take place somewhat infrequently. The teacher needs more regular and immediate feedback, evidence which is more readily available in the hour-by-hour activities of the classroom. Such evidence takes two basic forms— what the children write in their exercise books and what they say in response to his questions. At root the evidence on which the teacher relies is the child's ability to produce, in written or oral form, the right answer to the problems imposed by the teacher.

The teacher's reliance on right answers, and his desire to obtain plenty of them, indicates that from the pupil's point of view much of his behaviour is *answer-centred*. The teacher sets the problems and the task of the pupils is to find the right answer which will please the teacher. They know that the teacher knows the answer; it is there in the teacher's mind. Their job is to hunt around until it can be found. The focus is not so much on the problem itself as a problem, but on chasing the answer. The result is that schools encourage *producers*, the pupils who can get the 'right answers', and may thus be discouraging places for *thinkers*. The pupils who wrote *Letter to a Teacher* make the same point.

> During [oral] exams the whole class sinks either into laziness or terror. Even the boy being questioned wastes his time. He keeps taking cover, avoids what he understands least, keeps stressing the things he knows well. To make you happy we need know only how to sell our goods. And how to fill empty spaces with empty words. To repeat critical remarks read in [books by established critics], passing them off as our own and giving the impression that we have read the originals.

This means that the best strategy for the pupils is to find a technique which will successfully produce the right answers and please the teacher. Any technique which works, which produces right answers fast, will be a good one. Sometimes in order to find a successful technique the pupils must understand the problem. But at other times no real learning is necessary for the pupils can find a formula or a recipe which will produce the right answer but which does not require any understanding of the problem at all. In such a case the teacher infers that pupils are learning, for the answer was right. Approval is given and the use of the strategy is strengthened. Yet the learning is only *apparent* learning, for no understanding of the problem has taken place. The recipe is a substitute for real learning. All teachers have experience of this, though they may not recognize it as such. On Monday all pupils seem to be able to solve the problems. On Wednesday, when the same work is covered again, half the pupils get the answers wrong. The teacher tends to assume that the children are being lazy or forgetful or careless and he rebukes them accordingly. After all, this is the most obvious explanation. But what may often occur in such circumstances is that the children never really understood in the first place. They found a formula or recipe which worked on Monday, but which they have forgotten by Wednesday.

For many pupils pleasing teacher is not just an end in itself, a survival kit for passing through school unscathed. It is also a necessary part of passing examinations and obtaining some qualifications, either into a job or onto the next rung of the educational ladder. This forms one of the most important rewards which accrue to the pupil who tries to please the teacher. Without the incentive of the examinations the pressure to please teacher would be substantially diminished. As the pupil-authors of *Letter to a Teacher* write:

> But your pupils' own goal is also a mystery. Maybe it is non-existent; maybe it is just shoddy. Day in and day out they study for marks, for reports and diplomas. Meanwhile they lose interest in all the fine things they are studying. Languages, sciences, history—everything becomes purely pass marks. Behind those sheets of paper there is only a desire for personal gain. The diploma means money. Nobody mentions this, but give the bag a good squeeze and that's what comes out. To be a happy pupil in your schools you have to be a social climber at the age of twelve.

The art of pleasing teacher as we have so far described it is essentially the orientation to life in school of the middle-class pupil. The values derived from home are consonant with this orientation and he possesses the requisite values, attitudes and social skills—all of which have in recent years become of interest to sociologists of education— that enable him to learn the art with relative ease and to be successful in pleasing teacher. Sometimes he learns that art so naturally and so thoroughly that he is entirely identified with the 'good pupil' role. In other cases he is aware that the good pupil image which he adopts towards the teachers is to some degree a misrepresentation of his true character, but he is able to play his part without effort and without a sense of hypocrisy at being 'two-faced'. One might assume that the 'successful' working-class pupil undergoes a similar socialization at school, whether or not is is supported in this endeavour by his home life. Certainly large numbers of working-class pupils are handicapped in this aspect of life in school as in others, so it is not surprising that many of them conclude their school life in playing the game in a very half-hearted manner. Who in this world ever retains enthusiasm for a game in which one is a consistent loser?

There are, however, alternatives to pleasing teacher with varying degrees of eagerness. The first is the delinquent or 'delinquescent' orientation. Here the rules of pleasing teacher are turned upside-down and the principal objective becomes to *displease* the teacher. The underlying causes of this orientation are complex and I have tried to deal with some of them elsewhere (Hargreaves, 1967, 1971), but with respect to this argument it can be said to result from a persistent failure to please teacher successfully and a realization that for the pupil it is an unprofitable activity. The delinquent orientation is a very difficult game because the pupil cannot sustain a continuous and open rebellion against the teacher and the system, for to do so would be to provoke the teachers into calling into force the most severe penalties at their disposal, including corporal punishment. In

157

coming to terms with the reality of his life in school, the delinquent has to play a more subtle game so that, in practice, the situation is not so much one of pitched battle but of intermittent skirmishes, in which the occasional flouting of the school rules is detected and punished. The delinquent spends much of his time in school in terms of a sullen compliance to the rules of the game, not because he accepts the rules but because he fears excessive sanctions. Such compliance is regarded as legitimate by other members of the delinquent group who do not expect their friends to become martyrs. But this compliance is *expedient compliance*. When punishment for non-conformity is both certain and severe, then the delinquent complies. Where the probability of severe punishment is relatively low, as in the classes of a teacher with 'weak' discipline, the delinquent can and does flout the rules in an overt expression of his rejection of the system. From time to time the delinquent will also indulge in disobedience when apprehension and punishment seem certain and this will command the admiration of his fellows and enhance his peer group status to a greater degree than will non-conformity in more 'safe' situations. So the delinquent does not seek to displease the teacher indiscriminately. Rather he takes a calculated risk. With luck he may be able to express his resentment and rejection of the system with very little personal cost. The occasional severe punishment remains a small cost relative to the high rewards that have accrued to him, in the form of peer group status, in the interim.

The second alternative to pleasing teacher, and the most difficult to elaborate in detail, is what might be called the indifferent orientation. In this case the pupil desires neither to please nor to displease the teacher. He is simple 'not bothered'. School is neither gladly accepted nor bitterly rejected. If he is rewarded by the teacher, it gives him little pleasure. If he is punished, it is regarded as an unfortunate and unfair intrusion. Essentially it is an orientation of withdrawal or of 'serving one's sentence'. At times he appears to be trying to please the teacher, but the resemblance to the normal game is superficial. He makes no attempt on his own initiative to please the teacher, but when challenged by the teacher he reacts with the expected and pleasing answer not in order to receive a reward but in order to fend off a challenge or a potential punishment. This attitude is betrayed in the 'I don't know' strategy that is typical of the indifferent orientation. When challenged by the teacher, the pupil seems either not to know the 'right' response or lack the motivation to hunt around for the pleasing answer. He responds with an 'I don't know' as a relatively safe way out until the 'right' answer becomes obvious from the teacher's prompting. A good example of this is given in Barry Hines' masterly novel, *A Kestrel for a Knave* (1968) in which Billy Casper comes very close to the indifferent orientation.

'You were asleep weren't you? . . . Well? Speak up, lad!'

'I don't know, Sir.'

'Well I know. You were fast asleep on your feet. Weren't you?'

'Yes, Sir.'

'Fast asleep during the Lord's Prayer! I'll thrash you, you irreverent scoundrel!'

He demonstrated the act twice down the side of the lectern.

'Were you tired, lad?'

'I don't know, Sir.'

'Don't know? You wouldn't be tired if you'd get to bed at night instead of roaming the streets at all hours up to mischief!'

'No, Sir.'

'Or sitting up 'til dawn watching some tripe on television! Report to my room straight after assembly. You will be tired when I've finished with you, lad.'

'Casper!'

Billy sat up and put his hands away.

'What, Sir?'

'What, Sir. You'd know if you'd been listening. Have you been listening?'

'Yes, Sir.'

'Tell me what we've been talking about then.'

'Er . . . stories, Sir.'

'What kind of stories?'

'Er . . .'

'You don't know, do you?'

'No, Sir.'

'You haven't heard a word of what's been said, have you, Casper?'

'Yes, Sir—some of it.'

'Some of it. I'll bet you have. Stand up, lad.'

Billy sighed and pushed the chair away with the backs of his knees.

'Right, now you can do some work for a change. You're going to tell us any story about yourself, the same as Anderson did.'

'I don't know any, Sir.'

One of the most tragic aspects of the indifferent orientation is that the pupil reacts in a very defensive way against the teacher who, full of good intentions, tries to offer help. For instance, the teacher may try to find out what really interests the child by gentle questioning. Typically the pupil responds with the other standard techniques of 'I'm not bothered' or 'I don't mind' whenever the teacher tries to probe his interests or problems. This is easily interpreted by the teacher as apathy. But it may also be that the pupil is reluctant to commit himself or give his true view because he suspects (correctly), on the basis of past experience, that the teacher is asking from an ulterior motive, i.e. seeking a means of getting the pupil involved in school work. If the pupil does commit himself then he may find that he is 'conned' into something he would rather not do. It is simpler and safer to say, 'I'm not really bothered.'

These three orientations, the 'normal', the 'delinquent' and the 'indifferent' have been outlined at a fairly crude level. We need to know very much more about the variant forms of coming to terms with pleasing teacher, about the range of strategies and skills involved, and about the different interpretive schemes employed by the pupils. One of the main problems is that of showing how these pleasing teacher orientations develop and change during the career of pupils in the educational system, and in particular we need research on the ways in which and the means by which pupils acquire an orientation and its associated strategies during the early years of schooling. We need, in other words, an educational equivalent to Goffman's (1961) brilliant analysis of the career of the patient in a mental hospital.

Using the concept of pleasing teacher I have tried to outline one form of a more phenomenological approach to the study of teacher–pupil interaction which contrasts with the approaches of the inter-action analysts and the role theorists. This approach, which we have barely begun to explore, has several important advantages. First, it opens research to the amateur, the practising teacher. Most teachers think of educational research as a very specialized concern of certain non-teachers that we call professional researchers. Research is not, in other words, something that the ordinary teacher can do. Yet John Holt shows that research is not the exclusive preserve of professional researchers. Indeed, he is the best evidence I know of to justify the assertion that professional researchers are too far from the realities of the classroom. John Holt writes as a teacher, without rarefied techniques, without technical language, without elaborate conceptualization. Yet his work reveals an almost unique insight into the nature of teacher–pupil interaction and in particular into the nature of the pupil perspective. Second, this approach offers potentialities of real interdisciplinary research. The philosophers' work on phenomenology has influenced both sociology (e.g. Harold Garfinkel, Howard Becker, Aaron Cicourel, John Kitsuse, David Matza) and psychology (R. D. Laing, Carl Rogers), though at present most work has been done on deviant or abnormal behaviour. Third, this approach offers an interesting orientation for teaching education students about classroom interaction. We all agree on the importance of sensitivity in the art of being a teacher. This approach emphasizes the ability of the teacher to put himself in the pupils' shoes and to see classroom events from their perspective. It suggests, in other words, a justification for the training of teachers in empathy.

Recommended reading

E. J. AMIDON & J. B. HOUGH (eds), *Interaction Analysis: Theory, Research and Application*, Addison-Wesley, 1967.

J. HENRY, *Culture Against Man*, Tavistock, 1966.

J. HOLT, *How Children Fail*, Pitman, 1964 (Penguin, 1969).

P. W. JACKSON, *Life in Classrooms*, Holt, Rinehart & Winston, 1968.

W. WALLER, *The Sociology of Teaching*, Wiley, 1932.

School of Barbiana, *Letter to a Teacher*, Penguin, 1970.

7 Teacher–pupil relations: where are we going?

In the last chapter we were concerned with applying some theoretical concepts, especially those that are central in the symbolic interactionist perspective, to the analysis of teacher–pupil relationships in the classroom. This analysis was essentially descriptive. Implicitly it also contained a *diagnosis* of teacher–pupil relations. It is but a very short step from describing a situation to making a value-judgment upon it. Indeed, I would argue that it is impossible to separate the two in any sharp way, because the terms we use to describe events are never completely neutral—much as the social scientist strives to that end—but contain reflections of the values of the person who undertakes the description. As Lionel Trilling's (1970) incisive comments on the Kinsey Report show, it is when one tries hardest to be non-evaluative and non-prescriptive that one's concealed assumptions and prescriptions become most dangerous.

The implicit diagnosis of the last chapter suggests that all is not well in the world of the classroom; and many teachers would feel that it is so obvious a fact that they hardly need this book to inform them of it! In this chapter I want to examine some of the new directions in teaching which are being offered as a solution to that diagnosis. It will immediately become apparent that I am in general sympathy with these writers and take the view that they offer the greatest hope for improving the nature of schooling.

These writers, who are sometimes grouped together by commentators under the title of the New Romantics, began to write on the basis of their own experience of teaching. They write as teachers to teachers, not as academics to students. Their writings have a strong personal flavour; they quote many anecdotes from their own experience; they reveal their own feelings and their own observations. Quite often they refer to one another in their books, but they almost never quote any of the books or research by academics. It is perhaps for this reason that many academics dismiss their writings as 'popular journalism'. It is true that their writing is often highly emotive, betraying a lack of sustained, systematic and well documented argument. But the brilliance of their insights and their potential importance for future trends in teaching make them far too significant to ignore. I shall deal with just a few of the leading figures among the New Romantics. One, John Holt, we have already met in the last chapter. In this chapter I shall also take account of Herbert Kohl, Neil Postman and Carl Rogers—the last of whom is the only social scientist in the list.

One of the faults of the last chapter is that it tended to talk about '*the* teacher' as if there was only one kind of teacher in our schools. In some ways it is perhaps justifiable to talk about the typical teacher; but in looking towards future developments in teaching I now need to make a differentiation among teachers into a set of *types*. I could perhaps adopt Waller's suggestions, or even a classification based on the lists of sub-roles mentioned early in the last chapter. Neither of these seems very adequate to my task. An alternative would be to use the distinction I made between instructional and disciplinary sub-roles, especially if this were refined somewhat. For instance, in the analysis of 'pleasing teacher' it becomes clear that much teacher behaviour could be analysed in terms of his functions as *motivator* and *evaluator*. These two functions could be seen as two dimensions which cross-cut the instructional and disciplinary functions. Thus the teacher must evaluate the pupil's learning and academic progress (instructional role); and he must evaluate the pupil's behaviour in the classroom (disciplinary role). He must also motivate the pupil to work hard and to be interested in what he is learning (instructional role); and he must motivate the pupil to behave well and to conform to the rules of classroom conduct and procedure (disciplinary role). This fourfold scheme might make a useful basis for the development of a set of teacher types.

In fact I am going to work on a much simpler scheme. I shall consider most current teachers under the heading of two types and then contrast these with a third type, namely the New Romantic. But the reader must remember that these are 'ideal types' in Weber's sense of the term. I shall construct these types in terms of a set of characteristics. They are *artificial* constructions, derived from actual teachers, but the types are not to be found in this form in the real world. Each is thus a collection of fragments of real teachers, *but it would be a disastrous mistake to think that the teaching profession can be divided neatly into three groups*. Whilst some teachers may be much close to one type than to the others, many teachers are a complex mixture of the three types.

What, then, shall I call my first two types? When I survey the literature on types I find myself confronted on the one hand with long lists of types described in everyday terms (e.g. Waller, 1932; Hoyle, 1969) and on the other hand with dichotomous types suggested by researchers—such as 'autocratic–democratic', 'teacher-centred–pupil-centred', 'direct–indirect', 'dominative–integrative', 'progressive–traditional'. My objection here is that the terms are not neutral descriptions at all; there are clearly 'goodies' and 'baddies', and it is obvious that it is the first term in each pair which on the side of the angels and in the good books of the researcher. Even when more neutral terms are adopted, as in Type 1 and Type 2 of the N.F.E.R. report on streaming (Barker-Lunn, 1970) we can easily detect the 'good' one of the pair. I want terms, therefore, which do not necessarily involve a moral judgment on the teachers but which allow one to recognize that both types have strengths and weaknesses. At the same time, my own preference is for the New Romantic type where 'new' does have the implication of 'better'—but I am quite unprepared to discard the other two types in pejorative terms such as 'authoritarians' which is the line taken by some of the New Romantics themselves (e.g. Kohl, 1969). I shall thus give the first two types names which reflect some of the central elements in the different philosophies of education that they embody. They will be referred to as *liontamers* and *entertainers* (Hargreaves, 1972). These are terms which contrast with most academic terminology and which arouse in us a good-natured smile, which befits the parodied form in which I must describe them.

My first task is outline the three types in some detail. I shall do this by analysing them under a number of headings, which will emphasize their different conceptions of teacher and pupil roles and relationships.

1. Motives and incentives

Liontamers

This is essentially a nineteenth-century model—but it is surviving well. In this model the pupils are seen as wild, unsocialized creatures who must be tamed and domesticated through schooling. Education becomes a process of civilizing. The teacher knows a set of tricks, in the form of knowledge, principles and ideas that the pupil must learn. The pupils are seen as naturally lazy and unmotivated, and even as resistant to being educated. The task for the teacher is thus to make the pupils sufficiently tractable and docile that they will jump through the appropriate hoops, at the appropriate time and in the appropriate manner. In the classical form the teacher had to *drive* the pupils into learning with the crack of his whip, in the form of threats and punishments. In the more contemporary version, the liontamer has read Skinner and now conditions his pupils through reinforcement schedules. Thus a generation of educational psychologists make their reputations by providing a fine-sounding rationale for liontaming. However, it would be quite wrong to depict liontamers as old-fashioned 'authoritarians'. Modern liontamers, in the classroom as in the circus, have realized that overt cruelty is by no means always the best method of teaching.

Liontamers thus simply demand pupil motivation and if it is not forthcoming they are willing to induce it through fear, though for preference the pupils should not display their fear too openly. Liontamers put a heavy stress on those unfashionable concepts of will and duty. They take their own liontaming duty very seriously and believe that pupils must make great efforts of will if they are to succeed. They are fine examplars of the Protestant Ethic. Ultimately the pupils must learn what is required because the teacher says so and it is the pupils' duty to obey.

Entertainers

The basic assumption about pupil motivation is similar to that of the liontamers; pupils do not naturally want to learn. Education, however, is no longer seen as something that must be *driven in* but as something that must be *drawn out*, and educationists write purple passages about the meaning of the concept of education as derived from the Latin word *educere*. The means of drawing it out is high-class entertainment. What the teacher needs above all else is a good script that will capitalize on the interests of the pupils who can, on this basis, be cajoled into learning. If things go wrong, he does not blame human nature as the liontamer does, but his script. And he looks round for a new and better set of gags and stage business. In response to these teacher demands, there emerges a new set of impresarios and script-writers, going under the official name of curriculum developers, who act as the Bernard Delfont or the Simpson and Galton of the Great Educational Show.

The central incentive of entertainers is *fun*. Things are worth doing in school simply because they are so enjoyable. After all, the teacher has spent a lot of time basing the curriculum on the interests of the pupils—or what he takes to be interests of the pupils. The classroom is like a children's party. Everyone is having such a good time; no-one is allowed to spoil things by declining to join in. If the fun argument fails, then there is an appeal to the usefulness of what is being learned, though normally the appeal is to future rather than to present utility. Entertainers inject motivation like a drug, one which

165

contains a stimulant to produce a euphoria in learning and also an analgesic that will deaden the pain of it all.

New Romantics

The fundamental proposition of the New Romantics, which is in direct opposition to the liontamers and entertainers, is that the pupils are *naturally* motivated to learn. It is taken to be an inherent part of the human condition. What is taken by liontamers and entertainers to be a *lack* of motivation ('Jones is completely apathetic. He's no interest in anything at all.') is interpreted by the New Romantics as a *loss* of motivation to do what the teacher wants the pupil to do, and at the same time and in the manner that the teacher wants it done. Schools are thus regarded as places that easily inoculate many pupils against their natural desire to learn.

> I became very irritated with the notion that students must be 'motivated.' The young human being is intrinsically motivated to a high degree. Many elements of his environment constitute challenges for him. He is curious, eager to discover, eager to know, eager to solve problems. A sad part of most education is that by the time a child has spent a number of years in school this intrinsic motivation is pretty well dampened (Rogers, 1969).

> Nobody starts off stupid. You only have to watch babies and infants, and think seriously about what all of them learn and do, to see that, except for the most grossly retarded, they show a style of life, and a desire and ability to learn that in an older person we might well call genius. . . . But what happens, as we get older, to this extraordinary capacity for learning and intellectual growth? What happens is that it is destroyed, and more than by any other one thing, by the process we misname education (Holt, 1964).

The New Romantics interpret their task as *facilitating* learning; there is no need to try to inject any motivation, though there may be some problems in breaking through the blockages that inhibit the natural motivation. However, the New Romantics eschew any kind of pressure, in the form of punishments, threats or incentives, that might be put upon the pupil to get him to learn. Compulsion and education are seen as antithetical; if the pupil declines to learn in school, then that is his right. The teacher must wait patiently until the pupil decides that *he* wants to solve.

> The role of the teacher is not to control his pupils but rather to enable them to make choices and pursue what interests them (Kohl, 1969).

There is no way to help a learner to be disciplined, active and thoroughly engaged unless *he* perceives a problem to be a problem or whatever is to-be-learned as worth learning, and unless he plays an active role in determining the process of solution. That is the plain, unvarnished truth, and if it sounds like warmed-over 'progressive education', it is not any less true for it (Postman and Weingartner, 1969).

The New Romantics see the destruction of motivation as a common response to the overt compulsion and constraint exerted by the liontamer and the more subtle forms employed by the entertainer. A cornerstone of their philosophy becomes the principle of voluntarism. There is thus a special emphasis on the concepts of *freedom* and *choice*. We all know that these are dangerous words because they are both imprecise and emotive. The New Romantics, however, tend to be more concerned with the problems of maximizing freedom *in practice* rather than with problems of definition. The New Romantics attack the liontamers and entertainers for creating classrooms where there is an atmosphere which is highly threatening and which induces fear in the learners. As a result, they argue, motivation is stifled and learning impeded (Holt, 1964).

We adults destroy most of the intellectual and creative capacity of children by the things we do to them or make them do. We destroy this capacity above all by making them afraid, afraid of not doing what other people want, of not pleasing, of making mistakes, of failing, of being *wrong*. Thus we make them afraid to gamble, afraid to experiment, afraid to try the difficult and unknown. . . . We encourage children to act stupidly, not only by scaring and confusing them, but by boring them, by filling up their days with dull, repetitive tasks that make little or no claim on their attention or demands on their intelligence.

2. The content of the curriculum

Liontamers

The liontamers believe quite firmly that the content of the curriculum must be entirely in the hands of the teacher. He is the expert and by contrast the pupils are far too immature and inexperienced to decide what they should study. Not until they have learned my imposed curriculum, argues the liontamer, can the pupils be in a position to make realistic choices. Consequently he allows choice in only the most peripheral matters of schooling among younger children, and when pupils are older their choice is restricted to alternatives among curricula all of which are controlled in detail by the teacher.

167

The liontamer has a special regard for 'subjects' and the traditional 'disciplines'. The so-called basics—literacy and numeracy—assume a special importance, and in his contemporary secondary school form he complains bitterly that these are being neglected by primary schools with their 'new-fangled' approaches. He thus values drills and rote-learning, not so much as ends in themselves, but because they provide a 'solid basis' for further studies.

Entertainers

The main assumption is that of the liontamers, that the teacher is the best person to shape the content of the curriculum. On the other hand there is a distinct scepticism about 'subjects'—on the grounds that they tend to be boring—and a preference for thinking in terms of themes, topics and integrated subjects. There is a movement away from memorization and mastery towards discovery learning, though this is almost always pseudo-discovery since the teacher has carefully planned beforehand what it is that the pupils shall 'discover'.

Because of their emphasis on enjoyment, entertainers devote special efforts to making the curricula interesting and relevant. Thus history is taught with a local bias, mathematics with examples from cricket scores and gas bills, which hopefully will be as potentially useful as they are enthralling.

New Romantics

Since the pupil is given choice in what he wants to learn, there is a strong suspicion among the New Romantics of curricula which are pre-designed or pre-packaged. It is assumed that the teacher should not impose a curriculum on the pupils, who must make their own choices. As it is unlikely that a whole class of children will want to investigate the same topic, it is recognized that frequently the curriculum must be *individualized*. This produces enormous problems for the teacher who is used to 'teaching a class', though teachers who have experience of teaching 'mixed ability' classes can recognize that the difficulties, though great, are not insuperable.

The movement towards 'integration' among entertainers initiated some general questioning about the traditional subjects. The New Romantics develop this trend even further and suggest that the placement of many subjects on the traditional school curriculum seems arbitrary (Postman and Weingartner, 1969).

It is increasingly difficult to decide what subjects to include in a curriculum. Why history and geography? Why not cybernetics and ecology? Why economics and algebra? Why not anthropology and psycholinguistics? It is difficult to escape the feeling that a conventional curriculum is quite arbitrary in selecting the subjects to be studied. The implications of this are worth pondering.

For the New Romantics, then, the curriculum is constructed, often on an individual or small group basis, as a 'collaborative venture' between teacher and pupil, in which the teacher, since he often knows little about the topics the pupils wish to pursue, can no longer play an 'expert' role. His expertise resides more in being able to help in the defining of problems, the provision of resources, and the suggesting of possible lines of development. He tends not to believe in 'basics' being taught as a foundation, but assumes that many of the skills of literacy and numeracy will be 'picked up' in an almost incidental way by the pupil as he investigates the topics he has himself chosen. Holt (1972) and Postman (1970) make a radical attack on the teaching of reading, suggesting that perhaps we should not teach it at all and that our current obsession with reading standards is completely misdirected.

3. Teaching style

Liontamers

Talk and chalk are the staple methods of liontamers, usually with much more emphasis on the talk. Liontamers define themselves as experts, and believe that the best means of conveying their knowledge to the pupils is by means of telling or lecturing. It is the teacher's job to define the problem, explain the concepts, principles and methods involved, and provide most of the necessary information. The teacher then checks on whether or not the pupils have understood and learned by question-and-answer sessions, in which the teacher asks the questions and the pupils answer, and by written assignments.

Liontamers take a special pride in their classroom discipline, which they think of as 'firm'. Just as they emphasize their expertise in relation to the curriculum, so they emphasize their status in social matters. The teacher makes the rules, because the pupils are seen as too immature to make their own, and the pupil's job is to obey those rules without question. Failure to conform to the rules is heavily penalized. In this, the liontamer believes he is giving pupils a good preparation for future life in society where they will have to adjust and conform to the authority structures of the wider world.

Entertainers

Being aware of the potential limitations of their script, entertainers talk rather less; they resort instead to a set of supportive educational props—audio-visual aids, which make the material more interesting and real; films and television programmes, which widen the walls of the classroom and introduce better speakers; teaching machines, because they can be efficient and novel; packages of materials, which provide a rich source of things to use and explore. In short, the classroom becomes a veritable Palace of Varieties. Around the classroom of the entertainer arises a vast network of enterprises, as the *Times Educational Supplement* reveals. Script-writers, stage directors and impresarios run weekend, holiday and term-long courses to keep the entertainers up to date with the latest ideas and bandwagons, amongst which the teachers can frantically hop in the never-ending pursuit of the new and exciting. So the entertainers set little store on their expertise, but stress their enthusiasm and adaptability.

For the entertainers, as for the liontamers, discipline is a matter of 'keeping the pupils at it', but it is a matter of keeping them happy rather than keeping them down. Discipline problems are treated as a sign of teacher rather than pupil failure, and the answer lies in preparing a more interesting and more relevant curriculum. When this approach fails to solve discipline problems, the entertainer is reluctant to punish a pupil, for this interferes with the happy classroom atmosphere that he is trying to create. So he prefers to pressure pupils into conformity by appealing to the pupil that his conduct is spoiling things for everyone else. Whereas the liontamer is willing to alienate himself from the pupil by punishing him, the entertainer prefers to alienate the difficult pupil from his peers by turning them against him rather than the pupil against the teacher.

New Romantics

Believing that the pupils are naturally motivated and are capable of making responsible use of freedom of choice, the New Romantic's teaching aim is to create the conditions under which that choice can be exercised. He believes that the creation of the appropriate classroom atmosphere, namely one that is non-threatening and acceptant, springs directly from the kind of relationship he establishes with the pupils. This, it is argued, is a relationship characterized by *trust* (Rogers, 1969):

> If I distrust the human being then I *must* cram him with information of my own choosing, lest he go his own mistaken way. But if I trust the capacity of the human individual for developing his own potentiality, then I can provide him with many opportunities and permit him to choose his own way and his own direction in his learning. . . . It is a basic trust—a belief that this other person is somehow fundamentally trustworthy.

The difficulties involved in maintaining this attitude of trust are best exemplified if we consider possible pupil reactions to the freedom which is given them. Most pupils react to the teacher's unwillingness to compel them to follow a predetermined curriculum with disbelief. They think the teacher is playing some kind of trick or game. Their immediate reaction is to do nothing that the teacher would regard as 'educational' but instead to sit around reading comics or chatting—which certainly has the effect of testing just how trustful the teacher is! The New Romantic trusts that this reaction is short-lived, and that if he can resist trying to cajole the pupils into 'doing something useful' then their natural motivation will eventually reassert itself. The writings of the New Romantics suggest that for the vast majority of children this testing period lasts several weeks, and it is a period of acute agony for the teacher, who feels rejected and superfluous (see especially Rogers (1969), chapter 1). But eventually the pupils get bored with their gossip and comics and begin to discuss other projects and involve the teacher in them.

There is a second way in which the teacher finds it difficult to maintain his trust. When a pupil does select an area for study, he may show a very deep involvement in it. He may want to do nothing else for a week, or a month, or even several months. Not unnaturally the teacher may become concerned about this concentration on one topic to the exclusion of his 'general education'. The New Romantic believes that if this is what the pupil wants to do then it is right *for him* at this moment in time, and he must therefore be allowed to continue until he decides to change topic. And isn't this really what 'love of learning' is about? The New Romantic assumes that no amount of time spent in real, active learning is wasted time, for once the pupil *wants* to learn, then the skills he might like to develop subsequently as part of a task that matters to him can be acquired in a relatively short time. As the pupil gets older, he will realize the costs of excessive specialization on a single topic or subject. But ultimately the choice must be his. We cannot make all his choices for him and then wonder why he does not want to learn. Nor is this pattern necessarily incompatible with public examinations; what matters is that the pupil should actively choose to follow, say, an 'O' level course and then choose what he will study within it when he has examined and discussed the syllabus with the teachers.

The same attitude of trust marks the New Romantics' approach to discipline. Certain basic rules are established; the teacher cannot condone personal violence, severe damage to property or the interference by one pupil in another pupil's work. The freedom that is given is not a total licence, which would be so devoid of structure that it would be threatening. Rather, the New Romantic seeks to provide a minimum of structure which will avoid a threatening chaos on the one hand and an imposed set of rules on the other. Most important of all, this means that as few rules as possible must be imposed; all rules must be fully discussed with pupils, so that they can see the point of the rules and accept them as in the interests of all.

4. The pupil's role

Liontamers

The pupils of liontamers spend most of their time in school sitting and listening, for their main task is to absorb what the teacher tells them. Typically, the class is taught as a whole and for the most part the teacher in his talk is addressing the class as a unit. 'Individual work' consist of each pupil doing the same thing in a state of social isolation from other learners ('No talking whilst you are writing'). Thus the teacher spends much of his time checking that the pupils are paying attention (listening) and not talking to one another. It is the pupil who must adapt to the subject. If he cannot keep up with the pace, he must be transferred to another stream or another school.

Entertainers

The pupil has a more active role, for he spends less time in sheer listening, and much more time in looking—at the films and other audio-visual aids that the entertainer employs. More time is also spent in group work, where three or four pupils carry out joint projects. It is this willingness to abandon teaching the class as a single unit that has helped entertainers to adapt more easily to mixed ability groups, for they can stream within the class by means of small group projects. The entertainer, then, is much more prepared to adapt the subject to the pupil and it is this which accounts for his fondness for the concept of 'readiness'.

The lower amount of time spent in teaching the class as a whole and the marked increase in pupil–pupil talk during group projects create new problems. The teacher finds it more difficult to observe what is going on amongst the pupils and he has to check constantly that the pupil talk is in fact related to the project he has set them. With the liontamer almost any pupil–pupil talk is defined as deviant, whereas with the entertainer it is only some kinds of content rather than the talk itself which is deviant. Further, there is the problem that in any one group perhaps only one or two pupils are actually working, whilst the rest are simply being 'carried' by the motivated ones. Much of the entertainer's time is therefore spent moving around the room to ascertain exactly what the pupils are doing. Since this task is difficult, the teacher tells the pupils that he must trust them to work without his surveillance; but in practice the teacher's constant checking reveals that this trust is illusory. It is a trust which the teacher feels forced to invoke, not one which is genuinely given.

New Romantics

We saw in the last chapter that John Holt believes that the traditional methods of teaching induce in the pupils answer-centredness, memorizing, and the acquisition of defensive strategies for 'getting by' and 'getting away with things' instead of real learning. In a New Romantic classroom the pupil role is changed dramatically in that *not* working is no longer something that must be hidden from the teacher. The strategies of concealment become pointless. The pupil's task is no longer one of 'getting down' to what the teacher imposes, but of deciding whether or not he wants to learn and then precisely what he wants to learn. The pupil is, in a dramatic way, thrown back on himself and his own resources. Once the pupil has decided on a project, then his role is one of directing his own work, with the help of the teacher when this is sought. The pupil role is therefore much less dependent and more self-reliant. Essentially, he is made responsible for his own conduct.

Under the liontamers and the entertainers, the primary task for the pupil is to learn the content of the curriculum. Teacher and pupil roles are both structured to this end. Under the New Romantic, two rather different aspects of learning assume great significance. The first is the learning by the pupil *that* he wants to learn, for this is the essential prerequisite of discovering *what* he wants to learn. The second is the emphasis given to *learning how to learn.*

> Since we can't show what knowledge will be needed in the future, it is senseless to try to teach it in advance. Instead, we should try to turn out people who love learning so much and learn so well that they will be able to learn whatever needs to be learned (Holt, 1964).

> We are, in my view, faced with an entirely new situation in education where the goal of education, if we are to survive, is the *facilitation of change and learning.* The only man who is educated is the man who has learned how to learn; the man who has learned to adapt and change; the man who has realized that no knowledge is secure, that only the process of *seeking* knowledge gives a basis for security (Rogers, 1969).

As we have seen, the New Romantics tend to regard traditional school curricula as somewhat arbitrary; this, combined with the limitations of our present knowledge, leads them to encourage in pupils a *learning to question*. The pupil is helped to question the assumptions and the implicit values of the 'knowledge' that he meets in his explorations.

> Knowledge isn't just *there* in a book, waiting for someone to come along and 'learn' it. Knowledge is produced in response to questions. And new knowledge results from the asking of new questions; quite often new questions about old questions. Here is the point: once you have learned to ask questions—relevant and appropriate and substantial questions—you have learned how to learn and no one can keep you from learning whatever you want or need to know. . . . The most important and intellectual ability man has yet developed—the art and science of asking questions—is not taught in schools. . . . We believe that the schools must serve as the principal medium for developing in youth the attitudes and skills of social, political and culture criticism (Postman and Weingartner, 1969).

5. Evaluation

Liontamers

One of the main duties of the teacher, according to liontamers, is the systematic evaluation of what pupils do in school. The pupils' learning, both in the achievements they demonstrate in oral or written form and in the motivation they show in their work, must be measured against certain standards of excellence. The liontamer believes that education is a process of bringing pupils up to given standards which, unless he defends them, are under constant threat of erosion. The teacher, being the expert in his subject, knows what these standards are.

The means by which the liontamer performs this evaluation is through the use of marks or grades and verbal comments combined with them. These marks have several functions. They provide feedback to the pupils who then discover how accurate their learning has been. They serve as rewards and incentives for pupils, who through them are encouraged to maintain their achievements or increase their efforts. Additionally, marks provide feedback for the teacher, informing him how well he has taught; they act as measures of progress, allowing the teacher to keep cumulative records of pupil progress; they can be used for making comparisons between pupils, yielding an estimate of relative progress. Typically, marks serve both evaluative and motivational functions. Thus the teacher adds the comment to the mark: 'Good work' (evaluation) 'keep it up' (motivation). The liontamer thus sees dispensing marks as a central part of his job. They act as goads which push pupils towards the attainment of high standards.

A 'marks' approach is taken by the liontamer to oral work. He asks pupils questions and they answer. Most of these answers are seen in terms of being 'right' or 'wrong'. He sees his task as rewarding the right answers and correcting/disapproving the wrong answers. The typical sequence for the liontamer is thus: teacher's question —pupil's answer—teacher's evaluation, and then the cycle begins again. It is simply a replication at the oral level of the liontamer's approach to written work: teacher sets the problem—pupil writes an answer—teacher marks it.

The evaluation of academic work is entirely in the teacher's hands. The liontamer cannot allow the pupils to evaluate their own work, for they simply do not know enough to make an adequate judgment. In any case, experience has taught him that when he lets pupils mark their own work, they cheat and give themselves high marks. Indeed, this is one of the pieces of evidence which leads him to distrust pupils.

The liontamer takes a similar attitude towards evaluation in the disciplinary area. He believes that certain standards of conduct are highly important and that it is his job to develop such standards in his pupils. If they do not conform to these standards, they must be punished and shown the right way to behave. There are moral as well as academic standards; education is about the inculcation of both.

Entertainers

Broadly speaking, the entertainer shares the attitude of the liontamer to evaluation. He tends, however, to de-emphasize punishment in both the academic and disciplinary area, and prefers to stress the rewards given to those who conform. In this, he reflects some of the thinking of behaviourist psychologists such as Skinner. But a more profound reason is that punishment tends to upset pupils and this strikes at the root of the atmosphere of enjoyment which he is seeking to create in the classroom. The entertainer thus has a gentler style in his evaluations. He consoles the pupil who does not reach the necessary standards and encourages him to try harder next time. Giving a wrong answer is readily forgiven if it is clear that the pupil is trying.

With respect to evaluation, the entertainer differs from the liontamer in two ways; he assigns less importance to it as part of his teacher role and he is less likely to see it as an exclusively teacher function. This can be explicated by drawing on the pioneering work of Douglas Barnes (1969) on language in the classroom. The liontamer wants the pupils to learn the 'facts', so his questions tend to be

175

closed, that is, there is one and only one possible correct answer, which is available to a pupil if he can memorize and therefore replicate what is in the textbook or what the teacher has stated earlier in the lesson. Moreover, for the answer to be correct it must be stated in a particular form, namely the technical terms that are part of the discipline in the subject the teacher is teaching. The pupils of a liontamer come to appreciate that, in Barnes' words, 'to learn is to accept factual material passively and to reproduce it for matching against the teacher's model, to be judged right or wrong'. Oral sessions in the classroom of an entertainer have a different structure. Quizzes and games are more common, because they are 'fun', though it must be recognized, as the television games *University Challenge* and *Mastermind* demonstrate, these may well have a liontaming structure. However, entertainers do frequently change the structure in that they ask *open* questions, that is, ones in which there is more than one possible answer and which allow for the expression of value and opinion. The entertainer's emphasis on pupil participation and talk encourages the pupils to initiate their own questions, opinions and comments, to 'think aloud' publicly, to expand and develop on their own or other pupils' comments. The teacher's response to pupil statements is frequently less in terms of evaluating them as right or wrong, but more in terms of providing an opportunity for the teacher to get the pupil to clarify his statement ('What exactly do you mean?'), to amplify his point of view ('Can you explain that more fully?') or to justify his answer ('What leads you to think that?'). Aso the entertainer will encourage pupils to evaluate one another's answers, by asking other pupils to respond to a pupil contribution. One result of this widening of participation and evaluation is that the entertainer is more prepared to accept pupil answers in their own everyday words rather than in technical language. All this underpins Barnes' (1971) belief that 'language is a major means of learning, and that pupils' uses of language for learning are strongly influenced by the teacher's language, which prescribes for them their roles as learners'.

New Romantics

As we have seen earlier, especially in the writings of John Holt, it is a fundamental tenet of the New Romantics that it is the pervasiveness of evaluation in the classroom which induces fear and undermines motivation. The 'pleasing teacher' phenomenon which we discussed at length in the last chapter springs directly out of the teacher's obsession with evaluation, that is, with the meting out of approval and disapproval for appropriate academic or disciplinary conduct in pupils. The New Romantic indictment of schools is that, although it is not readily acknowledged by teachers, the pupils' desire to obtain approval becomes the dominant feature of the pupil perspective on life in the classroom, and paradoxically subverts the learning process it is intended to promote.

The solution to this problem would appear to lie in the abolition of evaluation and approval in the classroom. Yet can the New Romantics actually achieve this? I doubt very much whether we can abolish evaluation entirely in the classroom, not least because in some form the giving of approval is a universal feature of human relationships. Moreover it seems difficult to conceive of a form of teaching in which the teacher utterly declines to evaluate the pupil's learning. The problem then is not whether or not we can abolish it, but rather whether or not we can reduce, minimize or transform the nature of classroom evaluation.

The basic problem with approval is that it is *personal*. Whilst the teacher may intend to approve or disapprove the pupil's efforts or achievements or interests, it is difficult for him to do so without at the same time approving or disapproving the pupil as a person. When I tell John that his work is well done, I am also implying that John is a good person. The approval spills over from the activities to which the approval is directed to John as a whole. Similarly, if I tell John that his work is bad, the implication is that John as a person is being judged unfavourably. Approval becomes, from childhood, associated with feelings of liking and love. It is for this reason that it is exceptionally difficult for the teacher to give 'pure feedback' to a pupil with reference to his learning—to tell him whether he is right or wrong, succeeding or failing, progressing or regressing, without conveying his judgment of the person. In all these cases the teacher tends to reveal the extent to which he values the pupil as a person. It is only in an impersonal relationship that feedback in a pure form is possible—the only other case will be mentioned shortly. A teaching machine can give pure feedback because the machine does not form a personal relationship with the pupil. (Even in this case approval cannot be entirely absent, since the pupil may approve or disapprove himself when the machine tells him that he is making the right or wrong response.) Similarly it is often easier to accept criticism (negatively toned feedback) from a stranger than from an intimate. In contemporary schools, the problem is particularly acute, since the teachers are trained to make 'good personal relationships' with their pupils. In so doing, they *increase* the degree to which the feedback they offer to their pupils is loaded with approval. The more personal the teacher–pupil relationship is, the more approval-loaded the feedback becomes. In other words the cold impersonal teacher, ironically, is more able to offer the pupil feedback without valuing the pupil as a person.

The New Romantics see quite clearly that to change the nature and form of evaluation in the classroom requires a radical transformation of teacher and pupil roles and relationships. Simply trying to reduce the extent of evaluation without making wider changes in roles and relationships will merely make the process of approval-seeking and approval-giving more subtle. Thus when the teacher encourages pupils to assess one another's contributions to a discussion, one finds pupils glancing at the teacher to see which of the various opinions offered is receiving teacher approval, either in terms of teacher comments or in non-verbal ways such as a nod of agreement.

The New Romantic believes that we must move away from evaluations made by the teacher (or by peers) towards *self-evaluation* by the learner himself. But what kind of teacher–pupil relationship is needed within which self-evaluation might prosper? The most sophisticated answer to this question is that provided by Carl Rogers. His answer is derived originally from his experience as a psychotherapist and his development of non-directive or client-centred therapy. This method rests on the therapist's belief that the client (or patient) has within him a basic force working towards growth and the realization of his potentialities, and that this self-realization is promoted in a non-threatening climate. It is assumed that the client has within himself the capacity to understand the factors causing him distress and pain which make him ill or unable to function adequately and also that the client has the capacity to reorganize himself in such a way as to overcome the illness. These two assumptions are obviously very similar to those made by the New Romantics in relation to learning and education.

The therapist believes that these powers in the client will become effective if the therapist can create a relationship which is marked by respect, warmth and acceptance. The therapist no longer sees his task as doing something *to* the client—treating him, curing him, changing him; no longer is he concerned with evaluating the client's history or personality. Rather, he approaches the client in terms of *empathy*, that is, seeing the client as the client sees himself, standing in client's shoes and understanding the world from his perspective. His aim is not to direct, interpret, judge or evaluate, but to understand by empathy. Provided that the relationship is acceptant and non-evaluative, the client can let his hidden and suppressed thoughts and feelings come to light without fearing that he is going to be hurt or condemned. It is clear that this form of therapy has a Meadian basis. The client takes to himself the attitude that the therapist takes to him. Because the therapist accepts him, the client can accept himself. Once the client accepts his own thoughts and feelings, however terrible or unnatural they seem to be, then he is free to explore himself and to integrate the rejected or distorted aspects of his experience and re-orientate his life on more positive lines.

Now teaching is not the same as therapy. The class is not there merely to improve the mental health of the members. The principal objective of the school class is a different sort of learning. But both *are* learning situations. The implication is that if the teacher wishes to divest himself of his evaluative role, he must try to create a relationship with the pupils that is marked by *acceptance*, which differs very markedly from a relationship characterized by approval. Acceptance arises when one makes an active effort *not* to approve or disapprove but instead shows 'unconditional positive regard', trust and a non-threatening attitude to others. Approval on the other hand is threatening precisely because it is conditional. If you do x I will approve you, but if you do y I will disapprove you. Approval is something that is deserved or won; acceptance is something which is simply given.

It is difficult to achieve this relationship in therapeutic situations; it is obviously very much more difficult to achieve in educational contexts, where the 'clients' are frequently less co-operative because they are forced to be present. But the New Romantics believe that this is the kind of relationship that teachers should try to develop with their pupils. The development of this kind of relationship and the attempt to promote self-evaluation in place of teacher-based evaluation must go hand in hand. Experiments along these lines have already begun (Rogers, 1969). The average pupil feels very disturbed when asked to estimate the effort he has put into his work, or its quality or worth, for all his training has taught him that this is the teacher's job. Yet at the same time pupils are often in surprising agreement with teachers in assessing the work. Once the learner has been persuaded that he is in a position to make judgments about his own work, and that these judgments can be discussed harmoniously with the teacher—who only on very special occasions insists on having the final word—then the pupil can cease regarding the teacher as the fount of all approval. Instead, he becomes the person with whom the learner can discuss, and argue about, his achievements and progress; his intellectual difficulties; his problem of distraction, concentration and lack of interest. They can be discussed openly because the teacher accepts and trusts the pupil, who need no longer be afraid to discuss his work honestly because the relationship is no longer so heavily conditional. As a result, the strategies of 'pleasing teacher', or obtaining approval and deflecting disapproval, become irrelevant and superfluous.

Experiments in self-evaluation are not likely to succeed unless the teacher has created an acceptant relationship with the pupils. If the relationship is still approval oriented, then to initiate

179

self-evaluation is to invite the disaster of 'cheating'—as every lion-tamer discovers.

6. The teacher–pupil relationship

The previous five sections all embody, in different ways, aspects of the teacher–pupil relationship as embodied in the three models of teaching. In this last section, I wish to draw together some final threads in the argument.

Liontamers

Relationships between teachers and pupils are characterized by formality, coolness and distance. The relationship is one of conflict; at its worst this conflict is overt, at its best it is controlled conflict. It is a model of teaching that is enshrined in much of Waller's (1932) brilliant analysis. Liontamers do not wish to 'get involved' with their pupils; they aim to be admired (for their expertise) and respected (for their firmness). They do not expect schooling to be a particularly happy experience for pupils, for the process of acquiring the discipline of mastering a subject and the discipline of good conduct is hard. The gratitude of their pupils comes not now, but later, and they take a special pride in those occasions when former pupils return to convey their gratitude for having been made to 'get down to it' by the teachers. The pupils who do not return are, of course, forgotten.

The relationship between liontamers and their pupils is symbolized in the spatial structure of the classroom. The pupils sit in desks all of which face the 'front' of the room (Sommer, 1969):

> The straight rows tell the student to look ahead and ignore
> everyone except the teacher; the students are jammed so
> tightly together that psychological escape, much less physical
> separation, is impossible. The teacher has 50 times more free
> space than the students, with the mobility to move about. He
> writes important messages on the blackboard with his back to
> his students. The august figure can rise and walk among the
> lowly who lack the authority even to stand without explicit
> permission. Teacher and children may share the same classroom
> but they see it differently. From a student's eye level, the world
> is cluttered, disorganized, full of people's shoulders, heads and
> body movements. His world at ground level is colder than the
> teacher's world. He looms over the scene like a helicopter
> swooping down to ridicule or punish any wrongdoer. Like
> Gulliver in Lilliput the teacher has a clear view of what is going
> on. He sees order and organization and any deviation from it.

The aisles between the rows are sufficiently wide to allow the teacher to wander among the pupils and also wide enough to inhibit communication between pupils—'talking' and 'copying'.

This distribution of furniture and persons in the classroom reflects the teaching model and affects the conduct of teachers and pupils. In arranging the pupils in the form of a 'congregation'—as it were, with every alternate place left empty—the liontamer naturally becomes, in Richardson's (1967) words,

> the focus of all eyes, the central authority who tends to be asking all the questions or supplying all the answers, the presiding adult through whom all communications must go.

There are also some interesting effects on the pupils. The traditional seating arrangements can have a powerful influence on friendship formation (Byrne and Buehler, 1955; Byrne, 1961; Maisonneuve, 1952) and on what Sommer (1969) has called the ecology of participation, where his research shows that pupils at the front participate more than those at the back and those in central positions participate more than those at the sides. Participation is thus least in the corners at the back of the room.

Entertainers

In this model, formality gives way to informality, and coolness to friendliness. Entertainers seek to create a climate that is bright and cheerful. They do not mind being to some degree involved with their pupils, for knowing their pupils' problems provides the vital information which helps in the planning of lessons. They do not care overmuch about being admired and respected; they like to be liked.

The adaptability which is so important to an entertainer finds its expression in spatial arrangements. He prefers furniture which is moveable rather than stationary or even fixed to the floor—though this is usually resented by the caretaker and cleaners! He is more sensitive than the liontamer to the impact of space in that he recognizes that it is difficult to stage a successful discussion in which the pupils fully participate unless the pupils can actually see one another. So during discussion sessions the entertainer restructures his room into groups with pupils sitting round tables or desks placed in the form of a table. The teacher's desk typically remains at the 'front' of the classroom next to the blackboard, but he expresses his informal relationship with pupils by sitting on his desk or on one of the desks at the front of the room. The most fashionable entertainers are in favour of various forms of open-plan classrooms and schools.

181

New Romantics

Sometimes teachers show a remarkable sensitivity to spatial arrangements and their effects on interpersonal relations and classroom events. A good example is provided by Richardson (1967).

> Mr U. told me how he had deliberately used a certain ritual with chairs to symbolize two rather different roles in relation to the same sixth-form group. This was a school which recognized the near-adult status of its older pupils by providing for them a room quite unlike the conventional classroom and furnished with a large table instead of desks. It happened in one year that Mr U. had a sixth-form group both for 'A' level history and for current affairs, and that quite a number of boys were in both classes. In his history periods, which might have been described as directed seminars, he would sit at one end of the table and lead the discussion fairly strenuously. But in the current-affairs periods, which took the form of free discussion on agreed topics, he would sit half-way down one side of the table, and would expect more of the leadership to come from the boys. The boys who attended both these classes easily learned to associate the two chairs he occupied with the two somewhat different roles that he carried. As it turned out, they were also able to react spontaneously, and quite appropriately, to a sudden change of role in one of these situations.
>
> About half-way through the spring term, Mr U. handed over his current-affairs period to a student who was doing his teaching practice in the school and who had been observing this class for some weeks. As an observer the student, too, had sat at the table—on the opposite side to Mr U., near one corner. When the day came for the student to take over, nothing had actually been said about where he should sit; yet, without any pre-planning, Mr U. went over to the seat which had hitherto been occupied by the student, and the student, coming in a minute or two later, went equally naturally to the seat hitherto occupied by Mr U. The boys immediately accepted the student in the role of staff member, and only about half-way through the lesson realized that Mr U. was sitting at the table, quietly observing what was going on, as, up to that day, the student had been in the habit of doing.

It is, however, the New Romantics among practising teachers who have shown most sensitivity to spatial arrangements. Thus Kohl (1969) writes:

> The placement of objects in space is not arbitrary and rooms represent in physical form the spirit and soul of places and

institutions. A teacher's room tells us something about who he is and a great deal about what he is doing. Often we are not aware of the degree to which spaces we control give us away, nor conscious of how much we could learn of ourselves by looking at the spaces we live in.

Whilst the New Romantic is more sympathetic to the adaptable spatial arrangements of the entertainer than to those of the liontamer, he differs from the entertainer in declining to impose any structure at all on the classroom space. The arrangement of furniture and other resources is constantly changing, according to the needs of the members at particular times. But he does make an active effort to avoid arrangements which suggest or constrain relationships in the direction of liontamership (Kohl, 1969):

> The teacher's desk might also be anywhere. It might not even be the teacher's any more, the teacher settling for a desk like the pupils' and abandoning his privileged piece of furniture to some other use.

Such a spatial structure symbolizes the efforts of the New Romantic to de-emphasize the difference in status, power and authority between teacher and pupil.

The ways in which status and power are abrogated—rather than abdicated—in the interests of maximizing pupil freedom and responsibility form a central theme to New Romantic writing. Whereas liontamers are complaining bitterly about the loss of power among teachers—and finding support for their position among academic writers, including the *Black Papers*, Bantock and perhaps even Musgrove (1971)—the New Romantics are arguing that power conflicts between adults and young people are essentially mock battles (Holt, 1972):

> As a rule, we greatly exaggerate children's interest in power struggles with us. We are so concerned about maintaining our power over them that we think they are equally concerned about taking it away from us. . . . Most of the quarrels between adults and children that I see are needlessly provoked by the adults for no other reason than to prove what the child never for a minute doubts, that they are Boss.

The New Romantics believe that there is no necessary reason why schools must be, in Waller's famous phrase, 'a despotism in a state of perilous equilibrium', though this may be a perfectly just diagnosis of schools run by liontamers. So the New Romantics feel no need to assume an 'act' or 'façade' or (in Goffmanesque language) a 'false front' that typifies so many liontamers and entertainers. If the teacher is to communicate his trust in the pupils, he must be honest and genuine in his dealings with them.

> This trust is something which cannot be faked. It is not a technique (Rogers, 1969).

> We adults are not often honest with children, least of all in school. We tell them, not what we think, but what we feel they ought to think; or what other people feel or tell us they ought to think. . . . Even in the most non-controversial areas of our teaching, the books, and the textbooks we give our children present a dishonest and distorted picture of the world. . . . Worse yet, we are not honest about ourselves, our own fears, limitations, weaknesses, prejudices, motives. We present ourselves to children as if we were gods, all-knowing, all-powerful, always rational, always just, always right (Holt, 1964).

> The easiest way to bring this up in class was to tell the children exactly where they stood. I braced myself, and defying all precedent as well as my own misgivings, I performed the unforgivable act of showing the children what their reading and IQ scores were according to the record cards. I also taught a lesson on the definition of IQ and achievement scores. The children were angry and shocked; no one had ever come right out and told them they were failing. It was always put so nicely and evasively that the children never knew where they stood. After seeing the IQ scores—only two of which were above 100, the majority being in the 80 to 90 range—and the reading scores, which with few exceptions were below grade level, the children were furious. I asked them what they wanted to do about it (Kohl, 1967).

A teacher may feel that being genuine will conflict with being acceptant, for at times he will feel *un*acceptant. To be genuine, therefore, he must express his unacceptant feelings to the pupils. The difficulty is probably more apparent than real. If a teacher feels angry and desires to be genuine, then the important point is that he *tells* the pupils that he feels angry rather than merely *displaying* his anger in hasty actions. And this does not automatically undermine the acceptant relationship, for if the teacher has created a general and underlying acceptant relationship, then the anger which is expressed is by no means as threatening as it would be in a relationship that is generally unacceptant. The pupils can 'take it' because anger is so much more threatening when there are no acceptant roots to the relationship. The open expression of unacceptant feelings may, paradoxically, strengthen rather than weaken the general sense of being accepted by the teacher and may help the pupil to appreciate that he in his turn must learn to accept the teacher as a human being.

Inevitably, after all this, the New Romantic tends to display a relative loss of interest in teaching and an enhanced interest in learning. Whilst he does not deny that he knows many things the pupils do not, he recognizes that he knows little about many things in which the pupils are interested and that they know many things of which he is ignorant. He prefers to define himself in terms of being a fellow-learner (Rogers, 1969):

> Teaching is, for me, a relatively unimportant and vastly overvalued activity . . . I realize that I have lost interest in being a teacher. . . . When I try to teach . . . I am appalled by the results, which seem little more than inconsequential, because sometimes the teaching appears to succeed. When this happens I find that the results are damaging. It seems to cause the individual to distrust his own experience and to stifle significant learning. Hence, I have come to feel that the outcomes of teaching are either unimportant or hurtful.

It is perhaps the most disturbing of all the New Romantic contentions that it is the death of teaching which marks the birth of real learning.

The three types of teacher and their models of the teaching-learning process that I have outlined are not, of course, entirely distinct from schemes offered by other writers, though they tend to be more elaborate than most. It is perfectly possible to conceptualize them in more technical terminology than the everyday language of education (e.g. teaching, curriculum, learning, etc.) in which I have made the exposition. For example, in Bernstein's (1971) recently developed terms, classification and framing, which although clumsy and obscure are at least non-evaluative, the liontamer represents strong framing and strong classification (collection code); the New Romantic weak classification and weak framing (the integrated code type) with the entertainer falling somewhere between the two.

Rather than attempting such 'translation' exercises, I want to consider some of the problems which the three types of teacher present both currently and in the next few decades. Education is standing at a crossroads. In one respect education has never been as popular as it is today. The public clamours for more and more education, from the nursery level to postgraduate studies. The number of pupils staying on at school beyond the statutory leaving age has been rising for some years. Yet on the other hand, the raising of the school leaving age was not greeted with unalloyed enthusiasm by all teachers. The Schools Council *Enquiry I* (Morton-Williams and Finch, 1968) has shown that no more than a quarter of the teachers perceive RSLA as offering major opportunities only, and a mere one teacher in eight believed that virtually all pupils would benefit from a longer school course. Most of the opposition to RSLA has come from teachers in secondary modern and comprehensive schools in the poorer districts of large towns and cities. They were already fighting a daily, and often losing, battle to preserve some semblance of order and learning among classes of bored and sometimes recalcitrant teenage boys and girls, whose principal desire was to leave school at the earliest possible moment. These teachers felt alarm and dismay at the prospect of having to teach such pupils for a further year, during which the pupils would become increasingly bored and hostile—and in the case of boys both taller and stronger. Not unjustifiable fears of massive indiscipline, violence and truancy haunted these teachers.

The initial response of most teachers was, however, to give a massive boost to entertainership. Since boredom seemed to be the main problem, a careful preparation in entertainership offered the best hope of solving the problem. Time and money was devoted in large amounts to curriculum development and the construction of special 'Newsom blocks' where the pupils who would normally have left school could be housed. There is no doubt that many teachers have gained from this opportunity to rethink ideas and to develop more interesting courses, but one cannot help feeling that much of this has been a gigantic confidence trick. Too often the same old curricular material has been clothed in new forms in the hope that the pupils will be kept happy and quiet during their last years at school, whilst the rest of the pupils (who would have stayed anyway) could continue with their examination based courses.

The result has been that liontamers have been increasingly pressed into entertainer moulds, especially where they were in 'difficult' schools or had to teach 'difficult' pupils. Very little systematic thought was given to any fundamental rethinking or even to a questioning of the long-term consequences of entertainership. Only the New Romantics were suggesting that the school as a vast Music Hall would perhaps be a disastrous failure in the long run.

Paradoxically, RSLA brought the liontamers and New Romantics into a sudden and striking agreement. Both felt that it would be much wiser to *lower* the school leaving age. Their reasons, however, were very different. Liontamer-type teachers wanted to put reluctant teenagers out of school because they recognized that they would learn very little by staying in and that, more significantly, their presence would merely make the teacher's job so very much more difficult. In our present changing society liontaming is becoming less easy to operate, and it is the 'Newsom' pupils who offer the most serious challenge to it—though the new breed of sixth-former is by no means as tractable and docile as he was ten years ago.

The New Romantics favour lowering the school leaving age not because it has pragmatic value but because it forms a natural extension of his belief in freedom and choice and his opposition to compulsion. Having recognized that one cannot *compel* pupils to learn, the New Romantic becomes suspicious of any form of compulsory schooling, which not only makes life difficult for the teacher, but it also—and it is this which is given paramount importance—has a highly damaging effect on the pupil. At its worst, it actively inoculates pupils against any kind of formal learning and probably interferes with their natural motivation to learn.

The early works of the New Romantics are *reformist* in orientation. They asserted that schools could be changed from within if only teachers would change their assumptions and thus their practices. But then this movement was given a sudden jolt by the appearance of a group of writers who became known as the 'deschoolers'. The most celebrated of these is Ivan Illich in his book *Deschooling Society* (1971), though a book by his former colleague Everett Reimer (1971) also made some impact. Both made a systematic development of some ideas first expressed a decade earlier by Paul Goodman in his *Compulsory Miseducation* (1961), which foreshadowed both the New Romantic and deschooling movements.

Illich appears to accept the criticisms made by the New Romantics, but his critique is placed within a much wider indictment of the educational system and contemporary society. He sees Western Society as dominated by manipulative institutions which breed passivity and materialism so that we are reduced to being mere consumers. He argues that many of our plans for growth in formal education are economically unfeasible; that the present system is in any event highly inefficient; that education is socially divisive; that the working classes are subsidizing the middle classes and that our attempts at positive discrimination for the working classes (e.g. compensatory education programmes) are misdirected as well as unsuccessful. Perhaps his most serious indictment is that the school teaches a 'hidden curriculum'—a term which is defined in a related but nevertheless different way than when used by Jackson (1968) as discussed in the last chapter—by which pupils are constrained to believe that we cannot learn unless someone teaches us and that the only persons who can teach us are qualified teachers. School thus fosters the illusion that learning occurs only when one is taught by a particular kind of person (a teacher) in a particular kind of setting (a school).

Illich rejects the reformist position of the New Romantics and asserts that a *radical* change is required. Essentially this requires the abolition of the school, though he makes it clear that this could occur only as part of many wider changes in society in which all our major institutions also become 'deschooled'. Teachers, as we at present

187

understand that term, would also be abolished. Learning would take place through a system of 'networks' which would bring together peers who shared common interests; which would put learners in touch with 'skill models' (the new teachers who would *not* be professional pedagogues); which would give learners direct access to the things and resources which are needed for learning, but which in our present society are denied to the public; and which would provide a system of counsellors to advise prospective learners and assist them in making full use of all the networks.

This vision of education in the future is proving very attractive to many people, including many of those within education. It is generating a considerable amount of radical rethinking throughout the world as well as critical approaches (see, for example, Lister, 1974). Elsewhere I have elaborated my own reaction to this movement (Hargreaves, 1974); here I simply want to show that deschooling involves a natural extension to many of the assumptions of the New Romantics, who are now beginning to identify themselves with the deschooling movement (e.g. Holt, 1972).

In my own view we are a very long way from initiating a deschooled society. In the short-term we are likely to accept relatively modest reforms, such as lowering the school leaving age, though it has to be admitted that the main political parties seem more likely to raise the leaving age once again, if only to avoid the political embarrassment of unemployed teenagers. Serious attention may also soon be given to the 'credit' system of financing education, which is generally favoured by deschoolers. One objection against deschooling or voluntary schooling is that it is the working-class pupils who are most likely to opt out of the system and thus be even further deprived of opportunities in education than they are at present. Yet it can be argued that the progress we have made in widening opportunities for working-class children is in fact extremely small—as evidenced by the relative failure of compensatory education programmes to date; the unchanging proportion of working-class persons in higher education; the probable failure of comprehensive reorganization to achieve any fundamental restructuring of opportunities (see Ford, 1969). The introduction of a credit system, which gives all learners a fixed amount to spend on education in ways and at times that the learners themselves determine, combined with the abolition of compulsory schooling, would at least ensure that working-class children are not alienated from education, by being forced to attend schools, and would allow them to make use of educational facilities when they are older and perhaps then discover a need to learn. At present, working-class children who decide they want to learn when they are adults find it extremely difficult to get financial support to undertake serious study. Even the Open University, important a development as that is, still takes its students on a part-time basis. Given the enormous problems of evening study for working-class people, it is not surprising that the numbers of this group who have enrolled have been rather disappointing.

It is my belief that the number of teachers who espouse the New Romantic model of teaching and learning is increasing rapidly. The reasons for this are not difficult to find. Perhaps the most important is that it embodies and expresses much of the spirit of the age. The move away from liontamership towards entertainership was encouraged by the dramatic growth of informal relationships between teachers and pupils in schools during the 1960s. Since then our questioning of authority has deepened considerably; what was once scepticism has become opposition and rejection. The 'troubles' among students in higher education continue to be an expression of these changes—and students in teacher training do not remain unaffected. In my view the New Romantic model offers most hope for bridging the so-called 'generation gap' that arises as a result of the collision between some of the emergent values against our traditional values. It can also cope more adequately than can the liontamer or entertainer models with the demands of the young for greater freedom, greater power and greater participation, for it alone ensures that teachers can yield to these demands in that spirit of trust which is so absolutely essential if we want to obtain a responsible response from the young.

I am going to assume that over the next decade or so there will emerge within the teaching profession a significant minority who are more identified with the New Romantic than with liontamer or entertainer models. There are some, of course, already in our schools, especially in primary schools and colleges of further education. Other teachers, who are clinging rather reluctantly to the entertainer model, are ready to move towards the New Romantic model, but lack the opportunities and social support that are needed for such experimentation. For the most part, however, the converts to the New Romantic model will come from new members of the teaching profession. Most teachers do not read books on education —but students do. So some will enter the profession armed with ideas drawn from the writings of the New Romantics and deschoolers; and in this they may well be reacting against their tutors, most of whom were (and often still are) liontamers and entertainers. What then is likely to happen? What chances are there that these teachers will be able to put the New Romantic model into practice? What factors will facilitate or inhibit such experimentation? What will be the consequence of the presence of New Romantics in our schools?

It is in the primary school that these changes have been, and will continue to be, most obvious. A young New Romantic may find it fairly easy to find a school where the headteacher and staff are broadly sympathetic to such ideas. Moreover in a primary school the teacher takes a single class for most of the time. In consequence he has a high degree of autonomy, both over the content of the curriculum *and* over his teaching style. So there are relatively few constraints against the introduction of the New Romantic model. Even if he finds the headteacher and other members of staff very unsympathetic—for there are many primary school teachers who are liontamers—this autonomy means that he can still operate the New Romantic model *in secret*.

Kohl's (1969) advice to the aspiring New Romantic to act as a hidden subversive within the system hinges on this high degree of autonomy.

> Many teachers cannot stand the apparent disorder of an open classroom, but the problem is not so serious as it is with noise. They needn't see disorder if it upsets them. Often it is useful to place a drawing over the window looking into one's room and invite only sympathetic teachers to visit your class. So long as the freedom of your class doesn't spill out of your room many authoritarian teachers will let you go your own way. This is a melancholy fact, and one that some people can't put up with. The degree to which one pretends or refuses to conform is a matter for each teacher's conscience.

Recognizing that some persons (headteachers, supervisors, inspectors, advisers, etc.) have rights to observe the teacher at work in the classroom, Kohl makes some suggestions, inevitably involving a degree of hypocrisy, that might enable one to survive.

> —keep two sets of lesson plans, one for the supervisor that follows the curriculum and another for oneself that deals with the reality of the classroom
> —create a set of authoritarian lessons to use when supervisors observe
> —be polite and silent at (staff) meetings
> —seem to comply with administrative directives.

Experimentation with the New Romantic model is difficult enough even when sympathetic support from superiors is forthcoming (Rogers, 1969, chapter 1); Kohl's subversive alternative is likely to be fraught with dangers, especially for the young teacher who, not having earned the esteem of his colleagues by having demonstrated successful liontamership or entertainership, will find the inevitable early problems of introducing a New Romantic model interpreted by his sceptical colleagues as 'plain incompetence' rather than as 'transition troubles'.

At the *secondary* level, however, even Kohl's alternative is not really viable. Here the teacher typically teaches several different classes each day in blocks of forty minutes or so, and he is also expected to teach a 'subject' in which he is qualified and which is fixed on this timetable. He is free to operate the New Romantic model in a severely attenuated form. Only when the teacher demonstrates an interest in a group of pupils who are not being entered for public examinations, such as 'remedial groups', 'Newsom pupils' and 'the leavers' class', are the constraints of the timetable and a pre-structured curriculum likely to be inapplicable; only here, with the classes that most teachers do not want to teach, has the New Romantic in the secondary school the opportunity to put his philosophy into practice.

In an extremely important article, in which he makes a rare attempt to systematize many of the changes taking place in education, Basil Bernstein (1971) argues that the change from what he calls the collection code (liontamership) to an integrated code (roughly entertainership and some New Romantic elements) not only involves a change in conception of what counts as knowledge and how the curriculum is to be structured and evaluated, but also 'may well bring about a disturbance in the structure and distribution of power, in property relationships and in existing educational identities'. Bernstein's 'integrated code' is typified as the secondary level in those schools which integrate several subjects—for example, history, geography and English become 'Social Studies'—and introduce team-teaching both within departments and between departments. Yet in our present secondary schools such innovations are more likely to take place in line with the entertainer model than with the New Romantic model. In other words, I would argue that Bernstein's discussion, in spite of being a highly insightful analysis of the problems and consequences of many contemporary changes in education, does not deal in any depth with the emergent New Romantic model.

The New Romantic writers concern themselves with education at the primary level—with the exception of Rogers (1969) who deals with the higher education level. The secondary school tends to be ignored. Perhaps, then, I should try to examine what *in ideal form* a New Romantic secondary school would look like. I believe we would have to question three features which are universal in our secondary schools, features which to many teachers make schools recognizable as such. The first is the timetable. This springs from what I have called the Danish-sandwich theory of schooling. The school day is divided up into several layers of predetermined thickness of various predetermined foods, which most people would probably not prefer to eat in combination. (We are then surprised when the pupils get educational indigestion!) But the New Romantic

191

model requires that the public *choose* what they want to study, how they want to study it, and the time for which they want to study it. The notion of a timetable hinges on opposite assumptions—that the teachers decide the content of the curriculum and the way in which its teaching and learning is to be scheduled. In the New Romantic secondary school, the pupils would be free to choose traditional subjects or highly idiosyncratic 'topics' and they would be free to study them for as long as they saw fit.

The second feature is age-grading. This arises from our assumptions that pupils of the same age learn more easily together than children of different ages; that pupils are more easily taught if they are of similar rather than highly disparate ages; that the curriculum should be prestructured into age-related blocks which are followed according to a predetermined sequence. All these would be questioned by the New Romantic, who would argue that each individual pupil should construct his own curriculum and that the depth and sequence of study should be within his control (though doubtless with the advice and help of a teacher); and that if pupils of very different ages have a common interest in a certain subject or topic, then there is no reason at all why they should not learn together or teach one another.

The third feature is the availability of alternatives. In our present secondary schools, the pupil has no choice of teachers. At the higher levels, he can choose his subject specialism, and he may well choose one subject rather than another because he likes the teacher who teaches that subject. But he cannot choose his teachers at will. For the New Romantic, who accepts the principle of voluntarism, there is no reason at all why a pupil should not be free to consult the teacher of his choice. If some teachers end up with no pupils at all, then that merely indicates that the teacher is unsuited to teaching, at least in this context with this kind of pupil.

Clearly this would involve a very fundamental transformation of our present secondary schools. They would even have to be built in a different way, for they would need to be highly adaptable and would require a large number of small rooms, for tutorials with staff and for small group meetings of pupils with or without staff, and also many places where a single pupil could follow his own studies in relative privacy. Highly efficient resource centres, from which pupils could draw needed materials, equipment and books, would have an important role in the system. Teachers who would be prepared to advise on many topics apart from their own specialist subjects would have to be available. More controversially, some specialist staff would be assigned to schools on a temporary basis, since if few pupils choose to follow that subject, then their presence in the school would be superfluous.

In some respects the New Romantic secondary school might resemble the conventional secondary school. For instance, older pupils might very well opt to take public examinations. Naturally the form of such a course would change—the pupils would be presented with the syllabus and allowed to make their own selection of topics and their own pace and sequence of study. But they might well choose to organize discussions or study groups at particular times, producing a structure of study which outwardly resembles traditional class teaching. The difference is that it would be reached by a very different route. Another example might be science, and perhaps other subjects which entail the use of dangerous or expensive equipment, where groups of interested pupils would need to plan common meetings with the appropriate teacher.

The New Romantic secondary school will not arise by accident, by individual subversive innovators, and perhaps not by slow internal evolution. Such a school has to be designed and structured quite intentionally by the staff. Bernstein (1971) has noted that as we move away from liontamership (the collection code in his terms) we magnify the problem of *consensus* among the school staff. It is widely recognized, for example, that the problem of consensus is an important one in team teaching, where the members of the team have to agree on the content of the curriculum, the division of labour both between teachers and between teachers and pupils, and so on. Yet this is merely a minor symptom of a much wider problem of consensus in both school and society as a whole. We are coming to see our own society as pluralistic in nature; there is an emergent differentiation of values, attitudes and styles of life between various groups, subcultures and countercultures, and an ensuing debate about the extent to which such a differentiation is to be tolerated and accepted. Every social movement and liberation movement threatens some other group's values, assumptions and power. So there has arisen an inevitable questioning of the nature, structure and distribution of power and authority in society. In this respect the school reflects society. The school has its own version of pluralism, again creating problems of ideological consensus among teachers and conflicting views about the power and authority between teachers and headteachers and between teachers and pupils. The development of entertainership introduced a problem of consensus in that it challenged the once dominant ideology of liontamership. But the emergence of a significant minority of New Romantic sympathizers has created an educational version of 'the alternative society' which poses a challenge and threat to both liontamers and entertainers.

It can be argued, I think, that all schools have to some degree a problem of consensus. The easiest solution has been to ensure that a single school contains teachers of a single type or model. This might be called the solution of *self-selected recruitment*. Essentially, those who are responsible for staff recruitment allow onto the staff only those teachers who subscribe to the approved model. This is a common pattern in the public schools, where the headteachers ensure that applicants (of which they are never short) are of the appropriate type. If mistakes are made, then that teacher's contract can simply be terminated. But in the state schools, this is not possible. When a new head appears, he is faced with many different types of teacher, but he cannot dismiss at will those teachers who are of the 'wrong' type, for they have tenure in the school. The only equivalent examples within the state system are new schools, where the headteacher can appoint teachers of whom he approves. The first comprehensive schools were in this position—and it probably accounts for their success. Yet even here the system is subject to defects that do not occur within public schools, for in state schools the headteacher cannot remedy his 'mistakes' by dismissal and may well find that the governing body or local authority assigns to him teachers of whom he does not approve. The solution of self-selected recruitment is thus limited to the public schools.

An alternative solution, which is available to state schools, is the solution of *ruthless selection*. Here the headteacher ruthlessly pressures the governors and local authority to recruit new staff of the appropriate type and at the same time ruthlessly makes life so uncomfortable for those of his present staff who are not of the appropriate type that they resign. The latter element is a slow and difficult process; in my own experience there are more cases of unsuccessful attempts at this solution than there are actual successes.

A third solution is the solution by *conversion*. In this case the headteacher relies on his own charisma and skill to convert his existing staff from one type to another. This is usually never more than partially successful. The typical outcome is that the headteacher dies from over-exertion, or moves on somewhat less radically, that is to another school, or his proselytizing zeal fades with age.

The fourth and almost universal solution is that of *compromise and avoidance*. The impossibility of a general consensus is recognized. The teachers compromise, somewhat uneasily, about certain areas where it would be impossible for the school to operate at all in a state of dissensus, and in all other matters they avoid the problem by pretending it is not really there. Many difficulties arise, but they are resolved on an *ad hoc* basis that never exposes or treats the underlying problem of consensus. Overt conflicts are averted by means of the *professional norm of autonomy*, which enshrines a philosophy of live and let live. Each teacher proclaims as his oath to this norm: you do your own thing in your classroom as long as you don't interfere with me and don't rock the boat.

Typically the headteacher in this situation handles his staff in a manner designed to prevent the underlying dissensus from coming to the surface. In staff meetings the discussion is restricted to mundane and administrative matters, for if he allowed school or educational policy onto the agenda, then the lack of consensus would be fully exposed. From the safety of his study the head plays off the warring parties against one another; when it becomes essential, he plays the role of mediator between them. In some schools, the head openly sides with one faction, which is a dangerous ploy since it produces pro-head and anti-head factions—with a few canny double-agents in the middle. In effect, by avoiding the problem of consensus, the real issues of education are never discussed. Whilst the avoidance of overt tension has its advantages, many teachers tend to feel isolated, frustrated and unfulfilled.

At present there is relatively little differentiation between state schools in terms of the social and educational philosophies that determine organization, curriculum, teaching methods and social relationships in the school. It is true that some schools, especially at the primary school level, are more 'progressive' than others. Some schools 'stream' their pupils, others do not. Many schools contain small bands of teachers who are experimenting with new ideas, such as team teaching. But for the most part, this tells us relatively little about the school as a whole. It tells us that the school has a few teachers who are trying out new ideas, probably in face of sceptical non-co-operation if not outright opposition from other teachers on the same staff. More often, it tells us something about the head-teacher, who is trying to *impose* an innovation (e.g. non-streaming) on an unwilling staff (cf. Barker-Lunn, 1970, chapter 16). The avoidance reaction to the problem of consensus is everywhere to be seen. Despite what some politicians have asserted, there is no real choice between schools, because schools are not enabled by their structure to operate distinctive philosophies reached by consensus.

Real choice will be possible only when we devise a system in which schools are actively encouraged to develop particular educational approaches in a thorough-going way. In my view we need schools which practise a consistent model of teaching and learning. My own sympathies are obviously for schools which can be patterned on the New Romantic model—but I also want to see schools where teachers can practise liontamership and entertainership with pride and confidence. Our present system of schools based on compromise entails a destructive erosion of teacher commitment, co-operation and job satisfaction. As our teachers are emasculated, so the pupils suffer in their turn.

Yet it seems unlikely that in the near future we shall have such a differentiated system of schooling. The trend towards comprehensivization, especially when this is combined with the development of much larger schools, seems inimical to the provision of choice for teachers, parents and pupils among distinctive schools operating by consensus. Whatever the alleged advantages of larger schools—and I am suspicious about the validity of most of them—a major disadvantage may be an exacerbation of the solution by compromise and avoidance. The prospects for the New Romantic in the secondary school are gloomy. For this reason many who are attracted by this model will perhaps turn to primary schools and middle schools and colleges of further education. Those who remain in the secondary sector are going to find themselves deeply frustrated because, unlike the liontamer and entertainer, they cannot practise their philosophy within the norm of autonomy (doing one's own thing) which is in fact facilitated in some respects by the fragmented nature of the large comprehensive school. The New Romantic can operate only when basic changes are made in the structure of the school; the solution by compromise and avoidance powerfully inhibits such changes. The ensuing frustration for the New Romantic means that he persistently seeks to create a discussion of general policy. The effect of this is that the dissensus is maximized and conflicts which liontamers and entertainers would prefer to ignore are brought into the open.

I conclude that the growth of teachers of the New Romantic type will make the solution by compromise and avoidance less viable than it has been and that schools are moving towards a period of deep ideological conflicts among the staff. The interesting point is that these conflicts are frequently debated at the level of particular surface forms rather than at the level of the different basic assumptions held by staff which generate the different attitudes to the surface phenomena. A good example would be the conflicts about *ritual* in school. Bernstein, Elvin and Peters (1966) have distinguished between consensual and differentiating rituals.

Consensual rituals
> function so as to bind together all members of the school, staff and pupils as a moral community, as a distinct collectivity. These consensual rituals give the school continuity in time and place . . . [and] give the school its specific identity as a distinct and separate institution. . . . They assist in the integration of the various goals of the school, within a coherent set of shared values, so that the values of the school can become internalized and experienced as a unity.

Differentiating rituals
> are concerned to mark off groups within the school from each other, usually in terms of age, sex, age relation or social

function. The differentiating rituals deepen local attachment behaviour to, and detachment behaviour from, specific groups; they also deepen respect behaviour to those in various positions of authority and create order in time.

Many ritual events in school are both consensual and differentiating. The morning Assembly or 'morning prayers' typically brings together the whole staff and pupil bodies into a single place for a joint enterprise (singing hymns, saying prayers, etc.) and thus symbolizes the school as a unified community. At the same time, the school is clearly differentiated into a staff unit (on the platform) and a pupil unit (in the hall), and among the pupils into a prefect body (in special seats on the side) and into class and age-related groups (with junior forms at the front and senior forms at the back). Special emphasis is given to the status of the headteacher, who typically conducts proceedings and sits in a special chair at the centre of the platform. Often he is the last person to enter and the first to leave and the pupils stand in silence during his entry and exit.

Speech Days also combine consensual and differentiating rituals. The community is symbolized in the singing of the school song and the dominant values are reinforced in the giving of prizes to those pupils who are outstanding in those activities valued by the school—academic work, sports, some extra-curricular pursuits—and there are even prizes for loyalty. At the same time the staff emphasize their own status by the wearing of full academic dress. Also the giving of prizes to selected pupils differentiates those who succeed from those who are, relatively speaking, failing.

Such ritual occasions were most apparent in the public schools and in the pre-war grammar schools. Since then, the extension of grammar school entry to include great numbers of working-class children and the merging of grammar and secondary modern schools into comprehensive schools have produced school communities whose members are much less committed to a particular set of values. Moreover, there has been a growing scepticism about religion, which has traditionally been an important element in these rituals. Other movements within education, for instance the attempt to forge closer links between home and school, have made the boundaries which demarcate the school as a distinct community less sharp than they were. All these factors can be said to threaten the nature of assembly and speech day as consensual rituals, for the members of schools are increasingly less committed to a common body of values which can be ritually confirmed. The growth of the New Romantic movement puts a final nail in the coffin of such rituals, because the philosophy of the movement celebrates respect for individual differences rather than common values and actively opposes the making

197

of comparisons between the achievements of different individuals·
As we have seen, it de-emphasizes the distinctions between teachers
and pupils and between pupils of different ages. In the New Romantic
school the traditional ritual occasions would disappear since they
rest on presuppositions which conflict with the assumptions of the
New Romantic.

In our present schools, which contain a mixture of liontamers,
entertainers and New Romantics, the staff are willing to engage in
lengthy and often acrid debates about the point of assemblies and
speech days. The liontamer is most anxious that they be retained for
he typically believes that the school should be like our traditional
grammar school. The entertainer is somewhat less convinced, but
true to his philosophy he enjoys the spectacle and show of such
occasions. It is the New Romantic sympathizer who is most opposed.
It is he who is most likely to see the rituals as 'empty', irrelevant and
even as positively harmful. Sometimes the argument is about much
more minor rituals, such as that by which pupils stand when a teacher
enters a classroom, which symbolizes the difference in status between
teacher and pupil. Whatever the ritual at issue, the debate is rarely
seen as merely one expression of a much deeper underlying dissensus;
and thus it cannot be handled by the staff as such. As a result, the
debate gets diverted to other issues, such as whether or not the headteacher has the right to impose such rituals on the school.

I believe that the quality of relationships among staff has important
consequences for the quality of education and of teacher–pupil
relationships. I therefore want to conclude this chapter by making
some suggestions for the typical school which faces this problem. I
would argue that teachers in such a school must give up any hope that
they will in fact ever reach consensus. The differences between the
liontamer, entertainer and New Romantic models are too fundamental to permit resolution by compromise. But equally, I do not
think we shall improve schools by initiating a period of internecine
warfare between the different factions each of which is hoping to
win the day by defeating both the other factions. Such a battle would
in most cases merely exhaust the teachers and have a demoralizing
and damaging effect on the school as a whole.

As an interim solution—and it cannot be more than that—I would
suggest that we divert our energies into fighting for a more differentiated system of schooling, and into trying to achieve a real respect
between the proponents of different models. By this I mean the
development of a deep and genuine respect for models with which
one does not agree and perhaps even against which one has the most
profound objections. In *practical* terms this means, I think:

1. That the members of a school staff meet and talk. It means that
meetings between teachers should be directed not merely to passing

the time of day, to gossiping in the staffroom about pupils and the head, to making decisions of an administrative kind. These meetings must be devoted to discussing the most central questions in education. Such talk must not be the exclusive preserve of conferences and courses, where teachers are in a very real sense 'protected' from their colleagues, but must become an accepted part of staff activities. It means that we must have many more conferences in which the whole staff of a single school meet and talk to one another about the full range of educational issues.

2. That the teachers must be willing to talk about many matters that they would prefer to leave unsaid because others are likely to be upset by such talk. It means talking about those conflicts and problems which are typically hidden and suppressed. It means that teachers will require great courage to accept the arguments and quarrels which are probably an unavoidable part of the creation of a more profound encounter between teachers. Much of this talk between teachers must be directed to the basic assumptions which differentiate them. Perhaps then the arguments about the surface phenomena, such as the place of ritual, can be more profitably pursued. Perhaps I might add, as a New Romantic sympathizer myself, that I believe the New Romantics have overlooked the value of ritual. Schools towards which they are striving may well have problems of order, stability and identity which in our traditional schools were supported by traditional rituals. Certainly they have not, as far as I know, considered the desirability or feasibility of seeking to create new rituals to express the new kind of school and social relationships they are advocating.

3. That teachers should *listen* as well. It is often surprisingly difficult to listen to some other person's views, partly because we have already predecided what he has to say and partly because instead of listening we are in fact rehearsing our counter-arguments. To listen means really to hear and capture what the other person is actually saying and struggling to communicate, rather than hearing what we think we know he is saying. When one really hears someone, one is often quite shocked, for it shows him to be a different person than one thought he was. I need hardly add that the experience of really being heard is an important experience for us all.

4. That teachers must accept that their own favoured model has its weaknesses as well as its strengths, and that the models which one dislikes have their strengths as well as weaknesses. It means that there must be an active attempt by everyone to exorcize the arrogance that surrounds each position. The New Romantics, no less than lion-tamers and entertainers, display an inclination to caricature, to distort, and to impugn the integrity of, alternative models. Kohl's advice to young New Romantics to become subversives within the system is as

narrow as it is inconsistent. I would argue the opposite position, namely that just as the New Romantics wish to transform pupils and teacher–pupil relationships by creating conditions of trust, respect, acceptance and freedom of choice, so also must they be willing to extend that same attitude to colleagues. It will be possible to transform schools, pupils and teacher–pupil relationships only if teacher–teacher relationships are also transformed—and by the same methods.

5. That through the open expression of conflicts and disagreements in a spirit of mutual respect, there is some hope that the many important educational issues which are currently left unexamined by most teachers will assume a new significance in the life of the profession. If this can happen then perhaps teachers will take a new initiative in the moulding of our schools and our educational system, which to my mind is far too frequently left to the decision-making of politicians, civil servants, administrators and headteachers.

In this chapter we have moved some distance from the direct study of teacher–pupil relations in the classroom, the topic with which the social psychologist is most closely concerned. I hope the direction of the discussion demonstrates that teacher–pupil relationships must also be discussed in relation to a much wider set of problems within education and within society. If a social psychological approach omits this wider context, its analysis will be parochial and simplistic. But that applies equally to historical and sociological approaches which sometimes show an unwarranted neglect of the interpersonal aspects of education.

Recommended reading

B. BERNSTEIN, 'On the classification and framing of educational knowledge', in M. F. D. Young (ed.), *Knowledge and Control*, Collier-Macmillan, 1971.

I. ILLICH, *Deschooling Society*, Penguin, 1971.

H. R. KOHL, *The Open Classroom*, Methuen, 1970.

I. LISTER (ed.), *Deschooling: A Reader*, Cambridge University Press, 1974.

C. R. ROGERS, *Freedom to Learn*, Merrill, 1969.

8 Discipline

When it is said that a teacher has a 'discipline problem' the meaning usually intended is that the teacher has in some way failed to master the task of creating or maintaining order in his classroom. Yet every teacher, whether he is a 'success' or a 'failure'—in his own eyes or in the eyes of his colleagues or pupils—has a discipline problem in the sense that he must come to terms with the requirements of his disciplinarian role. We suggested that discipline comprises one of the teacher's two basic sub-roles for this very reason: no teacher can escape it. Most teachers, when asked to explain how one achieves or maintains discipline, find it difficult to give a very meaningful account. One is offered either trite and superficial accounts of incidents in the teacher's own experience ('Well, I always . . .' or 'I remember once when . . .') or vague generalizations that duck the question altogether ('It's all a matter of personality') and give no enlightenment to the seeker after knowledge. Tutors in Colleges and Departments of Education who are deeply involved in trying to help their students to cope with disciplinary difficulties with generous advice and criticism, know only too well how complex a phenomenon discipline is. For it seems to be of limited help to the students to tell them what or what not to do. Disciplinary 'tips for teachers' simply do not meet the needs of the novice. Discipline is a problem because we understand so little of the processes by which it is established or maintained, whether successfully or unsuccessfully. Although the way in which we evaluate the quality of a particular teacher's discipline depends very much on our own values and educational philosophy, we have little difficulty in recognizing 'good' and 'bad' forms of it. The difficulty is in analysing its composition. Here I shall be treating discipline basically from the point of view of the beginning teacher, though I hope nevertheless that the analysis will be of interest to the more experienced.

Discipline is of interest to a social psychologist because it is an *interpersonal* concept. Discipline refers to a set of rules or norms, specifying acceptable forms of classroom conduct, which is either imposed by teachers on pupils or agreed between them. It is a form of social control. Many of these rules are designed to regulate encounters between persons, between the teacher and the pupils and between pupil and pupil. So what we call discipline forms a major part of the 'definition of the situation' in the classroom. For this reason we cannot say very much about classrooms without encroaching into the territory of discipline, which is part of essence of life in the classroom for both teacher and pupil. Even to attempt to discuss discipline as distinct from the other basic feature of classroom behaviour that we call instruction is a dangerous pursuit. Discipline and instruction are the warp and woof of the fabric of classroom interaction; to pull out one for isolated inspection is to risk turning the whole into a meaningless bundle of threads. Yet that is a risk we intend to take.

Let us begin with a concrete example of a disciplinary situation, taken from Waugh (1928).

The masters went upstairs.

'That's your little mob in there,' said Grimes; 'you let them out at eleven.'

'But what am I to teach them?' said Paul in a sudden panic.

'Oh, I shouldn't try to *teach* them anything, not just yet, anyway. Just keep them quiet.'

'Now that's a thing I've never learned to do,' sighed Mr. Prendergast.

Paul watched him amble into his classroom at the end of the passage, where a burst of applause greeted his arrival. Dumb with terror he went into his own classroom.

Ten boys sat before him, their hands folded, their eyes bright with expectation.

'Good morning, sir,' said the one nearest him.

'Good morning,' said Paul.

'Good morning, sir,' said the next.

'Good morning,' said Paul.

'Good morning, sir,' said the next.

'Oh, shut up,' said Paul.

At this the boy took out a handkerchief and began to cry quietly.

'Oh, sir,' came a chorus of reproach, 'you've hurt his feelings. He's very sensitive; it's his Welsh blood, you know; it makes people very emotional. Say "Good morning" to him, sir, or he won't be happy all day. After all, it is a good morning, isn't it, sir?'

'Silence!' shouted Paul above the uproar, and for a few moments things were quieter.

'Please, sir,' said a small voice—Paul turned and saw a grave-looking youth holding up his hand—'please, sir, perhaps he's been smoking cigars and doesn't feel well.'

'Silence!' said Paul again.

The ten boys stopped talking and sat perfectly still staring at him. He felt himself getting hot and red under their scrutiny.

'I suppose the first thing I ought to do is to get your names clear. What is your name?' he asked, turning to the first boy.

'Tangent, sir.'

'And yours?'

'Tangent, sir,' said the next boy. Paul's heart sank.

'But you can't both be called Tangent.'

'No, sir. *I'm* Tangent. He's just trying to be funny.'

'I like that. *Me* trying to be funny! Please, sir, I'm Tangent, sir; really I am.'

'If it comes to that,' said Clutterbuck from the back of the room, 'there is only one Tangent here, and that is me. Anyone else can jolly well go to blazes.'

Paul felt desperate.

'Well, is there anyone who isn't Tangent?'

Four or five voices instantly arose.

'I'm not, sir; I'm not Tangent. I wouldn't be called Tangent, not on the end of a barge pole.'

In a few seconds the room had become divided into two parties; those who were Tangent and those who were not. Blows were already being exchanged, when the door opened and Grimes came in. There was a slight hush.

'I thought you might want this,' he said, handing Paul a walking stick. 'And if you take my advice, you'll set them something to do.'

He went out; and Paul firmly grasping the walking-stick, faced his form.

This entertaining, fictional account of a situation in a small private preparatory school many years ago captures in a masterly way the basic ingredients of the problem. We first notice that Paul, who is about to teach his first lesson, is nervous and apprehensive ('dumb with terror'). He does not know where to begin. He is the victim of the situation, unable to manipulate it to his own ends. He does not take the initiative in defining the situation, even though the pupils will expect and probably accept it if he does so. By his failure to take the initiative, the definition is given into the pupils' hands and they quickly turn it into a direction which is profitable to them, fun rather than work, but which is extremely costly to Paul as the situation becomes progressively worse.

The pupils gain control in defining the situation almost at once, before Paul has the chance to realize what is happening. Even as he enters the classroom, the pupils await him eagerly, 'their eyes bright with expectation'. Innocently he responds in a friendly way to the pupils' opening move of a 'Good morning' greeting, only to find himself trapped in a disconcerting chain reaction. A few minutes later the boys use the same technique successfully in response to Paul's attempt to discover their names. In not knowing how to define the situation, Paul hesitated, and was lost.

It is for this reason that most experienced teachers insist that the teacher must, if he is to survive, define the situation in his own terms at once. Basically this initial definition is not so much a statement of the rules that will govern behaviour in that class, but rather a clear indication that the teacher is completely in charge and not to be treated lightly. If the teacher can establish himself as the imperturbable lord and master of the classroom, who is not to be disobeyed or fooled, then all will be well. Once the teacher has thus exerted his authority, he can at a later stage create the kind of relationship with the pupils that his personal philosophy of education requires.

> You can't ever let them get the upper hand on you or you're
> finished. So I start out tough. The first day I got a new class
> in I let them know who's boss. You've got to start out
> tough, then you can ease up as you go along. If you start
> out easy-going, when you try to get tough they'll just look
> at you and laugh. (Becker, 1952)

> If you started with a mailed fist, you could later open that
> fist to reveal a velvet palm. If you let them step all over you
> at the beginning, there was no gaining control later.
> (Hunter, 1955)

> Either you murder them, or they'll murder you. Either you
> win or they win. And I'll tell you, mate, I'm the one that's
> going to win. (A teacher's comment to the author)

This is a lesson learned the hard way by countless generations of student teachers who, believing that the pupils ought to be treated with respect as mature persons, try to create a definition of the situation that is congruent with their beliefs. Almost always the result is disastrous. The pupils do not respond in the expected way. Soon the teacher finds himself only nominally in charge of a collection of noisy, disobedient, rude and irresponsible children, who are quite unwilling either to listen to the teacher or to work. It is a fascinating fact that pupils, even those in 'good' middle-class schools, respond so often in this way towards a teacher who is sincerely seeking to make life at school more pleasant for them. This is why so many student teachers fall so regularly into the trap. It seems incredible that the pupils should reject what is so clearly intended for their benefit. As we discussed in chapter 6 pupils like a teacher who is friendly, patient and humorous, who takes an interest in the pupils as individuals and who makes his lessons interesting. Why, then, should the pupils react so badly to a teacher who tries to live up to these ideals? Clearly the pupils' perspective or definition of the situation is not congruent with that of the teacher, whereas the student teacher assumes that it is. The teacher, finding his 'reasonable' assumption undermined, has to find some explanation of the pupils' behaviour. He can do this by switching to a common teacher assumption that 'kids are little devils' or by taking a view of human nature which suggests that children are essentially anti-social and need to be restrained and directed into acceptable social behaviour. From a social psychological view the problem is one of explaining the disjunction in teacher and pupil perspectives.

Perhaps part of the answer is that children do not like school very much, at least in the sense that they can think of preferable activities. This is not to say that they do not wish to learn, but rather that they do not wish to learn the subjects imposed by the teacher in the ways and at the time and place that the teacher demands. As has already been pointed out, unless we reorganize our schools very radically, the pupils are unlikely to find life at school rewarding for most of the time. Since the majority of the teachers manage to compel their pupils by various means, to do things they do not particularly like, they are in a sense constrained by the system to turn the lessons of a teacher who is unwilling or unable to achieve a dominant position over them into periods of rest and relaxation, or into 'fun'—anything that is not work. If this is the case, the teacher who is not prepared to be 'tough' is rejected not so much because the children do not want what he offers, but because his refusal to dominate serves as an emergency exit out of the prevailing boredom of school through which the pupils joyfully stampede. Such an interpretation might be confirmed by the fact that pupils do not usually give the teacher very much time to explain what he is offering them. As in the case of Paul above, the pupils are so eager to find a way out that they are unprepared, when they see one, to wait and see what things would be like if they stayed behind. And once a stampede has begun, it is difficult to stand still.

Other interpretations are possible. It may be that the pupils simply distrust the teacher who does not define the situation in terms of his own dominance. After all, since most of the other teachers dominate in the classroom successfully, it is only a matter of time before this teacher follows the customary pattern and becomes like the rest of them. In the meantime, the most profitable course for the pupils is to make hay while the sun shines—for it will be rain and storm very soon.

Whatever the causes, the phenomenon itself remains. If the teacher does not establish his own dominance, the children are likely to turn the classroom into a circus without a ringmaster and the teacher will become rapidly exhausted and demoralized. Many of the authorities on discipline interpret this situation as an attempt by the pupils to find the limits of the situation. In 'seeing how far they can go' the pupils are exploring what the teacher will allow and what he will forbid. I am sure there is much truth in this view, for it is natural enough that pupils whould try to discover a new teacher's code of acceptable behaviour, which will be unique to that teacher. But I am equally sure that this phenomenon is more complex than this view allows. My reason is that even the non-dominating teacher who makes his rules and expectations quite explicit in the very early stages seems to suffer the same unhappy fate as the vague non-dominating teacher. Every teacher, in short, is pressured by the pupils to exert his own dominance, sooner or later.

The pupils do this in a variety of ways. The whole class may appear to challenge the teacher with an uncanny, almost telepathic ability to co-operate against him. Alternatively, just one or two pupils may play the active role before an encouraging and appreciative audience. Sometimes a student or beginning teacher, finding the pupils polite and obedient, believes that all is well, that he is in control, and that the warnings of other teachers were but complaints of sadistic cynics. or even that he is such a good teacher that he has managed to avoid the trials and tribulations which the rest of us have to endure. Usually in such a case he has simply fallen for what I call the Disciplinary Illusion. The pupils do not always issue an immediate challenge to the teacher. Instead they play the game of watching and waiting. While the teacher imagines that he is firmly in control, the pupils are silently sizing him up. The first few minor infractions to test the situation are casually dismissed by the confident teacher, and then the infractions begin to assume major proportions. Soon the apparent discipline has been transformed into an obvious and uncontrollable indiscipline.

If the teacher feels that he must establish his dominance in the early stages of his first encounter with the students, he is faced with a problem of self-presentation. He must express himself in such a way that the pupils are correctly impressed that he is in charge and that he is a person not to be trifled with. At the first meeting with their new teacher the pupils are seeking to discover, either by a calculating silence or by tentative, probing assaults on the teacher's dominance, precisely what sort of person the teacher is and what sort of disciplinary regime is to be created. They are highly sensitive to the teacher's behaviour, to the expressions he gives and gives off. The 'first impressions' made by the teacher are thus especially important in establishing the definition of the situation. The teacher's image and the tone of all future interactions emerge within the first few minutes of the encounter. It is often thought by student teachers that the teacher's physical size is of great importance in this respect. This is without foundation.

The pupils are far too skilled in the character analysis of teachers to be misled by mere physical appearances. They can detect those clues to the teacher's real character, intentions and abilities with the cunning and patience of a wild animal stalking its prey. The advantage of the tall well-built teacher, like the disadvantage of small stature, lasts for a very short time, since the impression conveyed by the body is soon discredited (or confirmed) by other aspects of the teacher's self-presentation. What counts is not the single isolated 'bit' of the teacher's image, but the total, overall picture of himself constructed by the teacher in the fine detail of his behaviour. He must present himself as a unified whole to which all the bits, each congruent with the rest, contribute. Any bit which is discrepant with the whole will be identified by the pupils as a vulnerable chink in the armour and become the focal point of future attacks. Let us now consider the case of a teacher who, in contrast to the irresolute approach of Paul given above, is determined to impose his own 'tough' definition of the situation and tries to present himself accordingly. We join the teacher, Rick, as he receives his class on the first day of term (Hunter, 1955):

> he picked up his roll book and his briefcase, walked quickly to the steps, and mounted them with his shoulders back and his head high. He paused dramatically for a moment, and then began calling the roll in his best Sir Laurence Olivier voice.
>
> 'Abrahams,' and he saw movement out there in the seats, but he did not pause to focus the movement.
>
> 'Arretti,' and another blur of movement.
>
> 'Bonneli,' and 'Casey,' and 'Diaz,' and 'Di Zeffolo,' and 'Donato,' and 'Dover,' and 'Estes,' and on, and on, until he flipped over the last card in the book. There had not been a murmur while he spoke, and he was satisfied that he had been accorded the respect due to an English high-school teacher. He slapped the roll book shut, and walked

down the steps and then into the centre aisle, conscious of
the curious eyes of the kids upon him.

When he reached his official class the same curiosity was
reflected in their eyes.

'Follow me,' he said unsmiling. 'No talking on the way up.'

That, he figured, was the correct approach. Let them know
who's boss right from the start, just the way Small had
advised.

'Hey, teach,' one of the boys said, 'what did Mr. Halloran
say your name was?'

Rick turned his head sharply. The boy who'd spoken was
blond, and there was a vacuous smile on his face, and the
smile did not quite reach his eyes.

'I said no talking, and I meant it,' Rick snapped.

The boy was silent for a second, and then Rick heard
him say, 'Dig this cat. He's playin' it hard.'

He chose to ignore the comment. He walked along ahead
of the class, feeling excitement grow within him now, feeling
the same excitement he'd felt when he got the job, only
greater now, stronger, like the times at school when he'd
waited in the wings for his cue. Like that, only without the
curious butterflies in his stomach, and without the unconscious
dread that he would forget all his lines the moment he stepped
out on to the stage in front of all those people. He felt in
complete control of the situation, and yet there was this raging
excitement within him, as if there was something he had to do
and he simply could not wait to get it done ...

He led the class to the stairwell, and aside from a few
whisperers here and there, they were very orderly, and he felt
that everything was going well. . . .

When they reached the door to Room 206 he inserted the
key expertly, twisted it, removed it, and then pushed the door
back.

'Sit anywhere,' he said brusquely. 'We'll arrange seating
later.'

The boys filed in, still curious, still wondering what sort
of a duck this new bird with the Butch haircut was. They
seated themselves quickly and quietly, and Rick thought,
This is going even better than I expected.

He walked rapidly to his desk, pulled out his chair, but
did not sit. He looked out over the faces in the seats before
him, and then sniffed the air authoritatively, like a bloodhound
after a quarry. He cocked one eybrow and glanced at the
windows.

'What's your name?' he asked.

The boy looked frightened, as if he had been accused of something he hadn't done. 'Me?'

'Yes, what's your name?'

'Dover, I didn't do nothing, teach. Jeez . . .'

'Open some of the windows in here, Dover. It's a little stuffy.'

Dover smiled, his lips pulling back over bright white teeth. He got up from his seat and crossed behind Rick's desk, and Rick congratulated himself on having handled that perfectly. He had not simply given an order which would have resulted in a mad scramble to the windows. He had first chosen one of the boys, and then given the order. All according to the book. All fine and dandy. Damn, if things weren't going fine.

He turned and walked to the blackboard, located a piece of chalk on the runner, and wrote his name in big letters on the black surface.

MR. DADIER.

'That's my name,' he said. 'In case you missed it in the auditorium.' He paused. 'Mr. Dad-ee-yay,' he pronounced clearly.

Although Rick's troubles with this class are by no means over, his initial encounter with his pupils can be regarded as a success, at least insofar as he attempts to assert his own dominance. How has he done it? In the first place he shows considerable foresight in *planning ahead* against possible disruption which might undermine his control or upset his performance. He selects a single boy to open the windows; he prohibits talking before they set off from the hall to the class-room; he has a store of pencils readily available. Second, *he refuses to allow the pupils any opportunity of taking the initiative in defining the situation* from him. He silences at once the boy who asks for his name on the corridor, and who in so doing both makes the first assault on the rules ('No talking on the way up'), and seeks to tempt the teacher into the mine-field of an informal interaction. Third, in the very early stages of the interaction *he outlines a general code of expected behaviour.* He forbids shouting out without permission and fixes the modes of address. Fourth, he indicates that *he is not to be treated lightly.* He threatens a punishment at the first sign of inso-lence. Finally, and perhaps most important of all, *he tries to present himself generally in ways which are consonant with his total intentions.* He makes no attempt to give clues to a liberal, child-centred philo-sophy. He shows no sign of wishing to court popularity. He is cold and unsmiling; he speaks 'brusquely', 'coldly', 'gruffly'. His expres-sions make the right impression on the pupils—'Dig this cat. He's playin' it hard.'

There is a further contrast in the behaviour of Rick and Paul. Rick is very conscious that he is 'playing a part', that his behaviour is somewhat artificial and contrived. These feelings are so strong that he recalls actual performances in plays during his own schooldays. Paul, on the other hand, is 'being himself'; his behaviour is not staged. This raises the perennial problem of student teachers: is it right for the teacher to 'act a part'? Most beginning teachers rightly want to endow their relationships with their pupils with honesty and integrity, which seems inconsistent with pretending to be something one is not. To 'act a part' is associated with feelings of intense strain and guilt. I do not think the student teacher should worry about this problem. The contrived performance is a means to an end, namely the establishment of his dominance. It is essentially a *temporary* measure. For reasons we shall examine shortly, he will soon be able to drop his mask. The only danger is that of permanently 'playing a part' where the contrived performance becomes an end in itself. A few teachers do become life-long classroom actors, dreary cardboard caricatures who become incapable of any adequate and satisfying relationships with their pupils. But they are exceptions who are trapped by the opening move of the game; the majority advance to a much deeper personal involvement in the intricacies of educating children.

One of the essential features of 'playing a part' is an ability to make a simultaneous check on the effect of the act on the pupils. A contrived performance is extremely dangerous if the actor is so bound up in his art of presenting himself that he takes no account of the audience. It is essential that only a part of the self is involved in the act, whilst the more central self evaluates and guides the performer. This is fully exemplified in Rick's account. At times he stands back from his performance to see how well he is doing, to congratulate himself on his success, or warn himself that he is losing ground.

The second danger of 'playing a part' is that of failing to make the performance *convincing*. Unless the teacher is consistent in his performance, unless he attends to the minor details with the same care and attention that he lavishes on his general approach, then he will be 'seen through' by the pupils. A discredited act is worse than no act at all. It is for this reason that if the teacher is to play a part it must be of a simple unelaborate kind. If the act is too ambitiously conceived then he is almost certain to be unable to sustain it, especially if as is likely he is nervous and apprehensive about meeting the pupils. If the ambitious act breaks down, the teacher will look as foolish as the amateur actor who fluffs his lines or trips on the staircase and causes the set to collapse. Drama is soon turned into farce.

In advising student teachers to take the initiative in defining the situation in terms of their own dominance and to be prepared, if necessary, to 'play a part' to this end, I have been accused of being reactionary, Victorian and inconsistent with my own educational philosophy. Such accusations stem from a misunderstanding of my position. By 'tough' I do *not* mean to suggest a ruthless and punitive autocracy. A 'tough' approach is characterized by a maintenance of the teacher's dominance by firmness, clarity and consistency. In other words, the teacher must remain in charge, be firm and consistent in his treatment of the pupils and be prepared to punish pupils who call his bluff. This is *not* achieved, I might add, if the teacher's first action is to bring out the three largest pupils and punish them quite arbitrarily to prove that 'there will be no nonsense in my classroom'. In being 'tough' the teacher can, and should, be humane and reasonable.

My advice is also based on the fact that most state secondary schools, in which most of my students will teach, contain teachers whose attitudes are conservative and traditional rather than liberal and progressive. Their approach to the pupils will not be very 'tenderminded' or 'child-centred'. Any teacher who does not behave in accordance with the 'party line' is likely to be regarded as 'soft' and incompetent by both staff and pupils. Yet if the teacher is to survive in his chosen profession he must have a minimum of respect and support from his colleagues as well as from his pupils. Both pupils and staff are unlikely to respond favourably to his new ideas simply because they are so different to what is customary in that school and because they will not have been tried there. If the student or beginning teacher proclaims to a wary and cynical staff-room his childcentred theories (which in *their* eyes are irrelevant and impractical theories invented by people quite out of touch with the real world of teaching) and yet in the classroom cannot maintain even basic control, then his disciplinary failure will be seen as the perfect refutation of the theories. On the other hand, if the new teacher starts out 'tough' he has more chance of achieving adequate discipline in the classroom and of earning the esteem of the more experienced teachers.

Starting out with a 'tough' approach does not mean that the teacher must persist in maintaining such a regime for the rest of his career. Many teachers do so, for they know that the 'tough' approach works and gains the respect of colleagues and pupils. In consequence they become afraid to try any other approach, lose their ideals, and join those teachers who actively oppose any new policies. In truth, the 'tough' approach should be regarded not as a terminus, but as a point of departure. Once the pupils know that the teacher is in charge, that trying to 'play him up' is a profitless activity, the teacher can begin to put into practice his own ideas and ideals about how pupils should behave in the classroom. The situation is, in other words, open to redefinition. The pupils will probably respond with pleasure and gratitude, regarding the teacher's innovations as new and exciting privileges rather than as opportunities for having fun or for taking a rise out of the teacher. Such changes must, however, be introduced very slowly. A sudden change in regime is likely to have disastrous effects on the pupils, who will respond to the new uncertainties with misbehaviour and abuse of unfamiliar freedoms. The definition of the situation must be altered very gradually to allow the pupils to adapt to the new activities, new roles, new relationships and new codes of behaviour.

Many students who accept the necessity of an initial 'tough' approach are so keen on redefining the situation that they instigate the redefinition too quickly and long before it is due. In the term (or less) of a teaching practice there is barely time to establish the initial definition of the situation. Student teachers, in their impatience with the old ways and in their enthusiasm to try out the new, easily persuade themselves that the ground is adequately prepared for change. In this, I must confess, they are often encouraged by their tutors who share their disrespect for the conventional and surpass them in their eagerness to experiment with new ideas and teaching methods. It never ceases to surprise me that so many students do indeed succeed in assessing the situation in the classroom so well. Perhaps it is that they make a compromise between the conservatism of the serving teachers and the radicalism of the tutors, and the right course may well be somewhere between the two.

One of the most important reasons why the definition of the situation must be initially made in terms of the teacher's dominance is that the detailed definition takes some time to establish. It cannot all be done at the first meeting. In accomplishing his own dominance immediately, the teacher is ensuring that he has the right to make the rules that form the code of acceptable behaviour and also the power to enforce them. If the teacher fails to establish his dominance this process will be extremely difficult.

In the very first encounter the teacher will try to lay down some of the most basic rules of the code, covering such areas as modes of address, movement about the room, distribution of equipment and so on. It is obviously best if these basic rules are few in number. They should also be fairly comprehensive, though not so general as to offer little guidance in specific situations. (Making the first rule 'Love thy neighbour as thyself' will not help very much.) During the following weeks the teacher will have to ensure that these rules—and the reasons for the rules—are fully understood, learned and conformed to. Both teacher and pupils may find this difficult, for many of the rules may be specific, at least in their detailed application, to one particular teacher. No two teachers ever have precisely the same code of acceptable conduct, though there will probably be much in common. New teachers are frequently besieged by cries of 'But sir, Miss Smith always said . . .'

The rules which the teacher enjoins at the first meeting cannot be more than basic generalized rules. In the ensuing weeks these rules will be clarified with respect to particular events. The pupils will learn what behaviours are covered by the rules and in what ways. Further, the basic rules will not cover many eventualities. New rules will be promulgated and brought into force as relevant to the requirements of novel situations as they arise. Often the rules will be made in response to a pupil's misbehaviour. In such cases the rule arises to prevent the continuance and recurrence of something of which the teacher does not approve. In creating rules in response to pupil misbehaviours the teacher must beware of manufacturing a code that consists of a list of *don'ts*.

The definition of the situation takes some weeks to establish because the rules must be often created and always clarified in relation to concrete incidents where the rules are applicable; because the pupils need time to learn the rules and how they apply in given situations; and because the teacher must be able to demonstrate his power to enforce the rules and gain conformity to them. The definition of the situation is, in short, a progressive and cumulative process. It is built up, day by day, incident by incident, into a consistent whole.

Once the rules are mastered by the pupils, that is learned, understood and conformed to (at least by most of the pupils for most of the time), the teacher's relationship with his pupils can enter a new phase. The rules become part of the taken-for-granted aspect of life in the classroom. As the teacher has asserted his dominance and generated a set of clear-cut rules and penalties, there are unlikely to be any serious attempts to undermine the rules or to play up the teacher. So although the teacher will have to assert his own dominance, reiterate the rules and impose punishments from time to time, generally speaking his dominance can begin to fade into the background. The classroom situation and relationships are open to redefinition in accordance with the teacher's personal philosophy of education.

An important part of this change concerns the teacher's attempt to *legitimate* his authority. Hitherto the teacher's ability to establish and maintain discipline and order in the classroom has rested on his power to dominate and to impose sanctions. The teacher relied on his *formal* authority as the possessor of adult status, legal rights and so on. Now the teacher is in a position to change this to a more *personal* authority which is based on the teacher's personal qualities and the special relationship he develops with the pupils.

Whilst the teacher is concerned with his own dominance, the pupils comply to the teacher's demands and rules without in any way being necessarily committed to them. The pupils tend to be concerned with the effects of their behaviour on the teacher and comply largely to avoid punishments of various kinds. As the teacher moves to the exercise of personal authority, his formal power becomes increasingly less prominent. The sources of his new power are based on the pupils' desire to establish and maintain a good relationship with him, and on the liking, respect and admiration that the pupils have for him. The pupils are now less concerned with simply avoiding punishments and more concerned with maintaining their self-image as good pupils, worthy of the teacher's approval, and with abiding by values which are congruent with those of the teachers. They behave well, not because they are pressured to do so, but because they want to. On the surface the order and discipline of the classroom may appear to be unchanged; in fact, the sources of the teacher's power and the pupils' motives for conforming have been radically altered. We have moved from an obedience based on fear and the desire to survive unscathed to a relationship of deep trust and mutual concern. It is at this point that discipline has in a meaningful sense become self-discipline.

Redefining the situation in this way is, as all experienced successful teachers know, much more difficult and more an uneven process than it sounds. If it were easy, so many teachers would not become trapped for life in the stage of initial dominance or, even worse, of attempted dominance. The truth of the matter is that the seeds of the redefinition are sown in the initial stage of teacher dominance. It is absurd to expect a harvest if these seeds are not sown at the right time and in the right way. The way in which the redefinition is prepared for consists in the form of the dominance exerted by the teacher and the techniques he uses to attain it. Advice to be 'tough' at the outset is dangerous precisely because such advice rarely specifies in what ways the teacher should be 'tough'. Unless we can formulate further detail, the advice to be 'tough' will produce quite as many disasters as successes.

Educationists not infrequently tell their students that there is no discipline problem if the teacher's lessons interest the children. In my view this is pernicious nonsense. It is true, of course, that when the teacher's lessons are exciting to the children there are less likely to be infractions of the classroom code. Boredom is one of the major sources of minor infringements of the rules and fascinating lessons reduce boredom to a minimum. But boredom is not the only cause of rebellion and the ability to plan fascinating lessons is not the only skill required of the effective teacher. The 'discipline problem' is, as I have tried to show, a much more fundamental and pervasive issue than many educationists allow. When they argue that interesting lessons eliminate the discipline problem they ignore the wide variety of interpersonal skills that are the mark of the 'good' teacher. It is these interpersonal skills that we must now consider.

When a pupil breaks one of the rules, the teacher who is aware of this deviation is called upon to respond. Typically a wide range of actions is at the teacher's disposal, but only one or two of the possible responses are actually enacted. In selecting a particular response the teacher usually seeks to stop the deviation from the rules and inhibit its recurrence and its 'spread' to other pupils. Essentially, then, the teacher is attempting to *control* the pupil's behaviour by means of certain *techniques*. Following Redl (1951, 1952), we shall regard these control techniques as a kit of tools. Like tools they can be used properly or improperly. One can successfully use a chisel as a screwdriver, but in so doing one damages the chisel. The screwdriver might be used as a chisel without harming the screwdriver, but the wood will not escape serious damage. The same is true of control techniques. If they are used improperly, there will be deleterious effects on both the technique and on the pupil.

The 'good' teacher, presumably, is one who achieves morally commendable disciplinary objectives by the proper use of morally acceptable techniques. This is clearly a highly complex process by which the teacher solves the problems of what technique to use on what occasion in what way and for what reason. Thus there are four questions to be asked—which? when? how? why? *Which?* requires the teacher to select from his repertoire a technique that is appropriate to the particular misbehaviour committed, to the context in which the misbehaviour arises, and to the particular needs of the offending pupil. A technique cannot be regarded as appropriate or successful unless it has the desired effect. This requires that the teacher know how the pupil is likely to react to the technique in this particular situation, which calls for considerable imagination, insight and understanding on the part of the teacher. *When?* raises the matter of timing. Is this the right moment to intervene? Should action be postponed till later? The *how?* question is concerned with the manner in which the teacher applies the technique. For example, if the teacher decides to administer a rebuke, what tone of voice should the teacher use? Should the pupil be rebuked publicly or in private? *Why?* includes two questions. The first concerns the teacher's reason for wishing to apply the technique, his objectives in seeking to take action. Is it because he wants to help the pupil or is he motivated by anger or resentment or impatience? The second concerns the pupil's motives. Why did the pupil misbehave in the first place? Did his misbehaviour spring from ignorance or misunderstanding of the rules? from boredom? from frustration? from an attempt to annoy the teacher? from an attempt to gain popularity with his friends?

These questions are essentially *short-term* ones. They are concerned with the immediate situation, that is, with the issues involved in the teacher's selection of a control technique to deal with a classroom misbehaviour by a pupil. However, the appropriateness of a control technique is not determined by these short-term problems alone. It is equally important to consider a number of *long-term* objectives which are less closely related to the immediate situation. Neither the misbehaviour nor the control technique that is adopted by the teacher can be regarded as isolated incidents. Every action by the teacher must be seen in the light of the contribution it makes to the general, on-going relationship of teacher and pupil. So if a technique is to be appropriate it should make a positive contribution to that relationship or at least not damage it in any substantial way. This is *not* to say that the pupil must always be pleased with the control technique adopted by the teacher. Frequently the pupil will be displeased with and resentful of the teacher's action. Rather I am suggesting that the teacher must beware of using techniques which damage his relationship with the pupil in a more than momentary sense. This raises the problem of how a teacher calculates such effects of his actions, a problem to which we shall turn shortly. Secondly, it is important to consider the effect of a control technique on the pupil's relationship with his peers. It should not, for example, cause the pupil to feel degraded as a person or to lose the respect of his friends if this is avoidable. A third long-term objective concerns the pupil's attitudes —to school, to learning, to the curriculum. A control technique cannot be said to be satisfactory if it promotes in the pupil negative attitudes of dislike and avoidance to these.

In attempting to analyse the disciplinary skills of teachers we have soon found ourselves compelled to make value-judgments—to distinguish the 'good' from the 'bad' methods of achieving and maintaining order and discipline in the classroom. Yet the lack of a generally agreed definition of what comprises 'good' discipline is well known. To some teachers, 'good' discipline is defined in almost military terms, with domination by the teacher, unquestioning obedience from the pupils, and silent classrooms. Such a view is anathema to teachers of a progressive or child-centred approach. What is 'good' in one school of thought is very often the 'bad' of a different educational philosophy. The skills required to promote discipline according to those different views are probably not the same. The 'good' teacher that I am concerned with might be considered to be of a broadly child-centred persuasion—though in practice such a teacher might be very reluctant to describe himself in partisan terms. My analysis is based on the behaviour of many teachers whose classes I have observed and who have in common only the fact that they are teachers.

1. *The teacher possesses an extensive repertoire of control techniques that are readily available for use and that are effective.*

If the teacher is to be able to apply to a misbehaviour a control technique that is appropriate to the misbehaviour, the particular individual and to the context in which the misbehaviour occurs, then he must have at his disposal a wide range of readily available techniques. It is important that these techniques are not just 'theoretically' available. A knowledge of what *might* be done can be gained from books or from observation of other teachers, but such knowledge is useless unless it can be called upon in practice and will actually stop the misbehaviour.

The repertoires of many experienced teachers are remarkably limited. In such cases the majority of available techniques tend to be in the punishment area—rebukes, lectures, tirades, sarcasm, ridicule, detention, removal of privileges, extra work, corporal punishment. The popularity of such techniques derives, I suspect, from the fact that many teachers, especially early in their career, see a misbehaviour as highly threatening to their control and mastery of the situation and thus as a personal affront. Almost instinctively, therefore, counter-attack seems to be the best form of defence. Such a reaction on the part of the teacher is encouraged by advice to be 'tough' in the early stages, since this advice is almost invariably interpreted as a need to be punishing. Further, since these punishing counter-attacks are not uncommonly effective, that is they do stop the misbehaviour and inhibit further immediate outbreaks, they can easily become adopted by the insecure teacher as the natural and basic method of maintaining discipline. In this way they quickly become over-valued by the teacher, who precludes himself from experimenting with alternative methods.

From my own observations I concluded that there is a Punishment Illusion, which is akin to the Disciplinary Illusion discussed earlier. Punishing techniques *appear* to be effective because they often stop the misbehaviour. The teacher's attack, verbal or physical, on the offending pupil has a 'stunning' effect, which, like the sharp blow of a boxer, disables temporarily and hinders immediate retaliation. But rarely (perhaps never) does it get to the root of the misbehaviour and in consequence new forms of misbehaviour arise or the pupil smoulders in resentment and humiliation. Like the boxer, he recovers and returns to the fight wiser for the experience or retires from the ring angry at the inequality of the contest.

It is for this reason that more 'positive' techniques are an essential part of the teacher's repertoire. By 'positive' I mean techniques which aim to cure as well as to stop a misbehaviour, for cure is the only adequate means of preventing a recurrence. Without doubt the greatest exponent of these positive control techniques is Fritz Redl. His provocative, stimulating and highly practical discussions of disciplinary problems are unrivalled. Although my thinking has been considerably influenced by Redl (1952, 1966), and my debts to him are evident throughout this book, I wish to refer to his work directly at this point by recounting some of the control techniques he has identified, named and fully described. It is a sample to whet the appetite.

Signal interference. Many misbehaviours can be inhibited in their early stages if the teacher can bring an incipient act to the offender's attention and indicate that it is not acceptable. The most common methods of signal interference are catching the pupil's eye and clearing one's throat. Another form of the technique is for the teacher to prowl in the area of an offence until the pupil 'gets the message'. Of course, if this technique is to be effective the teacher must anticipate the misbehaviour or recognize the early stages. It is not a technique for inhibiting a serious misbehaviour that is in full flight.

Interest boosting. Since many misbehaviours arise from the pupil's boredom or frustration they can be eliminated by an effort by the teacher to rekindle the pupil's interest in the work. This is often much more effective than a reproof ('Pay attention', 'Get on with your work', 'Stop fidgeting', etc.) which often merely suggest to the child that his inattention is obvious and must be concealed.

Humorous decontamination. A slight lapse or even a threatening situation can often be controlled by an unexpected humorous reaction from the teacher. If the teacher makes a joke to break the tension it is important that it is done in a benign way, otherwise the humour becomes punishing (e.g. ridicule). At the same time, it must contain some hint of disapproval or the pupil may feel that his behaviour is not being taken seriously or even that it is being encouraged.

Non-punitive exile. Some misbehaviours can be overcome by sending the child out of the classroom. It is not a punitive technique ('Get outside and don't come back in here until you can behave') but rather an attempt to allow the child a strategic retreat in order to 'get over it'. It is particularly effective in cases of the 'giggles' where attempts to stifle the offence can actually increase it.

2. *The teacher employs control techniques that meet both short-term and long-term objectives.*

I have tried to suggest that it is not enough in selecting his control technique, for the teacher to find one that simply stops the misbehaviour. In most cases the misbehaviour can be stopped by a whole range of techniques and if the intention is merely to stop it then the 'functional equivalence' makes the choice of a particular technique quite arbitrary and subject to the whim of the moment. Almost any method, particularly if it is punishing, will do the trick. But if the technique is to be appropriate, it must be selected as the most fitting teacher response to the particular offence, the needs of the offender, the factors of the immediate situation, the pupil's relationship with the teacher and with his peers, and the child's attitudes to learning and to the curriculum.

Many subtle skills are involved in learning to choose appropriate control techniques. It usually takes some time for the beginning teacher to acquire the capacity to know what misbehaviour committed by which pupil in which situation is best dealt with by a stern rebuke or by laughing it off—or by any other technique. Much trial and error seems to be needed. Moreover, every particular technique can be applied in different ways. For example, let us suppose that the teacher decides that a stern rebuke is the best response to a pupil's infraction of the rules. The question then arises: how stern should the rebuke be? If the rebuke is insufficiently stern it will not be taken seriously by the offending pupil and the misbehaviour will not be stopped. If the rebuke is too stern then the teacher has gone beyond what is necessary. Again much trial and error learning is needed to acquire the skill of applying 'just enough' pressure to stop a misbehaviour. Beginning teachers tend to swing somewhat erratically between under- and over-reaction—typically over-reacting when they find that a previous under-reaction has not been effective. In my own observations I have seen student teachers abandon a technique as 'useless', that is, it did not achieve the desired end of stopping the misbehaviour, and then switch to another technique (usually more punishing) when in fact the first technique was indeed an appropriate one, but failed because its application was marred by under-reaction It is much more common, of course, for a teacher to conclude that a technique is useless as a result of an inappropriate application. The beginning teacher must beware of prematurely rejecting a technique before he has given himself the opportunity to assess its value by using it in an effective and appropriate way. It requires courage and persistence to continue to experiment with a technique which does not prove to be instantly successful until its usefulness can be fully assessed.

One of the most basic skills involved in choosing an appropriate technique is related to the teacher's *perception* of the offender. How the teacher reacts is in part a function of what motives and intentions the teacher infers and attributes to the pupil. Much less frequently than we imagine are we in possession of sufficient information to be certain of the causes of the child's behaviour because there are usually so few cues available to guide our inferences. Typically we fill in the gaps in our knowledge of the child's motives and intentions from our own assumptions of what might seem to be the *likely* or the most *reasonable* causes for the offence.

The process of control technique selection, then, is highly complex, entailing a consideration of the past (the sources of the pupil's misbehaviour), the present (the immediate consequences of the pupil's behaviour), and the future (the long-term consequences of the pupil's behaviour). Once the situation has been diagnosed with respect to the sources and consequences of the misbehaviour, certain possible control techniques can be eliminated as inappropriate. The selection of the actual control technique is then influenced by the teacher's estimation of the short-term and long-term effects of the remaining possible control techniques, as defined earlier in the chapter.

3. *The teacher gets feedback on his own behaviour and learns from experience.*

The ability to profit from experience is implicit in the previous two points. If the teacher is able to apply a wide range of techniques that achieve both short and long-term objectives, then he must be able to judge the effects of the control technique once it has been applied, and estimate the extent to which it is appropriate and successful. There is obviously little point in applying a technique and then assuming that it is effective. If the technique is not effective and the misbehaviour does not stop, then the teacher will have to strengthen his reaction or switch to another technique. If he has made a mistake by selecting an inappropriate technique or applying the right technique wrongly, then he must be able to recognize the error and learn to avoid making the same mistake again. A surprising number of student teachers persist in endless repetition of the same mistake because they fail to recognize it as such. Sometimes the source of the difficulty is a failure in *seeing it through*. Because he feels insecure, afraid and self-conscious when faced with a misbehaviour, the inexperienced teacher tends to hurry on to other matters without checking that the technique has been effective. Such a teacher must resist the temptation to undue haste and take his time in seeing it through. Suppose a teacher calls for silence. If he then moves on before complete silence is attained, further disruptions are inevitable. To see it through, he must wait until complete silence reigns, then pause for a few seconds, and then move on. Seeing it through is no mean skill, for there is no point in seeing through a technique that is doomed to failure from the beginning. The skill consists in recognizing at an early stage that the technique is going to work and then seeing it through.

Whilst it is relatively easy to assess the short-term effectiveness of a technique it is much more difficult to calculate the effectiveness or appropriateness of a technique in the long term. This is because long-term effects are inevitably dissociated in the teacher's mind from particular immediate situations. John may seem not to mind very much whenever the teacher says, 'Shut up—don't be such a chatter-box,' and it may inhibit John from further chatter, but may not his general apathy in lessons be the cumulative result of the teacher's having said this twice a day for three years without having ever got to the root of his talkativeness?

A whole set of skills is involved in getting feedback on one's own behaviour as a teacher. Perhaps the most important is a sensitivity to knowing what is going on 'out there' in the classroom. This awareness of what is going on is called *with-it-ness* by Jacob Kounin (1966). It means that the teacher must have the proverbial 'eyes in the back of his head'. The teacher must not be so absorbed in his own behaviour or so intent on executing his own predetermined lesson plans that he pays insufficient attention to how the pupils are reacting or behaving. In my view with-it-ness in its most subtle form consists of three elements: (i) close observation of the pupils; (ii) the pupils are not always aware that they are being observed, that is, the teacher is in fact observing them when he appears not to be; (iii) the teacher gives the children evidence that they have been observed. For example, if the teacher notices a misbehaviour, he does not always have to look at the child and tell him to stop. He can look in the *opposite* direction and then tell the pupil to put his comic away. When the offending pupil looks up he will see the teacher looking elsewhere and it will appear that the teacher can indeed see through the back of his head—and he will be duly impressed.

The new teacher may find it very hard to notice what is going on 'out there' because he is so preoccupied with other things. As he gains more experience, what initially passed unnoticed soon becomes very obvious. This change in the teacher's sensitivity to pupil behaviour is noted by Blishen (1955) in describing the more developed awareness of a teacher after several months' classroom experience.

> Williams was sniggering behind his hand. It was like an elephant trying to hide behind a rosebush. I felt sorry again. Concealment was impossible to them. Everything they did was huge and instantly perceptible. It would go on like that for a long time, until they learned adult techniques of camouflage. They couldn't even whisper. Jenkins was trying it now. His voice came out like a half-stifled klaxon. And Jimmy Green was pinching his twin brother's bottom in what was intended to be secrecy. The writhings of one, the malicious plunges of the other's arm, could have been seen clearly a hundred yards away.

An associated skill is the ability to recognize and distinguish a major from a minor deviance. The teacher who is so involved in explaining to Tom that he must not chew gum in lessons that he does not see or react to the fact that in the other corner Jim is busy tattooing with his pen the neck of an unwilling Mary, cannot be said to be with-it. In other words the teacher must never be involved in one activity to the exclusion of all others. He must be able to pay attention to one behaviour whilst continuing to monitor other activities. For example, when the teacher is marking work at his desk, he looks up regularly to check that all is well with the other pupils, that no one is seeking his attention or that no misbehaviour is brewing at the back. Occasionally new or student teachers discover, to their horror, that pupils have been taking photographs during the lesson or that an 'L' sign has been pinned on his back. Such ruses succeed because the inexperienced teacher has difficulty in *not* getting totally involved in one activity and in remembering to scan what is going on elsewhere. The experienced teacher keeps half an eye on activities and pupils that are not the immediate object of his attention. He can sense when mischief is in the making. Kounin calls this ability to pay attention simultaneously to two or more aspects of classroom activity *overlappingness*. The lack of this ability is obvious in the example of Blishen (1955).

I couldn't write on the blackboard without turning my back
on them, nor without putting my whole energy into the
business of being legible on a large scale. They knew at once
that when I turned to the board I was effectively absenting
myself from their midst. It was then that the trouble began.
'This sum . . .' I would say, and absent myself. There
would be a buzz. Then I would hear the tail-end of an improper joke. There would be a shriek, the crash of a desk.
But I would be lost in the complexities of handling chalk.
'Now, shut up!', I would murmur, but absent-mindedly,
with evident incapacity to pay much attention to what was
happening. When I did turn round, the class would no longer
be in an arithmetical frame of mind.

As with many social skills, the ability to get feedback is most easily demonstrated negatively, that is by illustrating a lack of it. Another brilliant example is provided in A. J. Wentworth, B.A., the ingenious invention of Ellis (1964).

'This morning,' I remarked, taking up my *Hall and Knight*,
'we will do problems,' and I told them at once that if there
was any more of that groaning they would do nothing but
problems for the next month. It is my experience, as an
assistant master of some years' standing, that if groaning is

not checked immediately it may swell to enormous proportions.
I make it my business to stamp on it.

Mason, a fair haired boy with glasses, remarked when the
groaning had died down that it would not be possible to do
problems for the next month, and on being asked why not,
replied that there were only three weeks more of term. This
was true and I decided to make no reply. He then asked if he
could have a mark for that. I said, 'No, Mason, you may not,'
and taking up my book and a piece of chalk, read out, 'I am
just half as old as my father and in twenty years I shall be
five years older than he was twenty years ago. How old am
I?' Atkins promptly replied, 'Forty-two.' I enquired of him
how, unless he was gifted with supernatural powers, he imagined
he could produce the answer without troubling to do any
working-out. He said, 'I saw it in the *Schools Yearbook*.' This
stupid reply caused a great deal of laughter, which I suppressed.

I should have spoken sharply to Atkins, but at this
moment I noticed that his neighbour Sapoulos, the Greek
boy, appeared to be eating toffee, a practice which is forbidden
at Burgrove during school hours. I ordered him to stand up.
'Sapoulos', I said, 'you are perhaps not quite used yet to our
English ways, and I shall not punish you this time for your
disobedience, but please understand that I will not have eating
in my class. You did not come here to eat but to learn. If you
try hard and pay attention, I do not altogether despair of
teaching you something, but if you do not wish to learn I
cannot help you. You might as well go back to your own
country.' Mason, without being given permission to speak,
cried excitedly, 'He can't, sir. Didn't you know? His father was
chased out of Greece in a revolution or something. A big man
with a black beard chased him for . . .'

'That will do, Mason,' I said. 'Who threw that?'

I am not, I hope a martinet, but I will not tolerate the
throwing of paper darts or other missiles in my algebra set.
Some of the boys make small pellets out of their blotting-
paper and flick them with their garters. This sort of thing
has to be put down with a firm hand or work becomes
impossible. I accordingly warned the boy responsible that
another offence would mean an imposition. He had the
impertinence to ask what sort of an imposition. I said it would
be a pretty stiff imposition, and if he wished to know more
exact details he had only to throw another dart to find out.
He thereupon threw another dart. I confess that at this point
I lost patience and threatened to keep the whole set in during
the afternoon if I had any more trouble.

Poor Wentworth simply cannot see that his expression is having quite a different impression on the pupils to the one he intends. If he only would (or could) recognize that, for example, his threats are not taken seriously by the pupils, then the uselessness of the technique would be exposed and he himself would be made aware of the need to try alternative approaches. Like many teachers who never master the discipline problem, Wentworth is his own worst enemy.

4. *The teacher is able to maintain momentum and smoothness.*

Disciplinary problems can arise because the teacher lacks certain general management skills in the running of the lesson. Kounin (1970) has brilliantly analysed these skills and shown that lack of them in the teacher is associated with disciplinary troubles and reduced work involvement. I shall focus on two areas, namely the skills of maintaining smoothness and momentum in the lesson.

To maintain smoothness is to manage the activity flow in a manner that avoids jerkiness. Smoothness is impeded by the occurrence of *thrusts, dangles* and *flip-flops*. A *thrust* occurs when the teacher 'bursts in' on pupil activities with an order, statement or question in a manner that demonstrates his insensitivity to the pupils' readiness to receive the message. It is like 'butting in' on a conversation without waiting to be noticed or to discover what is being talked about so that one can 'ease in' on the conversation. In a *dangle*, the teacher starts an activity and then leaves it suspended in mid-air. For example, the teacher begins one activity ('Let's do these arithmetic problems') but then suspends it whilst he takes up some irrelevant and intrusive theme ('By the way, does anyone know why Mary is absent today?'). The *flip-flop* occurs at transition points between activities. The teacher ends one activity, starts a new one, but then leaves that dangling by returning to the first activity. For instance, the teacher says, 'Right, put your arithmetic books away and take out your readers.' The pupils do so, but then the teacher says, 'Let's see now, who got all the arithmetic problems right?'

Momentum is concerned with the absence of *slowdowns* that impede the forward momentum of the lesson. One form of slow down is *overdwelling*, where the teacher dwells on an issue to an extent that is clearly beyond what is necessary, as in general 'nagging' or the preaching of elaborate sermons. Or the teacher may overelaborate instructions or explanations long after the pupils have understood so that the children are held back from the task by having to continue to listen to the teacher. Another slowdown is *fragmentation*, where the teacher breaks down an activity into subparts when the activity could easily be performed as a single unit.

A student who is prone to jerkiness and slowdowns may find it difficult to recognize what he is doing and how he is doing it. An observer may be in a good position to point them out, or the student may learn for himself if he can see himself in action in videotape recordings of his lessons.

5. *The teacher is able to make fast decisions.*

Earlier I tried to suggest the host of long-term and short-term objectives that must be satisfied if the control technique applied to a misbehaving pupil is to be regarded as appropriate. I do not imagine that anyone will dissent from these suggestions. The trouble is that when the teacher is faced with a disciplinary infringement in the classroom he must make an almost instant decision about how to react. Occasionally he has the opportunity to consider the problem, as when he can observe a minor misbehaviour in its early stages or when he asks a misbehaving pupil to come and see him at the end of the lesson. In such cases he can give some thought to the matter before taking action. But typically he must react at once. Classrooms are not like law courts. The teacher cannot hold a trial and then postpone judgment and sentence for a day or two. Even where the teacher postpones his final action until a later stage, the decision to postpone has to be taken at once, and must be a positive act rather than a lack of action based on indecisiveness. Moreover, the teacher has to decide whether he knows enough about the circumstances of the misbehaviour to act at once or to hold some sort of investigation into the precise details of the pupil's conduct and his motives for behaving so.

How can the teacher consider all the long-term and short-term objectives before he applies a control technique or holds a brief investigation? How can all this be accomplished in a few seconds? The answer is that the teacher does not consider all these matters—at least not consciously. The skill of good discipline is in some respects like the skill of riding a bicycle. When one rides a bicycle one does not have to think about where one's feet are, about how to turn the handlebars or about the delicate feat of maintaining one's balance. To the rider these skills are automatic. He simply *knows* how to ride the bicycle. Much of this knowledge is tacit (Polanyi, 1966). The rider, when asked for an explanation, does not find it easy to explain how he managed to control his feet, his balance, the handlebars, the brakes, etc., when he takes action to avoid a sudden obstacle. He can no more explain the details of his behaviour than can a pianist or a juggler.

The same is true of discipline. Ask an experienced teacher how he manages to make an appropriate reaction to a disciplinary infringement and he will probably tell you that it somehow seemed to be the right thing to do. The beginning teacher marvels, just as small children learning how to ride a bicycle admire the seemingly incredible skills of the experienced riders. In both cases a great deal of practice is required before the skill is achieved, before much of the necessary knowledge has become tacit and masked from our conscious thoughts. In both cases, some people seem to have more natural ability which helps them to learn faster than others. A few never learn. For them twenty years' experience is one year's experience repeated twenty times.

6. *The teacher is able to take prophylactic action.*

In other words, prevention is better than cure. Few misbehaviours arise in the classroom of a teacher who has mastered his disciplinary role because he takes action that prevents misbehaviours arising in the first place. Sometimes it *looks* as if there are no disciplinary problems. In reality, they have been forestalled. Many teachers seek to inhibit misbehaviours by establishing some basic rules at the first meeting with the pupils. Rules which are general enough to cover a variety of circumstances and specific enough to provide adequate guidance in a particular situation can prevent many of the misbehaviours which arise from ignorance about how to proceed rather than from a desire to flout the teacher's authority. A simple example of the value of planning ahead was given in Rick's story earlier. He asked one specific boy to open the window and avoided the chaos which might have resulted from a general request for fresh air. Similarly if the pupils are dismissed from a classroom row by row then a noisy stampede (and possible accidents or fighting) is easily prevented. Such examples may seem very mundane and obvious, but most beginning teachers take some time before they can put the obvious into practice. I have seen many student teachers distracted by incidents of the following type. The teacher tells the pupils to turn to page 24 of the textbook. His next words are drowned in a flurry of banging desk lids, raised hands, protests and mutterings—all because he had not checked that all the pupils possessed a copy of the book and they had it on the desks before them.

Yet it is by no means easy to take the necessary prophylactic action, as an example from Blishen (1969) shows. The teacher has taken his pupils on a visit to the Tate Gallery.

> at last we reached the gallery, and made our way up the steps; somehow like the great scene in *Battleship Potemkin* back to front. There was a moment when I expected to see the attendants come out of the revolving doors in a body, brandishing bayonets. I drew the boys together for a moment

with a quick flapping of my arms, and tried to give them a simple sharp summary of the proper etiquette for visiting a national art collection. 'If you feel strongly about anything, talk about it very quietly with a friend,' I said. 'Don't run. And don't touch anything.' I felt sure I'd missed several vital points, but by now we were on our way in. I *had* forgotten about the revolving doors, of course, and I had to stand by while they discovered one of the oldest of comic routines.

One aspect of this skill concerns the ability to recognize a misbehaviour in its early stages when it can be 'nipped in the bud'. Enormous problems can obviously accrue to the teacher who cannot recognize a misbehaviour until it is in full flower. The teacher who is aware of the early stages of boredom and frustration over work—and these are sources of much misbehaviour—can take remedial action before the misbehaviours actually arise.

7. *The teacher cares for and trusts his pupils.*

All the previous six factors we have discussed are skills rather than qualities. They can be learned—though I am not sure whether they can be taught, as so many students wish. They could have been described in quite different ways. To say that *sensitivity* and *flexibility* are the marks of the teacher with good discipline would simply be another way of saying the same thing. For example, Flanders (1964), describing the 'good' teacher (in general terms, not with special reference to discipline) writes:

First, the teacher was capable of providing a range of roles, spontaneously, that varied from fairly active, dominative supervision, on the one hand, to reflective, discriminating support, on the other hand. The teacher was able not only to achieve compliance but to support and encourage student initiative. Second, the teacher was able to control his own spontaneous behavior so that he could assume one role or another at will. Third, he had sufficient understanding of principles of teacher influence to make possible a logical bridge between his diagnosis of the present situation and the various actions he could take. Fourth, he was a sensitive, objective observer who could make valid diagnoses of current conditions. All of these skills, which seemed to characterise the most successful teachers, were superimposed upon a firm grasp of the subject matter being taught.

Caring for and trust in the child are not skills as such, but rather assumptions, attitudes or approaches taken by the teacher towards the pupil. Yet several social skills may be involved, especially in the way in which the teacher is able to *convey* his trust to the pupil and in the way in which the teacher is able to *sustain and develop* his assumptions. There is little point in trusting the pupil if the pupil does not realize that he is trusted or if the teacher's trust is short-lived. We saw in an earlier chapter that the student teacher tends to lose many of his ideals in teaching practice and during the early years of his life in the profession. One of the reasons for this may be that the teacher lacks the skills to put his attitude of caring and trust into effect. As a result he comes to change his assumptions because caring and trust yield little fruit. If the student teacher does care and trust then we must, in teacher training, help him to know how his assumptions can be used to good effect within his classroom teaching. We need, in other words, to define the skills associated with caring and trust and then train teachers in such skills.

We do not at present know very much about these associated skills. But it does not seem unreasonable to suggest that empathy is likely to be one of them. If the teacher can take the perspective of the pupil, if he can understand what it is like to be the pupil, then it is much easier to care. The teacher's generalized care and trust can be given a more specific focus, thus suggesting particular lines of conduct through which the teacher can express his care and trust. It is the teacher who cannot understand the pupil and who finds it impossible to take the pupil's perspective, who is most likely to condemn the child with an uncaring attitude. To train teachers in empathy would be to help them to develop their caring attitudes.

Let us try to clarify the concept of caring and trusting in relation to the problem of punishment. This is another concept which it is extremely difficult to define. I shall take it that any unpleasant experience imposed intentionally by a teacher on a pupil is a punishment. When we, as teachers, punish a pupil we like to think that we are doing it for the good of the child. But, if we are honest, we know that we often punish the pupil as a self-defence—because what the pupil has said or done is threatening to us. It is motivated by a spirit of angry revenge. It is as if we are saying, 'I'll get my own back and more. I'll make sure you don't do that again.' Sometimes we regret such punishments later, when our anger has cooled, when our resentment has evaporated or when our sense of dignity has been restored. We recognize that we punished in haste and without rational consideration. On other occasions we punish because we are frustrated by being unable to think of a non-punishing control technique that might work. We feel that we are at our wits' end, and the punishment we mete out is motivated by desperation. It is as if we are saying, 'You've got to learn and I can't think of any other way of doing it.' Some teachers wish to retain corporal punishment in schools, not because they like it, but because it can be a 'last resort'. They are afraid of meeting situations which they feel they cannot handle. Such types of punishment are common in schools because we have learned that, when we feel under attack or helpless, punishments are effective in the sense that they subdue and silence the pupil and give us a curious sense of satisfaction that we have won the day.

Most teachers at some stage in their careers are, I think, led to punish pupils on such grounds. But the teacher who cares about and trusts his pupils recognizes that he cannot justify such punishment and seeks to find alternative means of dealing with such situations. He knows that Fritz Redl is right when he suggests three conditions which must be fulfilled before a punishment can be justified. First, the child must know that he was wrong to behave in the way he did and understand the reasons why his behaviour was at fault. Otherwise the child, though technically guilty, is really innocent. Second, the pupil should see the punishment as fair. If we punish pupils who are innocent or pupils who feel they are being treated unfairly, then the punishment cannot possibly help the child. He will react with anger, resentment and hostility. It will lead the child merely to conceal future misbehaviours or refrain from future misbehaviour simply in order to avoid the punishment. In neither case has the punishment helped the child to recognize the wrongness of the behaviour or the reasons why he did it. It has not led the child to a self-examination through which he can overcome the desire to do it again or take measures to exert some control over his desires. I once heard a teacher say to a child, 'Either you apologize to Miss Smith or you go into detention. You can take your choice.' This teacher is really saying, 'Miss Smith wants an apology. You must go and make an insincere apology to her to make her happy or I shall make life unpleasant for you by putting you into detention.' I do not see how Miss Smith or the child could possibly benefit from such a course of action.

Redl's third condition is that the punisher should care for the child. In a sense the first two conditions are implicit in this third one, for if the teacher cares, then he would not seek to impose punishments which are unjust or which cannot help the pupil. If the teacher cares, the justification of the punishment is that it provides an unpleasant experience which leads the child to work through and try to cope with the sources of the misbehaviour. It is the uncaring teacher who justifies a punishment simply on the grounds that it reduces the probability of a recurrence or has a deterrent effect.

Finally, let me say that caring for the child does not mean being sloppy, sentimental or mawkish. On the contrary, teachers with sentimental attitudes tend to exploit the pupils to satisfy their own emotional needs. Caring for children means believing in them and trusting them, from the beginning. It is this fundamental trust which allows the new teacher to move from a 'tough' initial definition of the situation to later redefinition such as that advocated by the New Romantics, as discussed in the last chapter. The difficulty is that all teachers justify what they do on the grounds that it is for the ultimate benefit of the child—'This will hurt me more than it hurts you, Jones.' Even Mr Squeers believed that he had his pupils' interests at heart. We are all such experts in convincing ourselves of our altruism when in reality we are meeting our own needs. If the teacher is to act towards the pupils for their ultimate benefit, he cannot succeed without a ruthless self-honesty about his motives and intentions, both for the present and for the future. And that, as we well know, is the hardest thing in the world.

Recommended reading

R. FARLEY, *Secondary Modern Discipline*, Black, 1960.

J. S. KOUNIN, *Discipline and Group Management in Classrooms*, Holt, Rinehart & Winston, 1970.

F. REDL, *When We Deal with Children*, Free Press, 1966.

L. STENHOUSE, (ed.): *Discipline in Schools: A Symposium*, Pergamon, 1967.

W. WALLER, *The Sociology of Teaching*, Wiley, 1932 (Science Editions, Wiley, 1965).

9 The teacher and group dynamics

In most schools the total population of pupils is divided up into various classes or forms, each containing between twenty and forty pupils. Assignment to such classes may hinge on ability or attainment measures ('streams' and 'sets') or on other bases such as the first letter of the surname or home address ('mixed-ability groups' or 'non-streaming'). It is this class which forms the major pupil unit for both teaching and for administrative purposes. In a very real sense it is the pupil's 'home' within the school. It is part of his identity—'I'm Smith of 3B'. There are many other formal groupings in school—tutorial groups, House groups, clubs and societies, sporting teams, bands, year-groups and so on; but to the pupil, and perhaps to most teachers, it is the class which is *the* important formal group in school.

Each class is a distinctive entity with a name, character and identity of its own. Teachers can communicate with one another in terms of these classes, as when they say '4C are a real shower this year' or 'I've just had a very good lesson with 2A'. Much teacher–teacher talk is at this level; generalizations about classes are a common feature of staff-room gossip. In many schools each teacher has a special responsibility for a class (the 'form-teacher') and he may well develop a special relationship with that class. Towards most of the classes he teaches he will come to have distinctive feelings of attraction or dislike. At the same time, every teacher is conscious that each class is made up of distinctive *individuals*, each of which is quite unique. Each class may have its own distinctive climate and reputation, but it is also composed of individuals who are often strikingly different from one another. 'Getting to know a class' is the way in which teachers describe *both* the process of determining the climate and characteristics of the class as a unit *and* the process of learning to differentiate each individual pupil from the rest of his class-mates.

Most of the teacher's conduct towards pupils is at these two levels

—the class and the individuals within that class. During lessons he will frequently address the class as a whole and by its collective name —'Now listen to me for a moment, 3B'—and he will also spend a lot of time asking questions of individuals, giving orders to individuals, helping individuals.

The study of group dynamics sensitizes us to the fact that each class or formal group can develop its own culture and structure. But it also leads us to a more important point, namely that each class is often made up of even smaller groups—informal groups of friends or cliques—which also have a distinctive culture and structure. Each formal group is divided into informal groups. Yet very little attention is devoted by the teacher to these informal groups or cliques, for the simple reason that their existence seems irrelevant to the teaching and administrative duties which the teacher performs. Very rarely does he make use of these groups; and the structure of the class may be such that their existence is difficult to observe. It is probably for this reason that teachers in general are very poor at predicting the clique structure of their classes (Bonney, 1947; Gronlund, 1955).

In my own Lumley study (Hargreaves, 1967) I used some of the concepts of group dynamics to interpret and analyse the conduct of pupils in their fourth year at school. First of all I tried to discover the number, size and membership of the informal groups in each class. Second, I tried to examine the culture and structure of each clique. Finally, I looked at the relationship between different cliques. It appeared that most friendship groups were confined within a single class; there were very few friendships between pupils in different classes and almost none between pupils in different year-groups. It also emerged that whilst several cliques within the class betrayed some differences in culture, most of the cliques within one class shared something of a common culture, which might then be designated the class culture.

In the A stream there were three main distinctive cliques, with relatively few links between them. A few boys did not really belong to any of these groups. Most of the cliques in this class subscribed to a distinctive set of pro-school values. They valued academic achievement and hard work; 'fooling about' and other methods of failing to work hard and pay attention to the teachers were strictly forbidden. All of them wanted to do well at school and to pass their examinations. They also valued smart appearance, approving the wearing of sports jacket, tie and trousers. All wore their hair in a short well-groomed style. Since they were keen about school, these boys pressured one another into attendance. Boys who were ill were encouraged to return as soon as possible and playing truant for an afternoon was frowned upon. None of these boys smoked or had been involved in delinquency.

In the C stream there were three distinct cliques with no links at all between them. Two of these cliques shared the same group culture, which became the dominant class culture. In essence this was the opposite of the dominant culture in the A stream. The central value of these boys was to 'have fun' in school. It was normative to avoid work as far as possible, to 'mess about'. If work was demanded then the easiest way was to copy from someone who had worked. Clothes were an important aspect of this culture, but here it is the wearing of jeans that is normative. Hair was worn long, in the style promoted by the Beatles, the Rolling Stones and other pop groups. Any boy who came to school in a tie was ridiculed. Since they did not show any enthusiasm about school, clique members were free to absent themselves from school whenever they wished; it was assumed that most boys would truant from time to time. Most of them smoked, most indulged in regular petty thieving and most had a court record.

Here, then, within a single year-group in a school drawing on a single working-class community were two classes which in many respects were two very different worlds. Each class had its own dominant informal culture, but the one was in striking opposition to the other. In each class there was one clique which most fully exemplified the class culture. In the A stream, the dominant clique consisted of six boys with several peripheral fringe members. As can be inferred from a knowledge of the group culture, they were high in attainment, high in popularity and high in social power. A second clique of four boys formed a quiet 'intellectual' clique; they had a higher average attainment but the members were not so popular or so influential as the first group. The fourth clique was the group whose culture to some degree conflicted with the dominant class culture; it was one boy in this group who espoused values which were in many respects more like those of the boys in the C stream. Not surprisingly he was, as far as the members of the other cliques were concerned, the least popular and most rejected boy in the class.

In the C stream, two of the three cliques shared the dominant anti-school culture. The third clique, on the other hand, shared the culture of the A stream. Inevitably this group was strongly rejected by most of the other boys in the class. At the same time the major cliques made use of the deviant third clique, in that they were able to copy work from them. The pro-school clique were unable to resist this since the members were simply afraid of the other two groups.

The relationship between the structure and culture of each class is particularly marked among the leaders. Adrian, the leader of the A stream, was the Head Boy of the school. Clint, the leader of the C stream, was the school's leading delinquent and trouble-maker. Adrian was the most popular as well as the most influential member of the A stream. The resources he brought to the group—his formal position as Head Boy, his academic ability, his hard work (though he never obviously worked so hard that he could be called a 'swot'), his elegant appearance, his loyalty to the school, his exemplary behaviour, his outstanding ability at football, his friendly and cheerful personality, his sense of humour—all these combined to give him the highest sociometric and social power status.

Clint's leadership in the C stream takes a very different form. One of the principal values of this group was fighting ability. The boy with the greatest fighting ability was given the title 'cock'. Clint was able to maintain this position by his swaggering, threatening display as being 'hard' or tough and by the lack of challenge to his supremacy from other boys. Being the cock, Clint exercised the most influence. But although this valued fighting ability gave him social power, it did not elicit liking from the other boys. Most boys secretly disliked him. Other resources were required for this second dimension of status, and these Clint lacked. Indeed, his cold, vindictive personality and his arbitrary aggressive outbursts alienated the boys who succumbed to his influence. Yet they dared not resist Clint's influence, for to do so would be to incur his hostility. They were influenced through fear. Thus, Clint's power, unlike that of Adrian, can be regarded as coercive and illegitimate. His followers expressed this by calling him—though not to his face—a 'bighead'. Had he been challenged and beaten in a fight, the others would have been glad. Unfortunately the only potential pretender to the title of cock was Don, who being the sociometric star in the low stream, was aware of the difficulties in being a popular cock and never issued a challenge. It was thought that Don could beat Clint in a fight. Clint seems to have thought this too, for he scrupulously avoided antagonizing Don.

The teachers at this school were not entirely ignorant of the differences in class culture between the A and C streams. Yet at the same time, their knowledge of these class and informal group cultures was at best partial. In many respects their day-to-day dealing with each class was at the level of the class as a unit or at the level of individuals. They were simply not aware of the subtleties of the dynamics of these groups because the groups were of no immediate or obvious relevance to the teacher's teaching or administrative duties. They did not have the time or the interest that I as a researcher had to discover or work out the culture or structure of these groups. Nor did they have a systematic knowledge of group dynamics; they lacked the conceptual language which would sensitize them to ask certain questions, to search for answers to these questions and to frame what they could have observed in a particular form. So although the complex world of the detailed group dynamics was for the most part hidden from the teacher, the impact of the culture of these groups was to be felt constantly. From the teacher's point of view, this complexity became reduced to two simple facts: the A stream was a 'good' class and the C stream was a 'bad' class; and the A stream contained a few 'bad lads' and the C stream contained some boys who were 'quite good'. In other words, the teachers ignored those aspects of pupil life which did not appear to have any immediate relevance to them. When the impact of the informal group culture became apparent, it was conceptualized entirely from the teacher's perspective in traditional teacher language.

This tendency of teachers to see pupil conduct in particular ways is best exemplified in the teacher's concept of *leadership*. Most teachers interpret leadership as being of a particular kind; they think of generals or officers in armies; of politicians; of community leaders. In school, a leader among pupils is, to the teacher, someone who shares essentially the same values as the teacher, who shows what the teacher defines as a sense of responsibility, who accepts the authority structure of the school. Leaders, in other words, are the kinds of pupil that one appoints a prefect or to whom one gives a responsible and privileged position. I once visited a school, very like Lumley, to do some research on group dynamics and leadership. I explained what I was doing to the headmaster, who pointed out that I need only visit the A stream. 'All the leaders are in the A stream,' he said. 'There are no leaders in the other streams.'

To the social psychologist, as we have seen, leadership does not consist in the possession of particular traits or in the commitment to a particular set of values. Clint was a leader just as Adrian was a leader. Both exercised a high degree of social influence. Yet the teachers tended to think of Adrian as a leader whereas Clint was regarded as a 'thug' or a 'troublemaker', which tended to obscure the very real leadership he exercised in his class. His leadership was occasionally recognized in that he was sometimes referred to as the '*ring*-leader of the trouble-makers'. This interesting concept suggests that Clint's leadership is a perverted form of leadership rather than 'real' leadership. So teachers ensure that those pupils who share certain values are demonstrating a capacity for leadership and ensure that they are given formal leadership positions. When pupils are allowed to elect a class monitor or a prefect, the teacher is often ready to veto the pupil elected on the grounds that he 'is the wrong type who will never make a leader'. To the social psychologist, such a teacher is saying 'The class must not elect a pupil who is in fact their informal leader, but must elect the pupil who meets my definition of leadership and I do not care whether his status among the informal group is very low indeed.' Given this teacher perspective, it is hardly surprising that in a recent British study, Evan-Wong and Bagley (1970) found that there was no correlation at all between class leaders

235

nominated by teachers and the actual sociometric leaders. Most teachers simply do not see that they have to make an imaginative leap if they are to capture the pupil perspective and be in a position to perceive each pupil as other pupils see him.

The teacher's failure to make use of informal groups in his work, his ensuing ignorance of the dynamics of these groups, and his conception of leadership give the teacher a restricted and partial understanding of pupils. The teacher frequently believes that it is essential for him to understand each pupil as an individual, but he underestimates the impact and importance of the informal group. The individual pupil is indeed an individual—but he is an individual-within-a-group. He contributes to that group and sustains its culture; he is also affected by that group and his identity, values and conduct cannot be separated in any sharp sense from the group. The teacher who cannot or does not recognize this is liable to be involved in misperceptions and misunderstandings, which can then become the basis for actions that can have unintended and unfortunate consequences for teacher and pupil. Thus if the teacher appoints as a monitor or prefect a pupil who is well below average in informal status, then the rest of the pupils may actively resist the prefect's attempts to influence them and the prefect's informal status may decline even further. But the teacher may be unaware of these consequences on the prefect's informal status and may interpret the hostility to the prefect merely as a confirmation that many of his pupils are 'difficult'. At Lumley, to take another example, the teachers of the low streams did not seem to recognize that when they approved with glowing praise the behaviour of the minority of 'good' pupils, they were in fact alienating them still further from the majority of the class by emphasizing their failure to live up to the dominant informal anti-school values. Further, in punishing the outstandingly 'bad' boys, the teachers were not simply disapproving or controlling unacceptable classroom behaviour, but they were also confirming their high status in anti-school groups. Another example concerns the 'ripple effect' in classrooms (Kounin & Gump, 1958). When the teacher disciplines a particular child, it is often done in the presence of other children. Although the teacher's disciplinary action may be directed at the one pupil, there is an effect on the other pupils as well as on the target pupil. It is like the ripple effect caused by dropping a pebble in a pond—the whole water surface is affected, not just the point of impact. Gnagey (1960) showed that the peer group status of the target child in a disciplinary incident can influence the way in which the other pupils, who are subject to the ripple effect, perceive the teacher. When the target pupil submitted to the teacher, the teacher was seen as more powerful than when the pupil defied the teacher, but the effect was much stronger when the target pupil was of high rather than low status. When the high status pupil submitted, the teacher was also seen as more fair and more expert and the pupils actually learned more from the lesson, than when the high status pupil defied the teacher. There were no such differences between the submission and defiance conditions when the target pupil was of low status among the pupils.

The disjunction between teacher and pupil perspectives on events in the classroom, and the failure of the teacher to take into account the importance of informal groupings within the pupil perspective, is amply illustrated by an analysis of transferring a pupil from one stream to another. This is an almost universal procedure in schools which group by ability/attainment. At the end of a term or school year, the teachers decide to 'promote' pupils of the highest attainment into a higher stream and to 'demote' those of the poorest attainment into a lower stream. The teacher's major concern is with the academic development of pupils. The pupil who is promoted is perceived as 'not being sufficiently stretched' in his present class, and the one who is demoted is perceived as 'being out of his depth' in his present class. To the teacher, these academic judgments serve as adequate grounds to justify transfer from one stream to another. In this the teacher is devoting his exclusive attention to the formal groupings and to the official, academic criteria for assignment to classes. The pupil, on the other hand, may well be concerned with the *informal* ties that have grown up between himself and some of his classmates who have become his friends. He knows that if he is moved into another stream his opportunity for interaction with his friends will be severely diminished and that he will be able to maintain these friendships in out-of-class contexts and activities. There is a high probability that if he changes classes he will have to change friends.

A few years ago I asked a group of highly experienced teachers what they would say to a pupil to whom they had to break the news of a stream transfer. What the teachers said to the pupil was almost entirely concerned with the academic aspects of the transfer. When the pupil was promoted to a higher stream, typical comments by the teachers were:

> Congratulations on a good year's work. You are doing so well that the staff have recommended that you should be put in the A stream where you will be able to make even more progress. This should mean that eventually you will do well.

> Well, you have done extremely well this year and as a reward for your hard work and conscientiousness it's been decided to promote you to the A stream. As long as you maintain your present progress and attitude to work we all expect you to do very well.

237

You are to be moved into the A stream because the work will be more interesting for you and you will enjoy it more.

You have been promoted because we consider that you have the natural ability to progress in the top stream, but you must work hard in order to justify your promotion, because pure natural ability is not enough; diligence is also a necessary requirement and ingredient for success.

You are able enough and have done well enough to do very well in the A stream, so you are going up. We expect great things from you there.

Well done. But I don't think you are being extended in the B stream and feel that the competition in the A stream will be to your benefit.

In their remarks, these teachers express a congratulatory note; they are pleased with the pupil concerned. The promotion to a higher stream is offered as a reward. Note, too, how many of the teachers emit strong expectations of future success—a good illustration of the ways in which teachers communicate expectations that can create self-fulfilling prophecies. Most of the teachers seem to believe that the pupil will react to the news in the way *they* do, namely as good news that is to be accepted joyfully. A few show indications that the pupil may be a little apprehensive, so they emphasize that the pupil will enjoy his new class and that the transfer is in his own interest. Only one teacher in twenty, however, actually raised the topic of the peer group in his comments.

Next term you are to join the A class. You will find some nice boys in that class as friends and I hope you will find the work interesting.

Ninety-five per cent of the teachers never mentioned the question of friends.

When the pupil was 'demoted' to a lower stream, typical comments were:

Bad news for you. You're going into the C stream. I think you could have avoided this if you'd worked harder. Make a fresh start and perhaps you'll be promoted later.

I think you'll be happier in another class. Some of the work here doesn't seem to interest you. I'm going to put you in a class where there are kinds of work which may suit you more.

I'm sorry, but we've given you every chance to prove yourself. You seem to want to chat rather than work, so we have decided next term that you must go in Mr ——'s class. Perhaps there you will pull your socks up.

I know you've found it difficult to keep up with some of the work this year and as a result have been a little unhappy. Next year we are going to let you work in a class where you work a little slower and I am sure find things a little easier.

You seem to be struggling in this class, so we are going to put you in another class where the work isn't so hard. You should be able to do very well in this class and be at the top of it.

We are moving you to Mr ——'s class next term. He is organizing some projects that should interest you and we think you will enjoy yourself and do well.

The teachers' reactions can be divided into two main groups. In the first, the teacher commiserates with the pupil; in the second, the teacher treats the transfer as a punishment. In the first case, the teacher looks for some 'compensation' (a more interesting curriculum, the possibility of being top of the class) to minimize the impact of the news; in the second case, the teacher takes the opportunity to preach a short sermon to the pupil. All the teachers betray that they know that the pupil will see the transfer as 'bad news', as an occasion for disappointment or distress. Only one teacher in sixty mentioned the question of friends:

We are hoping to help you get down to work by moving you to the C class. Do you have any friends there? Do you know what work they have been doing there? I think you could do well with them.

It is clear that in both cases the majority of these experienced teachers paid little attention to the potential significance of informal friendships on the occasion of a transfer from one class to another.

The teachers were then told that the pupil looked very unhappy at the news, and were asked to list possible reasons for this. A very large number of possible explanations was offered, and one third of these were related to the question of friendship. This demonstrates that the teachers are to some degree aware of the problem for the pupil—but they do not take it into account until they are confronted by an unusual situation, such as a child's overt unhappiness. It is interesting that when the pupil was promoted, loss of friends was cited as a possible explanation of the pupil's unhappiness by 70 per cent of the teachers. But when the pupil was demoted, only 13 per cent of the teachers thought loss of friends a possible explanation. In this case the teachers thought 'a sense of disappointment' the most likely explanation.

It seems that most teachers do not take the topic of informal friendship groups into account in any systematic way. They are, of course, fully aware of the deleterious effects that a change of formal grouping can have on informal groups, for they know that a group of 'troublemakers' can often be effectively broken up by assigning the members to different classes. But in this case it is the nature of the friendship that is held to constitute the problem and it is natural that the teacher must take it into account in framing a solution. But for much of the time the significance of these friendship groups remains hidden from the teacher. In the Lumley study, teachers correctly perceived that an upper stream pupil could be induced to work harder under threat of demotion to a lower stream, for this was a threat to the pupil's self-image as 'bright' and 'hard-working'. They did not recognize that there was an additional incentive arising from the informal group life, whereby upper stream members wanted to remain with their friends and were extremely anxious to avoid being placed in a lower stream dominated by boys with incompatible values and norms. To the upper stream pupil, the lower streams were negative normative reference groups. With respect to the lower streams, the teachers believed that promotion to a higher stream was a reward for academic merit, and they tended to assume that the pupils in the lower stream would take the same view as themselves and as the upper stream pupils. They tended not to recognize that most of the lower stream boys treated the upper streams as negative normative reference groups and would actively avoid such a transfer on these grounds alone—even to the extent of intentionally under-performing in examinations to avert such an outcome. The teachers, locked in their own perspective, tended to misperceive the poor examination performance in academic terms, such as lack of ability, which was in some cases quite erroneous.

We can see, then, that although the typical teacher has some knowledge of dynamics of the informal groups in his class, this knowledge is partial and unsystematic. It is knowledge which is acquired in a piece-meal fashion—casually, incidentally, even accidentally as part of his work with the pupils. The implication of our discussion so far is that if the teacher had more extensive and more systematic knowledge, then he would be able to avoid making a number of errors of perception, judgment and action. A teacher who possessed such knowledge would presumably be able to answer the following five basic questions about a class of pupils.

1. What is the composition of the sub-groups or cliques within the class? Which pupils belong to which cliques?

2. What is the culture of each clique? What aspects of conduct are subject to the values and norms of each clique?

3. What is the structure of these cliques? How cohesive are they?

Who are the leaders? Who are the most popular (sociometric status)? Who are the most influential (social power status)? Who are the low status members?

4. What is the relationship between cliques? Do they overlap in membership? Do they share a common culture? Is there a hierarchy of cliques? Is there evidence of hostility between cliques?

5. Which pupils do not belong to a clique? Are they aspirants to a clique but for some reason lack the qualifications for acceptance? Are they actively rejected by members? Are they socially isolated because they do not want to belong to a clique? Do they belong to another clique outside the class?

These questions are, to anyone with a knowledge of group dynamics, fairly elementary. They are important initial questions if one accepts the assumption that we cannot understand the behaviour of a class or of the individual pupils within it unless we know something of the nature of the groups. Thus it would seem to be a sensible idea for teachers to study group dynamics. At the end of a suitable course the teacher will be in a position to ask the elementary questions posed above.

Yet presumably in giving teachers a course in group dynamics we do not merely want to provide them with the intellectual knowledge and skill required to ask the questions. We are, presumably, aiming beyond this, towards sensitizing teachers to recognizing the problems in the group behaviour of children and to asking the right questions at the right time, and towards providing them with methods whereby they can also answer the questions and apply what they know usefully within the classroom situation. If we cannot do this, then teachers can with justice claim that the knowledge is useless. I have met many teachers with training in the social sciences applied to education who believe that this training made them more sensitive teachers. I do not know to what extent they are right, but in general I am sceptical. Earlier I have mentioned what I call the Sociological Myth, where I suggest that informing teachers of the powerful influence of home environment on school performance may lead teachers to feel and believe that they can do little to mitigate the effects of environment on socially deprived children. In consequence the teachers lower their expectations so that the children do indeed reach the low levels of attainment predicted by sociological research. If there is any truth in the Sociological Myth, then it is the reverse of what training in sociology of education was intended to achieve. I am likewise sceptical that a knowledge of group dynamics will in itself sensitize a teacher to the group dynamics in the classrooms. Some teachers do have a 'natural' understanding of classroom group dynamics, though they cannot usually couch their understanding in technical language. Training in group dynamics might help them by allowing them to conceptualize their 'natural' knowledge more adequately and even to extend their skilled use of this knowledge. It may, on the other hand, have the reverse effect, as in the proverbial case of the centipede and his legs. To assume that a training in group dynamics for teachers without this 'natural' knowledge will in some way make them 'better' teachers seems quite unwarranted.

I shall postpone for the moment the question of the means by which the teacher furnishes answers to questions about group dynamics that he might want to ask. On the assumption the teacher possesses this knowledge, what practical use can he make of it? We can illustrate some applications of group dynamics in the classroom by taking three problem situations.

First problem

Two pupils in the class appear to lack friends and do not belong to any clique. Pupil A arrived in the class in the middle of the school year, her family having recently moved into the district She is a shy, quiet girl. Whilst she does not seem particularly unhappy, she rarely participates in lessons and wanders about on her own outside the classroom. Pupil B, on the other hand, is a *rejectee* rather than a *neglectee*. He 'hangs around' on the fringe of several cliques, but his noisy and aggressive manner hinders his acceptance by other pupils. He is constantly trying to bring attention to himself and to assert himself over others.

Clearly these two pupils require very different help from the teacher. Pupil A, the neglectee, has become socially isolated as a result of her late arrival in the class combined with her retiring personality. The teacher can help by providing greater opportunities for her to interact with other pupils, who can then come to recognize her qualities and thus absorb her into the informal group life. The teacher can ensure that she is able to display her talents to other pupils by placing her with appropriate pupils in 'group work' or project sessions; he can ask one or two pupils to help to familiarize her with the school, its physical layout and its routines; he can make sure that she is introduced to pupils who live close to her home. Pupil B presents much greater problems, because his attempts to join groups have been rebuffed and he has incurred the hostility of many pupils. His lack of social skills with and sensitivity towards other pupils cannot easily be cured by the teacher Any attempt by the teacher to make the pupil feel socially secure and valued are fraught with danger. For instance, if the teacher gives him a responsible job, such as a class monitor, then there is the possibility that he will carry out these duties badly and in addition this may exacerbate his tendency to be 'bossy' towards other pupils. There are no easy answers here: the diagnosis is easy and the cure is difficult. The teacher will have to experiment with different methods and be prepared to face the fact that no short-term solution is to be found.

Second problem

The pupil is the leader of an anti-school clique within the class. He is an able boy who obviously has the potential to do well in school. He is intelligent enough to be able to avoid direct confrontations with the teacher—yet the teacher knows that he is a powerful influence behind the disruptive and non-co-operative conduct of many of his followers. The teacher wishes, in the interests of the boy himself as well as in the interests of the class as a whole, that he should take a more favourable attitude to school and exercise a more positive influence on his friends. The teacher's knowledge of group dynamics informs him that he cannot expect such a change unless such pro-school behaviour will bring the pupil greater satisfactions than his present conduct and his present leadership of the anti-school group. How can the teacher effect this change? It is obvious that the leader will not be allowed by other group members to deviate from central group norms without losing his leadership position. The teacher with a knowledge of group dynamics knows, in theory, that it will probably be ineffective to lecture the pupil in private and counsel him to mend his ways, for group pressures to conformity will soon reassert themselves against any resolutions made by the boy, however, sincerely, to be a better pupil. The teacher can recognize that although the boy's anti-school behaviour seems irrational to him, to the boy it is rational, given that he wishes to retain his membership in and leadership of the group. A good example is given in Evan Hunter's *The Blackboard Jungle*. The teacher, Rick, is producing the school's Christmas show. In rehearsal, he finds that the leading anti-school pupil, Gregory Miller, is surprisingly co-operative. In the following English lesson Rick finds that Miller has reverted to his more usual pattern of behaviour.

> Rick blinked at Miller, not able to understand the change in the boy. Was this the same helpful co-operative kid who'd worked out the speech rhythms in the auditorium just a period ago? This wiseacre who had just now initiated a new series of jibes against the teacher? He couldn't believe it, and so he let it pass because he couldn't understand it. But in the days that followed he learned a basic fact and he also learned to live by it.
>
> He learned that Miller formulated all the rules of this game, and that the rules were complex and unbending. And just as Miller drew an arbitrary line before the start of each fifth-period

243

class—a line over which he would not step—he also drew a line which separated the show from anything academic.

It was a confusing situation. It was confusing because Rick really did get along with Miller at rehearsals. The student–teacher relationship seemed to vanish completely. They were just two people working for a common goal, and Miller took direction and offered helpful suggestions, and stood by shamefacedly whenever Rick blew his top about a bit of stage business or a fluffed line. Rick valued the boy's participation in the show, and most of all the way Miller led the sextet, helped Rick mould it into a unified, smoothly functioning acting and singing machine.

And then rehearsal would be over, and in class Miller drew his line again, and he pushed right up to that line, never stepping over it, always baiting Rick so far, always annoying him until Rick trespassed onto Miller's side of the line and Miller was faced with the choice of retreating or shoving over on to Rick's side of the line, and that he would never do. . . .

The English class was another matter. The other boys in the class considered English a senseless waste of time, a headless chicken, a blob without a goal. Miller may have felt the same way, though it was impossible to know just what he felt. But he sensed that approval lay in disorder, that leadership lay in misbehaviour. And so he drew his line, and he drew his second line, the line that told Rick, 'The show's one thing Chief, but English is another. So don't 'spect me to go kissin' your ass in class.'

This teacher discovered a group dynamics principle for himself. But how could Rick change the situation? He did not find a solution, nor does our present knowledge of group dynamics suggest any easy solutions to problems such as this. In short, a knowledge that the leader of a group is unlikely to adopt behaviour that is the opposite of that prescribed by group norms is largely *negative* knowledge—knowledge which tells us where solutions are not to be found, rather than where they are to be found. This may be no mean contribution of the group dynamics approach when one considers the amount of time spent by teachers in trying to solve problems by methods which are almost certainly doomed to failure from the beginning. But, quite rightly, the teacher wants positive solutions to his problems. In general such positive solutions are not available. Most research in group dynamics is not based on children's groups in school but on students in psychological laboratories and on small groups in industrial organizations. Whilst much of this research on other groups has yielded principles of group dynamics which can be applied to classroom groups, there is a desperate lack of research geared to analysing classroom problems with a group dynamics component, to examining the range of possible solutions to such problems, and to assessing the relative difficulty, merit and success of such solutions.

Third problem

Within the class there are two cliques which display a high degree of mutual hostility. The effect is to create friction and disruptiveness in lessons, often of a petty nature but (to the teacher) highly irritating. Further, the teacher's attempt to give the class as a whole a sense of community and solidarity are constantly vitiated. It is here that the important experimental work of Sherif (1966) becomes relevant. In a series of experiments, a number of white, Protestant, middle-class boys aged twelve were taken to a summer camp. The boys were unaware that they were the subjects of an experiment, and were not acquainted before the experiment. For a while the boys lived together, during which period friendships developed. The boys were then divided into two groups, living in separate cabins, in such a way that the majority of each boy's original friends were now in the other group. Within a short time all the boys made new friends within their own group. As they lived, worked and played together, each group developed its own norms, jargon, jokes, secrets and nicknames, and also a status structure with leaders and lieutenants. At this point, by means of games and other activities, the two groups were given a competitive relationship. This became associated with marked in-group solidarity and hostility towards the other group. Sherif then tried to restore the two groups to a friendly and co-operative relationship. Several ploys, such as the making of appeals for co-operation or arranging conferences between the two leaders, and including attempts to maximize contact between the two groups, failed to achieve this goal. Co-operation and friendly relationships developed only when the two groups were brought together under what Sherif calls a superordinate goal, by which the groups had to co-operate if either group was to achieve its goal. For example, Sherif arranged an 'accidental' breakdown of a truck on a picnic and a failure of the water supply, problems which could be solved only when the groups co-operated. The result was a reduction in the hostility between the groups and a restoration of friendship ties between members of the two different groups.

Once again, the teacher learns that some potential solutions—lecturing the two groups about co-operation, bringing the two groups together, etc.—are unlikely to bring much success in reducing the inter-group conflict. Yet the invention of situations in which a

245

superordinate goal can be introduced will undoubtedly require considerable ingenuity on the part of the teacher.

The ability to develop solutions to situations in the light of the teacher's knowledge of the dynamics of classroom groups presupposes that the teacher is in a position to acquire such knowledge in relation to the particular groups in his class. Research reports make the evidence look obvious and easy to acquire, but the researcher's sole function in the classroom is to explore the group dynamics and to this end he is able to use very sophisticated and time-consuming techniques. To the practising teacher, who is already very busy with the myriad problems of doing his job to the best of his ability, the group dynamics of the class are by no means obvious as he scans the thirty or so faces before him in the classroom or on the corridor or on the playground. He simply does not have a great deal of time to devote to the systematic investigation of the group dynamics. Moreover many of the measuring devices—sociometric and social power tests, questionnaires, interviews—are not always easy to use, analyse or interpret. Let me discuss a single example, the sociometric test. In its classical form, the investigator asks the pupils to nominate others with whom he would like to associate in certain situations such as the classroom, in the playground or on a holiday. Often the results are then plotted into a sociogram which displays the clique structure and the isolates. Strictly speaking, this is an improper use of the test. It is true that the sociometric test reveals the popularity structure of the class, both the popular 'stars' and the isolates who receive no choices at all. Yet the test is asking the pupils to make *ideal* choices. Those who have many friends will probably nominate them in the test. But those who have few friends or who have friends they do not like particularly will often choose pupils whom they admire but with whom they do not in fact associate. In this sense some of these choices are unrealistic, and the sociogram misrepresents the *actual* structure of social relationships within the form.

For the most part the majority of teachers will need to rely on observation for their knowledge. Yet this is a dangerous method. The teacher will find it difficult to observe in any systematic way. Rather, his observation must be incidental to his main task of teaching. It is very easy, therefore, for the teacher to jump to unjustified conclusions on the basis of such slender and casual observations. Moreover, John Holt's observation, noted in Chapter 6, that children tend to change when they are aware that they are being observed, makes the task doubly difficult. However, there is still much the teacher can do to enhance his own observations. In the assignment of places in the class, for example, if the pupils are allowed to select their own seats, most of the pupils will choose to sit near their friends. A close observation of seat selection will show that some pupils, usually the leaders, will take the initiative in the selection and lower status members of the group will tend to sit around these pupils. Again, a teacher on playground duty—usually regarded as an exceptionally boring chore—can use his time both for observing who is playing with whom, which pupils are exercising influence, and, if the teacher is prepared to watch and listen closely, the culture of these groups. The playground has the advantage that in this situation many children behave more 'naturally' than they do inside the school buildings. Thus the peer culture of the local environment can be revealed, for instance the significance of physical prowess and fighting ability among boys in certain areas. Whilst most teachers treat fighting incidents merely as something that must be stopped, an alert student of group dynamics may be helped to extend his knowledge through such incidents. In this respect, it is valuable if the teacher is familiar with studies of group dynamics which have studied young people *outside* school, such as the Sherifs' *Reference Groups* (1964), Wilmott's *Adolescent Boys in East London* (1966) or James Patrick's *A Glasgow Gang Observed* (1973).

Learning the principles of group dynamics does not in itself give the teacher the capacity to capture a pupil's perspective as a group member. In my view the ability of a teacher to capture the perspective of the individual-pupil-within-his-group is essentially the same ability as that required to capture any aspect of the pupil perspective, namely empathic understanding. If this is so, then it suggests that if teachers are to be taught the principles of group dynamics an essential part of their education would be training in empathy or sensitivity.

At present psychologists have done relatively little in the area of sensitivity training. The most important exception is the T-group approach, where the group studies itself in order to improve the sensitivity and social skills of its members (Bradford, Gibb & Benne, 1964). Some attempt has been made to organize T-group courses specially for teachers (Ottaway, 1966). A second exception is role-playing, where persons play the roles of others with whom they are likely to interact in order to improve sensitivity. Although this technique has been incorporated into a few conferences for teachers and headteachers, it is still not widely used nor has its effectiveness for teachers been assessed. A third approach, of which we are likely to see more in the coming years, is typified by the research of Jecker, Maccoby & Breitrose (1965) who have shown that teachers can be trained to judge accurately the facial expressions of pupils who are learning what they are being taught. A fourth development is the attempt by interaction analysis experts to use their methods to help teachers to achieve insight into and to obtain feedback on their own teaching behaviour (Amidon & Hough, 1967, Part III).

Unfortunately there are many trends within teacher education against such innovations. Colleges of Education, especially since the introduction of the B.Ed. degree, and University Departments of Education are still predominantly concerned with academic or subject training rather than the social skills of teaching. Even in 'education' courses, the stress is on the traditional educational disciplines of history, philosophy, psychology and sociology. Further, advanced diplomas and Master's degree courses in education are even more concerned with these and associated disciplines. It is the teachers who take these courses who tend to become the next generation of teacher trainers in the Colleges of Education and thus the academic tradition is perpetuated at the expense of the development of techniques designed to improve the social skills of teaching, which are assumed to be acquired through experience This is, in my view, a frightening abrogation of responsibility, yet University Departments of Education are under no pressure to change, for their clients are either students in initial training, who are not sure what is the most appropriate training for them, or experienced teachers (intending to leave schools for posts in Colleges of Education) competing for a place on the over-subscribed advanced courses whose academic content meets the needs of future lecturers in academic subjects. Teaching is a social process, yet we give so little guidance to teachers during training in the necessary social skills, and once they enter the profession they are left to achieve success in the isolation of the classroom on the basis of their 'natural' insight and skills, or, as in too many cases, without the necessary help being either available or acknowledged as important or essential. It is time that teachers began to recognize their own needs in this respect and relinquish their belief that every teacher is and should be self-taught—and that if he seems to be unable to teach himself then he is unteachable and must be tolerated as an unsuccessful member of the profession If they could take this step, then perhaps teacher trainers, the organizers of courses and conferences, and the staff of University Departments of Education would pay some attention and try to meet this need in addition to continuing their essential task of stimulating the academic study of education and curriculum development.

Recommended reading

DAVID H. HARGREAVES, *Social Relations in a Secondary School*, Routledge & Kegan Paul, 1967.

M. NORTHWAY, 'Outsiders', *Sociometry*, vol. 7, 1944, pp. 10–25.

J. PATRICK, *A Glasgow Gang Observed*, Eyre Methuen, 1973.

M. & C. W. SHERIF, *Reference Groups*, Harper, 1964 (Eyre Methuen, 1973).

Bibliographical index

Figures in square brackets refer to page numbers in the present book

ABRAVANEL, E. 'A psychological analysis of the concept of role', unpublished master's thesis, Swarthmore College, 1962, quoted in Brown, R., *Social Psychology*, Free Press, 1965. [30]

ALLEN, E. A. 'Attitudes to school and teachers in a secondary modern school', *British Journal of Educational Psychology*, vol. 31, 1961, pp. 106–9. [131]

AMIDON, E. J. & HOUGH, J. B. *Interaction Analysis: Theory Research and Application*, Addison-Wesley, 1967. [161, 247]

AMIS, KINGSLEY *I Want It Now*, Jonathan Cape, 1968. [84ff]

ANDERSON, H. H. & BREWER, H. M. 'Studies of teachers' classroom personalities', *Applied Psychology Monographs*, Stanford University Press, 1945, 1946. [115]

ARGYLE, M. *Social Interaction*, Methuen, 1966. [86]

ARGYLE, M. *The Psychology of Interpersonal Behaviour*, Penguin, 1967. [81]

ASCH, S. E. 'Forming impressions of personality', *Journal of Abnormal and Social Psychology*, vol. 41, 1946, pp. 258–90. [21f, 28]

ASCH, S. E. 'Effects of group pressure upon the modification and distortion of judgments' (1951), in Cartwright, D. & Zander, A. *Group Dynamics*, Tavistock, 1960 (2nd ed.). [95f]

ASCH, S. E. *Social Psychology*, Prentice-Hall, 1952. [70f]

BARBIANA, SCHOOL OF *Letter to a Teacher*, Penguin, 1970. [144, 156f, 161]

BARKER, R. G. & WRIGHT, H. F. *One Boy's Day*, Harper, 1951. [145]

BARKER LUNN, J. C. *Streaming in the Primary School*, N.F.E.R., 1970. [107f, 129, 164, 195]

BARNES, D. *et al. Language, the Learner and the School*, Penguin, 1969. [175]

BARNES, D. 'Language and learning in the classroom', *Journal of Curriculum Studies*, vol. 3, 1971, pp. 27–38. [176]

BARTLETT, F. C. *Remembering*, Cambridge, 1932. [19]

BECKER, H. S. 'Social class variations in pupil–teacher relationships', *Journal of Educational Sociology*, vol. 25, 1952, pp. 451–65. [204]

249

BERG, L. *Risinghill: Death of a Comprehensive School*, Penguin, 1968. [50f]

BERGER, P. L. *Invitation to Sociology*, 1963 (Penguin, 1966). [65]

BERNSTEIN, B. 'On the classification and framing of educational knowledge', in M. F. D. Young (ed.) *Knowledge and Control*, Collier-Macmillan, 1971. [185, 191, 193, 200]

BERNSTEIN, B., ELVIN, H. L. & PETERS, R. S. 'Ritual in education', in Cosin (1971). [196f]

BIDDLE, B. J. & THOMAS, E. J. (eds) *Role Theory: Concepts and Research*, Wiley, 1966. [61, 69]

BION, W. R. *Experiences in Groups*, Tavistock, 1961. [110]

BLISHEN, E. *Roaring Boys*, Thames & Hudson, 1955. [221f]

BLISHEN, E. *This Right Soft Lot*, Thames & Hudson, 1969. [226f]

BLUMER, H. 'Sociological analysis and the "variable" ', *American Sociological Review*, vol. 21, 1956, pp. 683–90. [7]

BLUMER, H. 'Society as symbolic interaction', in Rose (1962). [7]

BLUMER, H. 'Sociological implications of the thought of George Herbert Mead', *American Journal of Sociology*, vol. 71, 1966, pp. 535–48. [7, 14, 16]

BLYTH, W. A. C. *English Primary Education*, Routledge & Kegan Paul, 1965. [116]

BONNEY, M. E. 'Relationships between social success, family size, socio-economic home background, and intelligence among school children in grades III to V', *Sociometry*, vol. 7, 1944, pp. 26–39. [99]

BONNEY, M. E. 'Sociometric study of agreement between teacher judgements and student choices, in regard to the number of friends possessed by high school students', *Sociometry*, vol. 10, 1947, pp. 133–46. [232)

BRADFORD, L. P., GIBB, J. R. & BENNE, K. D. *T-group Theory and Laboratory Method*, Wiley, 1964. [247]

BROOKOVER, W. B., THOMAS, S. & PATTERSON, A. 'Self-concept of ability and scholastic achievement', *Sociology of Education*, vol. 37, 1964, pp. 271–8. [37]

BROPHY, J. E. & GOOD, T. L. 'Teachers' communication of differential expectations for children's classroom performance', *Journal of Educational Psychology*, vol. 61, 1970, pp. 365–74. [36]

BROWN, R. *Social Psychology*, Free Press, 1965.

BRUNER, J. S. *Toward a Theory of Instruction*, Norton, 1966. [145]

BRUNER, J. S., GOODNOW, J. J. & AUSTIN, G. A. *A Study of Thinking*, Wiley, 1956. [29]

BURSTALL, C. 'French in the primary school: some early findings', *Journal of Curriculum Studies*, vol. 2, 1970, pp. 48–58. [35]

BUSH, R. N. 'A study of student–teacher relationships', *Journal of Educational Research*, vol. 35, 1942, pp. 645–56. [131]

BUSH, R. N. *The Teacher-Pupil Relationship*, Prentice-Hall, 1954. [122, 127]

BYRNE, D. 'The influence of propinquity and opportunities for interaction on classroom relationships', *Human Relations*, vol. 14, 1961, pp. 63–9. [181]

BYRNE, D. & BUEHLER, J. A. 'A note on the influence of propinquity on acquaintanceships', *Journal of Abnormal and Social Psychology*, vol. 51, 1955, pp. 147–8. [181]

CARTWRIGHT, D. & ZANDER, A. *Group Dynamics*, Tavistock, 1963 and subsequent editions. [110]

CICOUREL, A. V. 'Basic and normative rules in the negotiation of status and role', in Dreitzel, H. P. (ed.), *Recent Sociology No. 2*, Macmillan, 1970, and in Cicourel, A. V. *Cognitive Sociology*, Penguin, 1973. [69]

CLAIBORN, W. L. 'Expectancy effect in the classroom: a failure to replicate', *Journal of Educational Psychology*, vol. 60, 1969, pp. 377–83. [35]

COHEN, A. K. *Delinquent Boys*, Free Press, 1955. [3]

COOLEY, C. H. *Human Nature and the Social Order*, Scribner, 1902. [5]

COSIN, B. R. *et al. School and Society: A Sociological Reader*, Routledge & Kegan Paul, 1971.

COULSON, M. 'Role: a redundant concept in sociology?', in Jackson, J. A. (ed.), *Role: Sociological Studies No. 4*, Cambridge University Press, 1972. [69]

CRUTCHFIELD, R. S. 'Conformity and character', *American Psychologist*, vol. 10, 1955, pp. 191–8. [96]

DAHLKE, H. O. 'Determinants of sociometric relations among children in elementary schools', *Sociometry*, vol. 16, 1953, pp. 327–38. [99]

DOUGLAS, J. W. B. *The Home and the School*, MacGibbon & Kee, 1964. [41, 129]

ELLIS, H. F. *The World of A. J. Wentworth, B.A.*, Penguin, 1964. [222f]

EMERSON, R. M. 'Power-dependence relations', *American Sociological Review*, vol. 27, 1962, pp. 31–40. [100]

EVANS, K. M. *Sociometry and Education*, Routledge & Kegan Paul, 1962. [99]

FARLEY, R. *Secondary Modern Discipline*, Black, 1960. [230]

FINLAYSON, D. S. & COHEN, L. 'The teacher's role: a comparative study of the conceptions of college of education students and head teachers', *British Journal of Educational Psychology*, vol. 37, 1967, pp. 22–31. [59f]

FLANDERS, N. A. 'Teacher influence in the classroom', in Amidon & Hough (1967). [227]

FORD, J. *Social Class and the Comprehensive School*, Routledge & Kegan Paul, 1969. [188]

FORSTER, E. M. *Aspects of the Novel*, 1927 (Penguin, 1962). [24]

FROM, F. *Perception of Other People*, Columbia University Press, 1971. [27, 43]

GETZELS, J. & GUBA, E. G. 'Social behaviour and the administrative process', *School Review*, vol. 65, 1957, pp. 423–41. [66]

GETZELS, J. & THELEN, H. A. 'The classroom as a unique social system', in Henry, N. B. (1960). [56]

GIBB, C. A. 'The principles and traits of leadership', *Journal of Abnormal and Social Psychology*, vol. 42, 1947, pp. 267–84. See also Gibb, C. A., *Leadership*, Penguin Modern Psychology Series, 1969. [105]

GNAGEY, W. J. 'Effects on classmates of a deviant student's power and response to a teacher-exerted control technique', *Journal of Educational Psychology*, vol. 51, 1960, pp. 1–8. [236]

GOFFMAN, E. *The Presentation of Self in Everyday Life*, Doubleday Anchor, 1959. [76ff, 86]

GOFFMAN, E. *Asylums*, Doubleday Anchor, 1961 (Penguin, 1971). [160]

GOFFMAN, E. *Encounters*, Bobbs-Merrill, 1961. [66]

GOFFMAN, E. *Behavior in Public Places*, Free Press, 1963. [80, 152]

GOLD, M. 'Power in the classroom', *Sociometry*, vol. 21, 1958, pp. 50–60. [104]

GOODMAN, P. *Compulsory Miseducation*, Horizon Press, 1962 (Penguin, 1972). [187]

GOULDNER, A. W. *The Coming Crisis of Western Sociology*, Heinemann, 1970. [14]

GRACE, G. R. *Role Conflict and the Teacher*, Routledge & Kegan Paul, 1972. [61]

GRONLUND, N. E. 'The relative ability of home-room teachers and special-subject teachers to judge the social acceptability of pre-adolescent pupils', *Journal of Educational Research*, vol. 48, 1955, pp. 381–91. [232]

GROSS, N., MASON, W. S. & MCEACHERN, A. W. *Explorations in Role Analysis*, Wiley, 1958. [61]

HALLWORTH, H. J. 'Sociometric relationships among grammar school boys and girls between the ages of eleven and sixteen years', *Sociometry*, vol. 16, 1953, pp. 39–70. [105]

HALLWORTH, H. J. 'Teachers' personality ratings of high school pupils', *Journal of Educational Psychology*, vol. 52, 1961, pp. 297–302. [127]

HALLWORTH, H. J. 'A teacher's perception of his pupils', *Educational Review*, vol. 14, 1962, pp. 124–33. [127]

HAMBLIN, R. L. 'Leadership and crises', *Sociometry*, vol. 21, 1958, pp. 322–335. [106]

HARGREAVES, D. H. *Social Relations in a Secondary School*, Routledge & Kegan Paul, 1967. [41f, 127, 157, 232ff, 248]

HARGREAVES, D. H. 'The delinquent subculture and the school', in Carson, W. G. & Wiles, P. (eds) *Crime and Delinquency in Britain*, Robertson, 1971. [157]

HARGREAVES, D. H. 'After the liontamers and entertainers', *Dudley Educational Journal*, vol. 1, no. 2, pp. 3–15, 1972. [164]

HARGREAVES, D. H. 'The deschoolers and the new romantics', in Flude, M. & Ahier, J. *Educability, Schools and Ideology*, Heath, 1974. [188]

HARRE, R. & SECORD, P. F. *The Explanation of Social Behaviour*, Blackwell, 1972. [68, 69]

HEBER, R. F. 'The relationship of intelligence and physical maturity to social status of children', *Journal of Educational Psychology*, vol. 47, 1956, pp. 158–62. [99]

HEIDER, F. *The Psychology of Interpersonal Relations*, Wiley, 1958. [23, 26]

HENRY, J. 'Docility, or giving teacher what she wants', *Journal of Social Issues*, vol. 11, 1955, pp. 33–41. [144]

HENRY, J. *Culture Against Man*, Tavistock, 1966. [147, 150f, 161]

HENRY, N. B. *Dynamics of Instructional Groups*, 59th Year Book of the National Society for the Study of Education, Chicago University Press, 1960.

HINES, B. *A Kestrel for a Knave*, Michael Joseph (Penguin, 1969). [158f]

HOLLANDER, E. P. 'Competence and conformity and acceptance of influence', *Journal of Abnormal and Social Psychology*, vol. 61, 1960, pp. 365–9. [109]

KLEIN, J. *The Study of Groups*, Routledge & Kegan Paul, 1956. [110]

KOHL, H. R. *Thirty-six Children*, Gollancz, 1967 (Penguin, 1972). [184]

KOHL, H. R. *The Open Classroom* (1969), Methuen, 1970. [164, 166, 182f, 190, 200]

KOUNIN, J. S. *Discipline and Group Management in Classrooms*, Holt, Rinehart & Winston, 1970. [224, 230]

KOUNIN, J. S. & GUMP, P. V. 'The ripple effect in discipline', *Elementary School Journal*, vol. 59, 1958, pp. 158–62. [236]

KOUNIN, J. S., FRIESEN, W. V. & NORTON, A. E. 'Managing emotionally disturbed children in regular classrooms', *Journal of Educational Psychology*, vol. 57, 1966, pp. 1–13. [221]

KUHN, M. H. 'The reference group reconsidered', *Sociological Quarterly*, vol. 5, 1964, pp. 6–21. [8]

LACEY, C. *Hightown Grammar*, Manchester University Press, 1970. [41]

LAING, R. D. *The Politics of Experience*, Penguin, 1967. [86]

LAMBERT, P. 'The "successful" child: some implications of teacher-stereotyping', *Journal of Educational Psychology*, vol. 56, 1963, pp. 551–3. [127]

LEMERT, E. M. 'Paranoia and the dynamics of exclusion', *Sociometry*, vol. 25, 1962, pp. 1–20. [33]

Letter to a Teacher, *see* Barbiana, School of

LIEBERMAN, S. 'The effects of changes in roles on the attitudes of role occupants', *Human Relations*, vol. 9, 1956, pp. 385–402. [52]

LINDESMITH, A. R. & STRAUSS, A. L. *Social Psychology*, Holt, Rinehart & Winston, 1949. [5]

LIPPITT, R., POLANSKY, N. & ROSEN, S. 'The dynamics of power', *Human Relations*, vol. 5, 1952, pp. 37–64. [100, 104]

LISTER, I. (ed.) *Deschooling: A Reader*, Cambridge University Press, 1974. [188, 200]

MACCOBY, E. E. 'Role-taking in childhood and its consequences for social learning', *Child Development*, vol. 30, 1959, pp. 239–52. [8]

MACCOBY, E. E. 'The taking of adult roles in middle childhood', *Journal of Abnormal and Social Psychology*, vol. 63, 1961, pp. 493–503. [8]

MACKENZIE, R. F. *The Sins of the Children*, Collins, 1967. [134]

MACMURRAY, J. *Persons in Relation*, Faber & Faber, 1961. [6]

MAISONNEUVE, J. 'Selective choices and propinquity', *Sociometry*, vol. 15, 1952, pp. 135–40 [181]

MANIS, J. G. & MELTZER, B. N. *Symbolic Interaction: A Reader in Social Psychology*, Allyn & Bacon, 1967. [5, 16]

MATZA, D. *Becoming Deviant*, Prentice-Hall, 1969. [142f]

MEAD, G. H. *Mind, Self and Society*, University of Chicago Press, 1934. [5ff, 17]

MEREI, F. 'Group leadership and institutionalization', *Human Relations*, vol. 2, 1949, pp. 23–39. [108]

MERTON, R. K. *Social Theory and Social Structure*, Free Press, 1949 (rev. ed., 1957). [13, 33]

MERTON, R. K. 'The role-set: problems in sociological theory', *British Journal of Sociology*, vol. 8, 1957, pp. 106–20. [47]

MICHAEL, W. B., HERROLD, E. E. & CRYAN, E. W. 'Survey of student-teacher relationships', *Journal of Educational Research*, vol. 44, 1951, pp. 657–74. [131]

MILES, M. B. 'The T-group and the classroom', in Bradford, Gibb & Benne (1964). [144]

MORTON-WILLIAMS, R. & FINCH, S. *Schools Council Enquiry I: Young School Leavers*, H.M.S.O., 1968. [185]

MUSGROVE, F. 'Parents' expectations of the junior school', *Sociological Review*, vol. 9, 1961, pp. 167–80. [50]

MUSGROVE, F. *Patterns of Power and Authority in English Education*, Methuen, 1971. [183]

MUSGROVE, F. & TAYLOR, P. H. 'Teachers' and parents' conception of the teacher's role', *British Journal of Educational Psychology*, vol. 35, 1965, pp. 171–8. [49]

MUSGROVE, F. & TAYLOR, P. H. *Society and the Teacher's Role*, Routledge & Kegan Paul, 1969. [49]

MUSS, R. E. 'Differential effects of studying versus teaching on teachers' attitudes', *Journal of Educational Research*, vol. 63, 1969, pp. 185–9. [60]

NASH, R. *Classrooms Observed*, Routledge & Kegan Paul, 1973. [35, 42, 57, 128]

NEWCOMB, T. M. *Social Psychology*, Dryden Press, 1950. [13]

NORTHWAY, M. L. 'Outsiders', *Sociometry*, vol. 7, 1944, pp. 10–25. [248]

OLMSTED, M. *The Small Group*, Random House, 1959. [110]

OTTAWAY, A. K. C. *Learning Through Group Experience*, Routledge & Kegan Paul, 1966. [247]

PALARDY, J. 'What teachers believe—what children achieve', *Elementary School Journal*, vol. 69, 1969, pp. 370–4. [35]

PARSONS, T. 'The school class as a social system: some of its functions in American society', *Harvard Educational Review*, vol. 29, 1959, pp. 297–318; reprinted in Halsey, A. H., Floud, J. & Anderson, C. A. *Education, Economy and Society*, Free Press, 1961, and in Grinder, R. E. (ed.) *Studies in Adolescence*, Macmillan, 1963. [12, 125]

PARTRIDGE, J. *Middle School*, Gollancz, 1966; published also by Penguin Books under the title *Life in a Secondary Modern School*. [41]

PATRICK, J. *A Glasgow Gang Observed*, Eyre Methuen, 1973. [247f]

PIAGET, J. *The Moral Judgment of the Child*, Routledge & Kegan Paul (1932), 1968. [10]

PIDGEON, D. A. *Expectation and Pupil Performance*, N.F.E.R., 1970. [43]

POLANYI, M. *The Tacit Dimension*, Routledge & Kegan Paul, 1966. [225]

POSTMAN, N. 'The politics of reading', *Harvard Educational Review*, vol. 40, 1970, pp. 244–53. [169]

POSTMAN, N. & WEINGARTNER, C. *Teaching as a Subversive Activity*, Delacorte Press, 1969 (Penguin, 1972). [167f, 174]

PROCTOR, C. H. & LOOMIS, C. P. 'Analysis of sociometric data', in Jahoda, M., Deutsch, M. & Cook S. W. (eds) *Research Methods in Social Relations*, Dryden Press, 1951. [99]

RABINOWITZ, W. & ROSENBAUM, I. 'Teaching experience and teachers' attitudes', *Elementary School Journal*, vol. 60, 1960, pp. 313–19. [59]

REDL, F. *When We Deal with Children*, Free Press, 1966. [218, 230]

SNOW, R. 'Unfinished Pygmalion', *Contemporary Psychology*, vol. 14, 1969, pp. 197–9. [35]

SOLES, S. 'Teacher role expectations and the internal organization of secondary schools', *Journal of Educational Research*, vol. 57, 1964, pp. 227–35. [122]

SOMMER, R. *Personal Space*, Prentice-Hall, 1969. [180f]

SORENSON, A. G., HUSEK, T. R. & YU, C. 'Divergent concepts of teacher role: an approach to the measurement of teacher effectiveness', *Journal of Educational Psychology*, vol. 54, 1963, pp. 287–94. [116]

SPARK, MURIEL *The Prime of Miss Jean Brodie*, Macmillan, 1961. [56]

SPROTT, W. J. H. *Human Groups*, Penguin, 1958. [87, 110]

STENHOUSE, L. (ed.) *Discipline in Schools: A Symposium*, Pergamon, 1967. [230]

SULLIVAN, H. S. *Conceptions of Modern Psychiatry*, White Psychiatric Foundation, 1940. [8, 15]

TAYLOR, C. 'The expectations of Pygmalion's creators', *Educational Leadership*, vol. 28, 1970, pp. 161–4. [35]

TAYLOR, P. H. 'Children's evaluations of the characteristics of the good teacher', *British Journal of Educational Psychology*, vol. 32, 1962, pp. 258–66. [131f]

TERSON, P. 'The tragedy of the worn-out games teacher', *Guardian*, 20 July 1967. [53f]

THELEN, H. A. *Dynamics of Groups at Work*, Chicago, 1954. [122, 123f]

THOMAS, W. I. *The Child in America*, Knopf, 1928. [33, 73]

THOMAS, W. I. *The Unadjusted Girl*, Little, Brown, 1931. [73]

THORNDIKE, R. L. Review of 'Pygmalion in the classroom', *AERA Journal*, vol. 5, 1968, pp. 708–11. [35]

THORPE, J. G. 'An investigation into correlates of sociometric status within school classes', *Sociometry*, vol. 18, 1955, pp. 49–55. [99]

TIEDEMAN, S. C. 'A study of pupil–teacher relationships', *Journal of Educational Research*, vol. 35, 1942, pp. 657–64. [131]

TINBERGEN, N. *The Study of Instinct*, Clarendon Press, 1951. [6]

TOOGOOD, J. E. 'The selection of children for responsibility in the junior school', unpublished dissertation for the Diploma in Educational Guidance, University of Manchester, 1967. [127]

TRILLING, L. *The Liberal Imagination*, Secker & Warburg, 1951. [162]

TROW, W. C. 'Role function of the teacher in the instructional group', in Henry, N. B. (1960). [116]

TURNER, R. H. 'Role-taking, role standpoint and reference-group behaviour', *American Journal of Sociology*, vol. 61, 1956, pp. 316–28, and in Biddle & Thomas (1966). [12]

TURNER, R. H. 'Role-taking: process versus conformity', in Rose, 1962. [69]

WALLBERG, H. J. 'Personality-role conflict and self-conception in urban practice teachers', *School Review*, vol. 76, 1968, pp. 41–9. [60]

WALLER, W. *The Sociology of Teaching*, Wiley, 1932. [118, 120, 122f, 139, 142, 161, 164, 180, 230]

WAUGH, EVELYN *Decline and Fall*, 1928 (Penguin, 1937). [202f]

WHYTE, W. F. *Street Corner Society*, Chicago, 1943. [95, 106f, 109]

WICKMAN, E. K. *Children's Behaviour and Teachers' Attitudes*, Commonwealth Fund, 1928. [126]

WILLANS, G. & SEARLE, R. *Down with Skool!*, Parrish, 1958. [149f]

WILLIAMS, J. R. & KNECHT, W. W. 'Teachers' ratings of high school students on "likeability" and their relation to measures of ability and achievement', *Journal of Educational Research*, vol. 56, 1962, pp. 152–9. [126]

WILMOTT, P. *Adolescent Boys of East London*, Routledge & Kegan Paul, 1966. [247]

WONG, L. EVAN, & BAGLEY, C. 'Conformity, attitude change, and group membership in adolescent girls', *Moral Education*, vol. 2, 1970, pp. 115–121. [235]

WRIGHT, B. D. & TUSKA, S. A. 'From dream to life in the psychology of becoming a teacher', *School Review*, vol. 76, 1968, pp. 253–93. [59]

WRIGHT, D. S. 'A comparative study of the adolescent's conceptions of his parents and teachers', *Educational Review*, vol. 14, 1962, pp. 226–32. [37]

YABLONSKY, L. 'An operational theory of roles', *Sociometry*, vol. 16, 1953, pp. 349–56. [66]

Subject index